"Every book Owen Strachan writes is worth the cover price, but *Reenchanting Humanity* doubly so. Strachan tackles the pressing biblical, theological, and cultural issues pertaining to human existence and experience. As he does, Strachan is resolutely orthodox, helpfully prescient, and unmistakably clear. Strachan offers the reader a guided tour through biblical anthropology, and any who desires to engage these issues owes it to himself to buy and read this book."

—Jason K. Allen
president, Midwestern Baptist Theological
Seminary, Kansas City, Missouri

"In the late modern West, we constantly face challenges to the Bible's description of what a human being is. The order of the day is what sociologists call expressive individualism, which means that human identity and meaning are self-constructed, not God-constructed. In this context, Owen Strachan's *Reenchanting Humanity* is a breath of fresh biblical air. Strachan offers a theological anthropology that defines human identity and meaning in light of God's original creation design. This book is a deep well issuing forth a fountain of biblical insight about what it means to be a human being created in the image of God. Drink deeply from this wonderful book."

—Denny Burk
professor of biblical studies, director, Center for Gospel and Culture,
The Southern Baptist Theological Seminary, Louisville, Kentucky,
and president, Council on Biblical Manhood & Womanhood

"This book is timely and important, providing an antidote for the cynical, disillusioned, misguided, and confused perspectives on the nature and purpose of mankind that pervade this age. Strachan has ably written to strengthen God's church, and he helpfully and articulately synthesizes a theocentric, biblical, and Christological view of humanity that celebrates our creation in God's image, takes seriously our depravity through sin, and celebrates how we can move from being fully human in Adam to truly human in Christ. Strachan tackles head-on our vocational and ethical responsibility in God's world, our complementary human sexuality as male and female, our limited and dependent and deteriorating human nature, and our eschatological and teleological hope if we are in Christ. This book supplies a doctrine of mankind that is derived from God's Word, that is both Christological and covenantal, and that celebrates that our chief end is to glorify God by enjoying him forever. *Reenchanting Humanity* is a gift to the church in the twenty-first century."

—**Jason S. DeRouchie**
research professor of Old Testament and biblical theology,
Midwestern Baptist Theological Seminary, Kansas City, Missouri

"An important area of systematic theology that is necessarily receiving renewed attention in our own time is theological anthropology: the study of the biblical doctrine of humanity. Our age is characterized by confusion at the definitional level. What is a human? What is a man? What is a woman? Furthermore, we are seeing a historical reckoning in our time, with, for instance, the failure of much of the Bible-believing church to do at least practical justice to the scriptural doctrine of the imago Dei, the image of God in man, in the face of slavery, segregation, and discrimination in the US, and apartheid in South Africa. I predict that we will benefit from sustained attention to this theological locus by scholars in the foreseeable future. Thus, I welcome this entry from a Dr. Owen Strachan, a respected and prolific theologian and churchman who writes from an unapologetically convictional, scriptural, and historical perspective. Strachan not only addresses traditional core issues like the imago Dei and harmartiology, but also tackles, for example, race and ethnicity, technology, and justice. Not only is Strachan enjoyable to read, but I find that he helps me communicate traditional systematic assertions in arresting and memorable ways. I commend this volume to scholars, seminarians, and pastors as we seek to reflect faithfully on and teach clearly about all that God says in the Scriptures about man."

—**J. Ligon Duncan III**
chancellor and CEO, Reformed Theological
Seminary, Jackson, Mississippi

"This book is filled with rich, scripturally grounded insight that will give every reader an increased appreciation for the great honor and significance of existing as a human being made in the image of God. Strachan courageously and persuasively challenges the deceptive views of modern secular culture regarding such topics as sexuality, equality, work, manhood and womanhood, race, and justice, reaching sound conclusions on every topic. Highly recommended!"

—**Wayne Grudem**
distinguished research professor of theology and biblical
studies, Phoenix Seminary, Phoenix, Arizona

"In this 'humble attempt to see humanity afresh through biblical eyes,' Owen Strachan asks, and brilliantly answers, questions such as 'Does the human person live in an ordered cosmos and have an appointed identity, or does he make his own identity in a world without God?' *Reenchanting Humanity* could not be more timely. In this Christological anthropology, Strachan offers a holistic vision of humanity for our disenchanted age. Who says anthropology has to be boring?"

—**Andreas J. Köstenberger**
research professor of New Testament and biblical theology,
director, Center for Biblical Studies, Midwestern Baptist
Theological Seminary, Kansas City, Missouri

"The recovery of a truly Christian, truly biblical, truly engaging doctrine of humanity is one of the greatest needs of our time. Everywhere we look, human dignity is threatened and the culture around us is increasingly hostile to the only adequate grounding of human dignity—biblical Christianity. Owen Strachan is one of the bright lights of scholarship in the evangelical world today. *Reenchanting Humanity* is an important book that is both timely and deeply thoughtful, and I am thankful for its arrival."

—**R. Albert Mohler Jr.**
president, The Southern Baptist Theological
Seminary, Louisville, Kentucky

"Charles Taylor explains modern secularization in terms of a growing disenchantment with our world, a loss of any sense that human existence, which according to science is nothing more than clothed matter in motion, is meaningful. This is the backdrop for Owen Strachan's retrieval of a biblically rich theological anthropology, according to which human life is much more than Hamlet's 'tale told by an idiot . . . signifying nothing.' Whereas contemporary thinkers find it difficult to specify how humans differ from higher primates, Strachan identifies nine aspects of theological anthropology that enable him to give an appropriately thick description of what it is to be human. Contra much fashionable thinking, the human being is not plastic, to be molded according to individual desires, but personal: what gives humans dignity is their ability to be addressed by, and enter into relation with, the God whose image they bear. Strachan effectively argues that we rightly reenchant humanity, and thus come to see the truth, goodness, and beauty of humanity, only when we view it in relation to the end for which it was created: conformity to Jesus Christ, the meaning of life made flesh."

—**Kevin J. Vanhoozer**
research professor of systematic theology, Trinity
Evangelical Divinity School, Deerfield, Illinois

"This great work by Owen Strachan proves that theological books must continue to be written to address old themes. Strachan uses the Bible as a magnifying lens and looks at mankind in the context of this anthropocentric, narcissistic, sin-ridden, self-sufficient, self-defined, and high-tech generation and has given us, not only his analysis of the problem, but also its cause and its cure. The book is wide in scope, deep in content, beautiful in prose, convincing in reasoning, and highly significant for the moral revolution we find ourselves in. I love the way the author begins with the image of God and ends with Christ, as the God-man who reenchants our humanity. This is a must-read."

—**Miguel Nuñez**
senior pastor, International Baptist Church,
Santo Domingo, Dominican Republic

"Someone once told me that where the battle rages hottest, there we must speak. Not retreat to silence and safety, but courageously yet winsomely speak—with grace and truth. In our generation, the battle for ideas is centered on the issues of humanness. What is a human being? Having lost our vision for God in previous generations, our vision for humanity is up for grabs. Consequently, the doctrine of humanity needs fresh and clear articulation in the church and in the culture. It is heartening to see young scholars like Owen Strachan take up this challenge in his book *Reenchanting Humanity*."

—**Don Sweeting**
president, Colorado Christian University, Lakewood, Colorado

"Evangelicals have all too often approached anthropological questions with either shallow worldview materials or narrow Biblical exegesis. Strachan's book offers us an alternative: a biblically grounded, theologically rich, thoroughly researched, and holistic account of the human person. As new challenges continue to arise in the twenty-first century, evangelicals need to have a theological framework that can speak to all aspects of the human condition. This book is a giant leap in that direction."

—**David Talcott**
assistant professor of philosophy, The King's College, New York City

"There is not a single issue in the news today that is not profoundly shaped by one's definition of humanity. A person's definition of a human being is at the heart of his views on politics, economics, parenting, education, gender, sports, the arts, bioethics, climate change, abortion, sexual ethics, religious freedom, war, poverty, and a host of other issues. There is a desperate need for Christians to have a clear, comprehensive, biblically grounded, God-centered, definition of humanity, and for that definition to transform the way we live, love, and minister. Owen Strachan has wonderfully met this need in *Reenchanting Humanity*. I hope that this important book has the deep and wide influence it deserves!"

—**K. Erik Thoennes**
professor and chair of theology, Biola University, and pastor,
Grace Evangelical Free Church, La Miranda, California

"The sad irony of our current context is that in seeking to dethrone the glorious triune God from the center of our thinking, worship, and obedience, we have lost the meaning of who we are as humans, and the very reason for our existence. God's 'death' in our culture has led to our 'death' as well. As a consequence, we are now reaping the whirlwind in every aspect of what it means to be human. We no longer know why humans have value and dignity. We have no reason to value our work and to truly live. What God created good and beautiful in human sexuality, marriage, and the family, we have turned to ashes. In such a situation, what the church desperately needs is to reject the disastrous thinking of our day and to return once again to think rightly about ourselves as God's image-bearers, created to know him and to serve one another. Owen Strachan has done precisely this in this insightful and well-written corrective to the mess of pottage of our day. If you want to know who you are in light of Scripture, and learn how to speak good news to our poor lost world, this book is must reading. From Scripture and faithful theological reasoning, Strachan carefully and wisely answers some of the most significant questions of our day. In this book we have the antidote to the diseased thinking of our day: a sound theological and Christocentric anthropology."

—**Steve Wellum**
professor of Christian theology, The Southern Baptist
Theological Seminary, Louisville, Kentucky

REENCHANTING HUMANITY

A THEOLOGY OF MANKIND

OWEN STRACHAN

MENTOR

Copyright © Owen Strachan 2019

paperback ISBN 978-1-5271-0502-7
epub ISBN 978-1-5271-0503-4
mobi ISBN 978-1-5271-0504-1

10 9 8 7 6 5 4 3 2 1

Published in 2019
in the Mentor imprint
by
Christian Focus Publications Ltd,
Geanies House, Fearn, Ross-shire,
IV20 1TW, Great Britain.
www.christianfocus.com

Cover illustration by Chiara Fedele / Astound

Printed in the USA

Dedication

To Bruce Ware, my father-in-law, who trained me in the classroom to love the Word of God, and whose example as a man of God points to one greater still.

is accipiet propriam mercedem novissimo die

"He shall be rewarded on the last day."

CONTENTS

INTRODUCTION

Some years ago, I encountered a word—a single word—that caught my eye. It was from a book by Charles Taylor. It was the concept of *enchantment* of our secular age.[1] Taylor put the term to use for his own ends in his illuminating study of secularism; for my part, as I delved into the doctrine of humanity in order to teach it faithfully to seminarians and churches, I saw that this word elegantly captured the effect of the Christic remaking of the human person. This, I realized, is what the human race desperately needs in our skeptical, secularist era: we need to see humanity afresh. We have been told that we people are the chance result of impersonal chaos working its dark magic on the universe; we have no divine origin, there is no design or *telos* (τέλος) to our bodies and

---

[1] Charles Taylor, *A Secular Age* (Cambridge, MA: Belknap Press, 2007), 27.

identities, and—this last part is taken almost for granted today—
there is no God. The outcome of such thinking? Humanity is *disenchanted*. We are not made by God, we have no greater purpose
in life, spirituality is just mystic make-believe for the emotively
oriented, children are a burden, and on the desultory creed goes.

But this is not the biblical account of man. In biblical anthropology—the doctrine of humanity—we are made by God, our
bodies are crucial components of our identities, there is immense
and even grandiose potential and dignity in our persons, and we
find happiness and fulfillment in God. If we wanted to say it more
simply, we might use aesthetic language. God, the beautiful one,
made the human race as his capstone work, his corporeal masterpiece (Ps 8:3–6; 27:4). The Lord did not make a great cathedral
or castle or war machine on the sixth day. He made a man, and
from the man he made a woman. If we have been trained to see
such biblical material as poetic reflection on a mythical moment,
we may be surprised to discover that the Scripture presents this
making in historical terms. God actually made humanity; God
actually gave humanity infinite dignity and worth, though we
have gambled our futures away in a bid for godlikeness.

What follows in these pages is a humble attempt to see
humanity afresh through biblical eyes. It is my hope that
Reenchanting Humanity will give the future pastors of Christ's
church great confidence in the doctrine of man; it is my further
hope that present shepherds of God's flock, those facing many
challenges to this doctrine from inside and outside the church,
will gain strength from our rigorously biblical and theological

study of theocentric anthropology. Beyond specific content, I pray that the method and hermeneutical approach will lend strength to readers. We proceed in the following chapters knowing with certainty that the Bible is true, that biblical teaching is not only true but is good for us, and that our greatest needs in ministry and life are to believe and love this God-given truth (see Luke 1:4; John 8:32; 2 Pet 1:3). I have taken great effort to include voices of the Christian past from whom I have learned much, and to show that this biblical doctrine is that which the church has loved long before our generation. Yet our authority is and must be the Word of God itself. This little book, then, is an exercise in biblical confidence and biblical hermeneutics.

The culture rages on these points. If the major issue of the sixteenth century was that of *acceptance* (how man may be forgiven by God), and the major issue of the twentieth century was that of *authority* (whether the Bible is inerrant), then the major issue of our time is that of *anthropology*. Does the human person live in an ordered cosmos and have an appointed identity, or does he make his own identity in a world without God? Beyond the finer points of the various debates we face today, this is the question of our age. So it is that I offer up this material as biblical anthropology for the twenty-first century. Much of what I will sketch in these pages would have been taken for granted by not only many Christians, but many Westerners (in an elementary, nonsalvific way). But a fallen culture changes on a dime, and ours has moved swiftly indeed on these matters, making the biblical doctrine of man quite distinct from a secular one.

We find ourselves in a contest of anthropological visions: Christianity vs. neopaganism. By this I do not refer primarily to politics, although politics is enlisted in this contest, but to theology and philosophy. We are fighting the same battles in all these realms, but with different language and different audiences. My task is to equip the church to give an answer for the hope that lies within all who are in Christ. In the end, God's preferred apologetic is not a chatbot or a code but a covenant people, a blood-bought church of sinners who personally testify to the grace of God that has renewed and reenchanted them. Christianity is, after all, a personal faith; it is not abstract. God is a *personal* being; we are *persons*; we know God intimately, in our very souls; the way back to God for hell-bound sinners is through the *person* and work of Jesus Christ.

We shall begin our study on these grounds. We will see the irreversibly spiritual nature of humankind in chapter 1. The *imago dei* marks out humanity as an enchanted race. Tragically, humanity disenchanted itself by following the anti-wisdom of the serpent, the subject of chapter 2. Despite this truth, we find great meaning and joy in working unto God, the theme of chapter 3. It is our call to live as godly men and godly women, though our secularized culture encourages us to eschew order and downplay design. More than any other challenge to Christianity today, the church faces continual pressure to downgrade its doctrine of sexuality and to repristinate homosexuality and transgender in particular. All this we cover in chapter 4.

The church has unity in Jesus Christ, though we often use our God-made diversity to separate ourselves from fellow image-bearers. Chapter 5 surveys the biblical material on race and ethnicity. In chapter 6, we consider the promise and peril of technology, distinguishing Christian humanism from transhumanism and posthumanism. In chapter 7, we think deeply about the doctrine of divine justice, an issue on which the church is frequently challenged today. We show that so far from defeating our faith, the justice of God gives us hope in a fallen cosmos. In chapter 8, we treat the matter of human contingency, looking at our limitations, our temporalness, and our mortality in biblical perspective. We conclude the anthropology by studying Christ the true man, thus ensuring that this is properly a Christological anthropology. In this sense, I believe that we have a stunning body of material—a holistic vision of humanity—to offer our disenchanted age, which sees mankind as a cosmic accident and not a being made by God for eternal fellowship.

A word on terminology as we begin. In this book, I use a range of terms to refer to the human race—*humanity* (most commonly), *humankind*, *mankind*, and also the traditional *man* as, for example, the special creation of God. I use each of these without hesitation or personal difficulty. The man, as I make plain in these pages, was created first by God and has a representational role in the presence of God.[2] This we cannot miss nor elide. This

---

[2] See *New Dictionary of Biblical Theology: Exploring the Unity and Diversity of Scripture*, ed. T. Desmond Alexander et al. (Downers Grove,

being said, I have no problem using more generic and modern terms, as you shall see.

This text is written to engage fellow theologians and to instruct seminarians, pastors, and those engaging these matters in the church and public square. It is a work of systematic theology, and I have written it in conversation with a guild of fellow systematicians. It has been a joy to teach systematics for nearly a decade, and I hope this book will lend insight and strength to the church's doctrine of man. If we have assumed in past days that the church of Christ held a meaningful anthropology, and that our children learned what they needed to know simply by ecclesial and cultural osmosis, let us be clear that we may hold this assumption no longer. Now is not the time to play down our doctrine of mankind; now is the time to teach it with confidence and with joy, seeking to be witnesses to fellow sinners and guides to all God's flock.

As we begin our study, we can scarcely do better than the words of Ps 8:4–5, which capture both the wonder and the promise and the eternal beauty of man, God's greatest creation:

> what is a human being that you remember him,
> a son of man that you look after him?
> You made him little less than God
> and crowned him with glory and honor.

IL: InterVarsity, 2000), s.v. "Adam and Eve." The Hebrew term for man, *adam* (אדמ), speaks of both an individual man and the human race more broadly. The theological significance of the term *man*—drawn from the Hebrew—cannot be underplayed or lost.

CHAPTER 1

IMAGE

Fifty years ago, the question landed like a bombshell on the cover of *Time* magazine: "Is God Dead?" In truth, death-of-God theology had debuted many decades prior (and atheism was no new phenomenon in the West), but the April 1966 coverage of this trend made the conversation a public one. It was change in Protestant doctrine through the work of theologians such as Thomas J. J. Altizer, William H. Hamilton, and Paul van Buren that made the broader conversation possible.[1] Not to be

---

[1] See Thomas J. J. Altizer and William Hamilton, *Radical Theology and the Death of God* (Indianapolis: Bobbs-Merrill, 1966); Thomas J. J. Altizer, *Living the Death of God: A Theological Memoir* (Albany, NY: SUNY Press, 2006); Paul van Buren, *The Secular Meaning of the Gospel:*

outdone, one professor inspired a new liturgy for the age marking God's death:

> He was our guide and our stay
> He walked with us beside still waters
> He was our help in ages past
> . . . He is gone, He is stolen by darkness
> . . . Heaven is empty.[2]

Apparently, the so-called death of God necessitated the rewriting of the beloved Psalm 23. This revisionism advanced primarily on college and university campuses as students reared in religious homes, in many cases, walked into classrooms aimed at deconstructing their spiritual formation. In time, through such pedagogy, it became not only possible but even fashionable to identify as an atheist, or at the very least as a skeptic, in the West.

In 2019, a new question has emerged in the West: "Is Man Dead?" Over the last fifty years, Western society has reenvisioned the human person. For millennia, humanity was understood in light of God; mankind was made in the image of God, and thus humans had certain duties before God and were fundamentally spiritual beings. But with the rise of the death-of-God theology,

---

Based on *Analysis of Its Language* (1963; repr., New York: Macmillan, 1966).

[2] Quoted in Leigh Eric Schmidt, "Is God Dead? A TIME Cover Turns 50," *Religion and Politics*, April 5, 2016, https://religionandpolitics .org/2016/04/05/is-god-dead-a-time-cover-turns-50.

mankind is no longer seen as the creation of God.[3] The prevailing view in critical circles today is that mankind is a blank slate, evolved from an eons-old combustion of gases. Humanity has no divine origin, but an accidental one. No creative figure guided the human race's formation or shaped the human person's identity. Chaos and randomness account for the order (such as it is) that we find before us. The human race is not really distinct from the beasts; we are a higher animal, nothing more. We have no greater story, no *telos* (τέλος), no ordained end to which we are traveling.[4] Atoms collide, and so does mankind.

Because of our godless origin, we have no greater body of ethics, no summons to a certain code of conduct. We are here;

---

[3] One of the original articles covering the death of God made the link between divinity and humanity explicit: "A group of radical Protestant thinkers . . . say that the word *God* is meaningless and that even if there once was a God, He no longer speaks to man. True Christianity, they say, is an affirmation of the secular world in the style of the man Jesus, and has no relation to traditional church practices such as worship, the sacraments and prayer." "'New' Theologians See Christianity Without God," *New York Times*, October 17, 1965, 85.

[4] "The death of God in 1965 also made the feminist theology of the 1970s possible as ideology, if not convincing as theology, because it removed the masculine-aggressive principle from the Christian drama of redemption." William Hamilton, "In Piam Memoriam: The Death of God After Ten Years," *Christian Century*, October 8, 1975, 872–73. The connection between secularized theology proper and a radicalized doctrine of humanity here is a fruitful one, for the revising of the doctrine of God made the revising of human identity possible, albeit to a contemporary degree that would have been scarcely conceivable to many half a century ago.

we die; we dissolve into nothingness. Nothingness is whence we came; nothingness is whither we go. Until then, we create our realities; we become who we want to be.

I do not suggest that most people believe humanity is a collective zombie, the walking dead. Humanity continues to exist, but in terms of a religious or traditional or merely stable conception of the human person, consensus is proving harder and harder to reach. The old view of humanity is outmoded in many circles. It is in this sense that we may say man is dead today. The theological vision of the human race—in some form the view of the ages—has dissipated. The West finds itself in a brave new moment, a moment of revision and redefinition of the human person. This change comes on the heels of our collective revision of the divine persons.

Our age features a confusing blend of perspectives on humanity, but it is hard to deny that the preceding sketch sums up the prevailing view among the Western intelligentsia. If it was normal to believe in God for most of human history, now it is normal among the highbrow crowd not to believe in God.[5] This does not mean that everyone is atheist today—far from it. Outside of the academy and numerous outspoken professors, people traffic in a strange and often nonlogical range of beliefs, a number of them "spiritual," some of them religious. The average person is pressured to espouse these beliefs: human persons are largely blank slates. Our identities are not fixed and stable. Any participation we might have in bigger structures or mediating

---

[5] This language is a variation of that introduced by Charles Taylor, *A Secular Age* (see intro., n. 1), 3, 25, 539.

institutions should not inhibit our rights to express the self, be authentic to our individuated beings, and act in total freedom. No code, creed, or doctrine should shape us more than our self-conceptions shape us; such epistemic interference would violate our humanity. We are free and freed.

Earlier we glimpsed a death-of-God liturgy. Here are fourteen modern humanistic mantras:

- I am capable.
- I know who I am and I am enough.
- I choose to be present in all that I do.
- I choose to think thoughts that serve me well.
- I choose to reach for a better feeling.
- I share my happiness with those around me.
- My body is my vehicle in life; I choose to fill it with goodness.
- I feel energetic and alive.
- My life is unfolding beautifully.
- I am confident.
- I always observe before reacting.
- I know with time and effort I can achieve.
- I love challenges and what I learn from overcoming them.
- Each step is taking me to where I want to be.[6]

---

[6] Belinda Anderson, "14 Mantras to Help You Build Positive Self-Talk," Mind Body Green, accessed January 15, 2019, https://www.mind bodygreen.com/0-12637/14-mantras-to-help-you-build-positive-selftalk .html.

There are twenty-five uses here of *I*, *me*, or *my*. The perspective here is of one of self-determination and self-authenticity. I determine my fate, I am the subject and object, and I am the judge of my life. The great need of my existence is not to honor someone or even something beyond me; it is effectively to honor myself. I need to be true to me. There is not very much that I can discover beyond myself; I am the one who maps meaning onto myself or finds it within me.

The Christian doctrine of humanity starts from an opposite perspective. It is not that believers reject any sense of agency or volition or "self-discovery." Christians know that we may only know ourselves if God has enabled us to know ourselves. In other words, a good deal of information that we need in order to know who we are does not come from any attempt to dig into our truest selves, but rather from studying the will of God for his special creation, both natural and supernatural.

If we wish to know ourselves, then we must look beyond ourselves. "No man," said Calvin, "can survey himself without forthwith turning his thoughts toward the God in whom he lives and moves; because it is perfectly obvious, that the endowments which we possess cannot possibly be from ourselves; nay, that our very being is nothing else than subsistence in God alone."[7] The witness of the Scripture and of the church that loves the Scripture is not that the knowledge of God helps in our formations of self-knowledge. The witness of Scripture is that we

---

[7] John Calvin, *Institutes of the Christian Religion*, ed. Anthony Uyl, trans. Henry Beveridge (Ingersoll, ON: Devoted, 2016), 18.

cannot know ourselves without knowing God. Carl F. H. Henry concurs with Calvin: "Divine revelation is the starting point of all human knowledge."[8] To know God and his intentions for humanity, we must start where the Scripture starts: Genesis 1. Many Christians derive their doctrine of origins from this chapter. This landmark text, however, offers not simply knowledge of God's creative work, but knowledge of God's design of humanity.

As we turn to this text, we enter another world—the theistic world, the God-made world. It is as if we have been wandering through a confusing building, shadowy and foreboding, only to enter C. S. Lewis's wardrobe and pass into a Narnian realm of wonder and discovery.

Mankind: A God-Stamped Creature

Then God said, "Let us make man in our image, according to our likeness. They will rule the fish of the sea, the birds of the sky, the livestock, the whole earth, and the creatures that crawl on the earth."

So God created man
in his own image;
he created him in the image of God;
he created them male and female. (Gen 1:26–27)

---

[8] Carl F. H. Henry, *God, Revelation, and Authority*, vol. 2, *God Who Speaks and Shows: Fifteen Theses, Part One* (1976; repr., Wheaton, IL: Crossway Books, 1999), 133.

It was on the sixth day that God made man, the day just before the Lord rested.[9] He had made the heavens; he had made the earth; he had made the sun; he had made the moon. He had made a spectacular pluriformity of living things—tiny fish and diving birds and trees hundreds of feet tall—but the apex of his work was not the terra firma of this planet, the dazzling sun in the sky, or the sea creature known as Leviathan. From time immemorial, the Lord had planned this moment, the moment when he would produce his greatest creation, his masterwork, the only being made in the "image" (*tselem*, Heb. צֶלֶם) and carrying the "likeness" (*demuth*, Heb. דְּמוּת) of God himself.[10] This was not true of the animals, marvelous as they are; it was not true of the celestial bodies, brilliant as they are; it was not true of the oceans, much as they roar. Humanity is the pièce de résistance of the holy work of God. Creatures roughly six feet tall with two eyes, two ears, and one nose, confined to the ground without wings to send them into the skies, unable to swim in the vast depths of the seas, formed on the sixth day.

---

[9] We need to read the six days of creation in conjunction with Exod 20:11. For an incisive survey of the historical discussion on the age of the earth, see William VanDoodewaard, *The Quest for the Historical Adam: Genesis, Hermeneutics, and Human Origins* (Grand Rapids: Reformation Heritage Books, 2015).

[10] See John F. Kilner, *Dignity and Destiny: Humanity in the Image of God* (Grand Rapids: Eerdmans, 2015), 128. I concur that we should not draw a strong distinction between the Hebrew terms for "image" and "likeness" in this text.

It is the speech of God that begets the man and the woman, not a cosmic accident.[11] The text focuses our attention on the nobility and beauty of the human race. The Lord already has given the call to "multiply" to the living creatures on the fifth day, and he calls his image-bearers to the same task. But the man's charge is unique: he must "rule" the living creatures, a commission that extends to the "whole earth," and one which advances as his seed multiplies. Mankind is not God; he is a mere creature, but a creature with a limitless charter. This small, nonflying, ungilled being has great responsibility and explosive potential. He is made by God to display God to the world God has formed. To one another, to the birds, to the heavens themselves, the human race is a testament to the reality of divinity. To look at man is to confront, however distantly, the Almighty.[12]

The first biblical words about the human race define the first man and woman in undeniably theological terms. Humanity is not made for the earth but is the creation of God; man is not an evolved product of the other creatures but is made by God

---

[11] "Gen 1, by further affirming the unique status of man, his place in the divine program, and God's care for him, gives a hope to mankind that atheistic philosophies can never legitimately supply." Gordon J. Wenham, *Genesis 1–15*, Word Biblical Commentary, vol. 1 (Dallas: Word, 1998), 40.

[12] "Gen. 1:26 is simply saying that to be human is to bear the image of God." Victor P. Hamilton, *The Book of Genesis: Chapters 1–17*, The New International Commentary on the Old Testament, vol. 1 (Grand Rapids: Eerdmans, 1990), 137. This is on the right track.

himself (Gen 2:7, 22). The Genesis account draws a clear and unmistakable line between the beasts of the field, the birds of the air, and the fish of the sea on the one hand and mankind on the other.[13] The former are made on one day; humanity is made on another.[14] Genesis 1 distinguishes between God-made creatures and does not draw genetic linkage of any kind between animal and mankind.[15]

It is nonetheless true that all beings have a common origin of existence: God's speech. The Word of God bears the very power of God. Life happens when God speaks. We are right to speak of creation ex nihilo, "from nothing," but we must also speak of

---

[13] Just as we must speak of a Creator-creature distinction (because this concept is the very first teaching of the Bible), so we must speak of a creature-creature or image-creature distinction. Man is not made to bludgeon the animal kingdom; he is the steward of it. To steward the other creatures, he must see himself as distinct from them. There is no animal or nonhuman creature "fit for him" (Gen 2:20).

[14] "Unlike animals, *man* is not broken down into species (i.e., 'according to their kinds' or 'all kinds of'), but rather is designated by sexuality: *male and female he created them.*" Hamilton, *The Book of Genesis*, 138. This points to the essential nature of sex in human identity.

[15] For an enthusiastic and thoughtful representation of the "hominid view," see Matthew Levering, *Engaging the Doctrine of Creation: Cosmos, Creatures, and the Wise and Good Creator* (Grand Rapids: Baker Academic, 2017), 155–63. Some theologians, seeking to bind together evolutionary science and the biblical creation account, have argued that the Lord may have allowed the hominid population to develop for thousands of years, only to choose a hominid couple for ensouling. This is a creative solution to the challenges of reconciling the natural world with the biblical account, but it fails to capture the direct nature of the formation of the first man and woman by God.

creation *in verbo*, "by word." There is no source of existence other than the revelation of the divine. From the words of God come the living things and the human race. Thus, the common origin between beast and man is not a gaseous pool in a Precambrian cosmos or any form of interspecies physical evolution. All things proceed from and inhere in God. His Word rules the day—more than this, it *makes* the day.

The Scripture has already drawn sharp ontological boundaries. This is true of humanity and the animals; it is also true of God and his creation. In this text, the created order is brimming with vitality and exploding with possibility. The world as made by God is not cold and lifeless, waiting for someone to bring a spark and a flame to unlit caverns. The world as made by God flashes with color and bursts with action. But this vibrant place is not God itself. The creation is distinct from the divine. Mankind, the apex of God's creative work, bears God's image and is God's own masterpiece; but humanity is not God, neither is the sun, the moon, the salamander, nor the volcano. And nowhere does the text indicate that God himself is in the created order. God's speech yields discrete beings and substances. Genesis 1 does not allow us to conclude that the thriving planet formed by the Creator *is* the Creator or is *in* the Creator in ontological terms, or that the Creator is himself in the planet. Taking the text at its word, God is God, the world is uniquely the world, and the creatures are discrete creatures.[16]

---

[16] This order is peaceable and tranquil, as Eugene Roop notes: "We find no strife in the world God is creating, no antagonism among the

All that is made belongs to God, but only God is God. Take away God, and nothing has form or shape. One of the chief ironies of an evolutionary approach to reality is that it inadvertently yields a cosmos that is self-directed. The non–higher power ends up being very much like a higher power; the propulsive force of evolution unintentionally functions as a quasi-theistic figure. Granted, the atheist does not personalize this force, but their principle of evolution becomes, at the very least, an impersonal law of life. Perhaps due to the vastness of the world and the universe beyond, it is extremely difficult to capture the origins of such a bustling system without reference to a transcendent force, whether personal or impersonal.

God himself made the human race. Such an affirmation may sound like a fairy tale or wishful thinking to some, but is this theory of planetary beginnings and, for our special purposes, human origins really that far-fetched? To be sure, Christianity requires faith. We confess this without apology or embarrassment. The Christian now sees "by faith, not by sight" (2 Cor 5:6–7). Of course, evolution requires far more faith than biblical

---

living creatures. In this picture of the peaceable kingdom, living creatures do not kill and eat other living creatures. Other texts describe differently the relationship between plants, animals, and people (e.g., Genesis 9). Nevertheless, this text affirms straightforwardly: God is creating a world without violence. Hence the concluding statement of assessment also serves as a benediction: *And God saw all that he made, and behold, it was very good* (v. 31)." Eugene F. Roop, *Believers Church Bible Commentary*, ed. Douglas B. Miller, vol. 1, *Genesis* (Scottdale, PA: Herald, 1987), 31–32.

Christianity.[17] In a Darwinian framework, mankind is not made or formed by any kind of higher intelligence. Mankind has no purpose. Man and woman, united but distinct, are cosmic accidents. There is no sharp differentiation between humanity and the animals, or humanity and any life-form. There can be no code of ethics or law of morality or purposeful spirituality to guide our conduct. There is no one to whom we may pray, no reason to be thankful for anything, and no hope at all of ultimate peaceful resolution.

In such a system, hope itself has no logical basis, neither does positivity, love, nor confidence in anything. Evolution is a well-worked-out and seemingly sturdy system of thought, but it is, as some have said, a closed box.[18] If there is no intention—or Intender, as it goes—behind the world, there is nothing higher than the world. There is only the world, and in the world, there is only the law of the jungle. If there appears to be "wonder" and "beauty" in the cosmos, this is only atoms colliding, symptomatic of nothing greater, nothing higher.

Although the logical basis for real affections seems suspect, many evolutionists live life as if it does have meaning and

---

[17] I think of the clever philosophical concept of a "properly basic belief" promoted by Alvin Plantinga, "Reason and Belief in God," in *Faith and Rationality*, ed. Alvin Plantinga and Nicholas Wolterstorff (Notre Dame, IN: Univ. of Notre Dame, 1983), 73–78.

[18] See the discussion in James Sire, *The Universe Next Door: A Basic Worldview Catalog*, 4th ed. (Downers Grove, IL: InterVarsity, 2004), 59–86. Sire interacts with Carl Sagan, Stephen Hawking, Julien Offray de la Mettrie, and others—and scores numerous points.

purpose. They love their children. They work hard. They sacrifice their own interests for no discernible gain. Freighted with sadness, they care for their fathers or mothers as their lives ebb, doing so without any real benefit to themselves.[19] The reason for such behavior is that mankind is made by God. We are not dust in the wind; we are not mere atoms colliding; we are not the products of chance. We are image-bearers. God made us.

This is the central truth of our existence, the first principle of our days. Our first father and mother heard the Lord commission them to rule and take dominion of all the earth. Ever since, humanity has heard a far-off echo of this holy mandate. We strive upward. We labor to carve our names in the earth. We try to "leave the world a better place than we found it." The image of God cannot help but image God: we relentlessly create and reproduce and subdue the earth, albeit in profoundly broken ways (more on this to come). We give ourselves over to love and care for others; we quest for the great answers of our world, despite the fact that twenty-first-century conventional wisdom has already told us there are no great answers to be found. There is only a purposeless, designless cosmos.

Although many mouth secularist cosmological and personal formulations, in their hearts they cheat. They treasure the

---

[19] I think of the example of utilitarian philosopher Peter Singer, who famously made the case for "nonhumans" but then lovingly cared for his mother when her faculties diminished due to Alzheimer's disease. See Peter Singer, *Practical Ethics* (Cambridge: Cambridge Univ. Press, 1993), 85–87; Michael Specter, "The Dangerous Philosopher," *New Yorker*, September 6, 1999, 46–50, 52–55.

wonder and mystery of this place, and act as if life is purposeful and meaningful. They do so because we are the image of God, and no one can erase this truth. We are stamped by God, and no one can scratch out the seal of God's making. Genesis 1 tells us why we were made, who made us, and what marks us out among all the living creatures.[20]

The Soul of Humanity

The moment Adam comes to life is mysterious and moving. In Gen 2:7, the Lord first forms the body of the man from the "dust" of the earth. Then he breathes life into him:

> Then the LORD God formed the man out of the dust from the ground and breathed the breath of life into his nostrils, and the man became a living being.

Notice the intention of the Lord's action here. Although some take these elegiac words as fictional poetry, they surely speak to the actual formation of Adam. God himself made Adam. The omnipotent one made a being from raw earthly material.[21] He

---

[20] "Gen 1, by further affirming the unique status of man, his place in the divine program, and God's care for him, gives a hope to mankind that atheistic philosophies can never legitimately supply." Wenham, *Genesis 1–15*, 40 (see intro., n. 11).

[21] "'Dust' as constitutive of human existence anticipates 3:19, where the penalty for the man's sin is his return to 'dust' (e.g., Job 34:15). While 'dust' may also show that man is fragile physically (e.g., Job 10:8–9; Ps

breathed into the body he made; the shape of the man's body reflected the Creator's interaction with him. He had nostrils so that God could breathe life into them. Adam was made according to the will and design of the Lord. His existence was God-derived, God-dependent, Godward in every sense.[22] By extension, mankind has a mind so that we may know the Lord.

It is only when the Lord breathed into this physical body that the man became a *nephesh* (נֶפֶשׁ) *haya* (הָיָה), a "living being." Here we learn as a surety that humanity is more than joints and bones, ventricles and pores. The man is not alive when he has structure and shape; he is alive when God breathes into him. The Lord does not breathe into the rabbit, the river, or the rising sun. The animals are "living beings" and have the "breath of life" (Gen 1:24, 30), but the man alone is an embodied soul who receives the breath of God. The man has a body formed by God himself. He is a soul, and the action of God breathes into him directly and personally.[23] This implies no tension or

---

103:14), the intent of the passage is the association of human life and the basic substance of our making." Kenneth A. Mathews, *Genesis 1–11:26*, The New American Commentary, vol. 1A (Nashville: B&H, 1996), 196.

[22] I concur with John Hartley, who notes, "'breath' establishes that humans continually and uniquely depend on God for their life force (Job 27:3). Whenever God takes the breath away, that person dies (Ps. 104:29–30)." John E. Hartley, *Genesis*, Understanding the Bible Commentary Series, vol. 1 (Peabody, MA: Hendrickson, 2000), 59.

[23] John Walton draws a parallel between Israelite and Egyptian cosmology on this point: "This idea occurs in early Egyptian literature, where the god Re puts breath into the nostrils of man, and in a late Egyptian text (second century AD), in which the breath of life causes all

ranking between body and soul, as was common in ages past, with the body being seen as evil. The fact that man is body and soul per the creative work of God means that Christians cannot adopt any gnostic vision that renders corporeality bad and the soul good. To the contrary, to state that we are an embodied soul is not to demean the body, but to recognize the importance of *both* the body and the soul.[24]

Theologians and exegetes have enjoyed a lively debate over this matter. Is the human person dichotomous—possessing a body and a soul—or trichotomous—possessing body, soul, and spirit? Jesus's words in Matt 10:28 and Mark 12:30 point us to the former conclusion, while Paul's words in 1 Thess 5:23 direct us to the latter. Though one's position on this matter should not

---

things to exist. The latter is similar to Israelite thinking, where people and animals both have the breath of life (Gen. 7:22)." John H. Walton, *Zondervan Illustrated Bible Backgrounds Commentary*, vol. 1, *Genesis, Exodus, Leviticus, Numbers, Deuteronomy* (Grand Rapids: Zondervan, 2009), 27.

[24] In recent years, some theologians have argued that humanity does not have a soul at all. Nancey Murphy argued for "nonreductive physicalism," the view that the human person is essentially physical, and that activities and properties commonly ascribed to the soul should be understood as "brain functions" in addition to other factors. See Nancey Murphy, *Beyond Liberalism and Fundamentalism: How Modern and Postmodern Philosophy Set the Theological Agenda* (Harrisburg, PA: Trinity, 1996), 135–53. Although Gregg Allison does not respond directly to Murphy's comments, his survey of positions regarding the composition of the human person is beneficial. See Gregg R. Allison, *Historical Theology: An Introduction to Christian Doctrine* (Grand Rapids: Zondervan, 2011), 321–41.

divide Christians and keep them from ecclesial fellowship, I believe it is best to understand humanity in dichotomous terms, as stated above.[25] It seems likely that Paul's comment to the Thessalonian church is not intended to introduce a third element of humanity, but to capture the totality of human experience. In a similar vein, when Jesus directs us to love the Lord with "heart, soul, mind, and strength," it seems unlikely that we should view "strength" as a fourth part of the human person.[26] Instead, Jesus is evoking different parts of our beings—we who are embodied souls—to capture just how devoted our love to God should be.[27]

However one understands this issue, Genesis 2 signals to us the dependence of humanity upon the Creator. From the outset, Scripture shows us that humanity's origin owes to God, and that our vitality—literally our inhalation and exhalation—comes from God.[28] Unless we dismiss Genesis 1–2 as fiction,

[25] Leon Morris says of the Matthew passage, "the whole person is body and soul," an instructive comment. Leon Morris, *The Gospel according to Matthew*, The Pillar New Testament Commentary (Grand Rapids: Eerdmans, 1992), 263.

[26] Mark Strauss notes that there is "significant overlap" among the terms Jesus uses, and that "it would be a mistake to distinguish sharply their meanings." This seems like a sound conclusion given other texts. Mark L. Strauss, *Exegetical Commentary on the New Testament*, ed. Clinton E. Arnold, vol. 2, *Mark* (Grand Rapids: Zondervan, 2014), 542.

[27] "Popular theology . . . thinks in terms of mankind *having* a soul, but the text (here and elsewhere) declares that he *is* a soul." Eugene H. Merrill, *Everlasting Dominion: A Theology of the Old Testament* (Nashville: B&H, 2006), 176.

[28] "Just as creation in the image of God marked the human beings as unique in the first creation account (1:26), the bestowal of the breath

we cannot miss the distinctly theocentric nature of humanity. In these chapters, we learn not only about the first moments of the human race, but we glean that we cannot understand humanity apart from the will and working of God. Our existence—both in terms of initiation and sustenance—depends upon the divine. We will say more in chapter 2, but it is important to note at this juncture that humanity is a covenantal race. The human person is a covenantal creature. We are made by God for relationship with God. Adam depended on the Lord and was never called to transcend this bond. Humanity was not made for isolation but for covenantal knowing, knowledge in the deepest and most joyous sense.

The Ontological Nature of the Image

Thus far we have sought to understand the nature of humanity by virtue of Genesis 1–2. We have seen that God personally made the man and tenderly gave him breath, bringing him to full vitality. Now, though, we need to probe the concept of the *tselem* (צֶלֶם), the "image." What, precisely, does our "image-ness" mean for our doctrine of humanity? Let us consider several leading views on the nature of image-bearing and suggest a synthesis.

---

of God brought them into a much closer relationship with God and rendered them compatible with him at a level enjoyed by no other creature." James McKeown, *Genesis*, The Two Horizons Old Testament Commentary, vol. 1 (Grand Rapids: Eerdmans, 2008), 32.

Theologians have several positions on the image. The first position is called the *substantive view*. According to advocates such as Millard Erickson, the image is a "definite characteristic or quality within the makeup of the human."[29] Various candidates come to the fore as the key "characteristic or quality" here: rationality, spirituality, morality, volitional freedom, and psychological similarity, for example. John Calvin offered the following as the "chief seat of the Divine image": "In the mind perfect intelligence flourished and reigned, uprightness attended as its companion, and all the senses were prepared and molded for due obedience to reason; and in the body there was a suitable correspondence with this internal order."[30] The mind is made for God, Calvin argued, and the body is formed for submission to God and fulfillment of divine tasks. Calvin's vision of rationality accords with the view held by Aquinas. "Rationality unto true knowledge" marks the human person as distinct from all other created beings.[31]

The second position is the *relational view*. According to theologians such as Karl Barth, man's image-bearing makes him uniquely fitted for relationship. Drawing off of the divine word in Gen 1:26—"let us make man in *our* image"—advocates argue

---

[29] Millard J. Erickson, *Christian Theology*, 3rd ed. (Grand Rapids: Baker Books, 2013), 460.

[30] John Calvin, *Genesis*, The Crossway Classic Commentaries (Wheaton, IL: Crossway Books, 2001), 24.

[31] Aquinas, *Summa Theologica: First Part of the Second Part*, ed. Anthony Uyl (Woodstock, ON, Devoted, 2018), 385–88. For a helpful synthesis of Aquinas's view, see Levering, *Doctrine of Creation*, 174–81.

that just as the three persons of the Trinity share relationship with one another, so humanity somewhat experiences what it means to be made in God's image through relationships. Barth wrote, "In God's own being and sphere there is a counterpart: a genuine but harmonious self-encounter and self-discovery; a free co-existence and co-operation; an open confrontation and reciprocity. Man is the repetition of this divine form of life; its copy and reflection." Because of this divine design, "these two male and female are to Him 'man' because they are one to Him."[32] God is fundamentally in relationship as a Trinity of persons; so human persons, made by the Trinitarian God, are by definition relational beings. Barth's foremost focus here was marriage, the man and the woman becoming "one flesh" per Gen 2:24.

The third position I call the *representative view* because it emphasizes that image-bearing means ruling the earth as a "vice-regent" of God. Theologians connect the command to rule in Gen 1:28 to the nature of mankind, and thus underline the conscious and intentional nature of human work as distinct from, say, the squirrel's industriousness. G. K. Beale connects the ancient Near East concept of image to the rule that God expected from mankind:

Ancient kings would set up images of themselves in distant lands over which they ruled in order to represent

---

[32] Karl Barth, *Church Dogmatics*, ed. G. W. Bromiley and T. F. Torrance, trans. J. W. Edwards, O. Bussey, and H. Knight, vol. 3, *Doctrine of Creation* (1958; New York: T & T Clark, 2007), 1:185.

their sovereign presence. For example, after conquering a new territory, the Assyrian king Shalmanesar "fashioned a mighty image of my majesty" that he "set up" on a black obelisk, and then he virtually equates his "image" with that of "the glory of Assur" his god. . . . Likewise, Adam was created as the image of the divine king to indicate that earth was ruled over by Yahweh.[33]

In Beale's handling, mankind *is* the image of God, the representative of God's authority in all the earth. But this is not a static representation; instead, the God-made man is to take dominion of all things, effectively putting representation into action. Adam and Eve reflected God's own activity by "subduing," "ruling," and "resting" according to Beale.[34]

Anthony Hoekema concurs to a significant degree with Beale. He argues that man was made to mirror and represent God. "When one looks at a human being," Hoekema avows, "one ought to see in him or her a certain reflection of God. . . . Man, then, was created in God's image so that he or she might represent God, like an ambassador from a foreign country."[35] Elsewhere Hoekema suggests that both the "structure" and the "functioning"

---

[33] G. K. Beale, *The Temple and the Church's Mission: A Biblical Theology of the Dwelling Place of God*, New Studies in Biblical Theology (Downers Grove, IL: InterVarsity, 2004), 82.

[34] G. K. Beale, *We Become What We Worship: A Biblical Theology of Idolatry* (Downers Grove, IL: InterVarsity, 2008), 128.

[35] Anthony A. Hoekema, *Created in God's Image* (Grand Rapids: Eerdmans, 1986), 67.

of humanity flavors our understanding of the image, which should "be seen as involving both the structure of man (his gifts, capacities, and endowments) and the functioning of man (his actions, his relationships to God and to others, and the way he uses his gifts). To stress either of these at the expense of the other is to be one-sided."[36]

We could delve into other notable perspectives—the Lutheran emphasis on righteousness lost and regained in Christ, for example—but the three previous perspectives possess primary relevance for the conversation at hand.[37] Beale and Hoekema have their own precise material on the relationship between identity and role, but both argue that "representation" explains the essence of the image. In my view, we best understand the image of God as an ontological reality that leads into function. Mankind is the representative of God on earth; to see a man or a woman is to see the only living creature made in the image of God. John Kilner captures this truth when he writes that in the ancient world, "the image represented someone or something, with significant implications for how the image should be viewed and treated."[38] The image, then, is not fundamentally a trait or attribute. Rather, humanity is made in the image of God. To see humanity is to see the likeness of God. The human race is

---

[36] Hoekema, 73.

[37] For a helpful distillation of Luther's view, see Marc Cortez, *Christological Anthropology in Historical Perspective: Ancient Contemporary Approaches to Theological Anthropology* (Grand Rapids: Zondervan, 2016), 83–109.

[38] Kilner, *Dignity and Destiny*, 120.

a living testimony to its Creator. The lordly nature of the human race in all the creation owes to the race's God-revealing status: "man's splendour is his likeness to God."[39]

The image, then, is not a quality which may wax or wane in a human person. The image is not dependent on a rationality-nurturing environment, for the image does not reduce to intelligence or powers of reason. The image is not inhibited by physical deficiencies, for the image does not derive from a certain bodily state. The image is not unlocked when a person gets married, for the image does not flow from personal relationship. Neither can we say that the image is lost or obscured or marred or in any way compromised by the fall of Adam, deformative as the fall is. Mankind is made in the image of God. The human race may recognize, celebrate, hate, or ignore this truth. It matters not. The human race is the race made to display the glory of God in all the earth in a special way. The human race reflects and represents the person of God even after the fall (Gen 5:1–2, 9). One person is no more an "image-bearer" than any other.[40]

In a closely related vein, we persons are not more or less human depending on our conduct, our views of God, or our moment-by-moment thinking. We may not feel as if we represent God on the earth, but we do. We may not believe that we display the excellency of the Creator in our being, but we do.

---

[39] D. J. A. Clines, "The Image of God in Man," *Tyndale Bulletin* 19 (1968): 54. We may observe a fruitful connection between the ideas of David Clines and those of Beale.

[40] For views that fall prey to this problem, see Kilner, *Dignity and Destiny*, 19–30.

We may not even wish to image God's glory—we may live as heathens, as animals, in ongoing projects of self-destruction— but such self-abnegation does not diminish our image-bearing nature or make us less human. Our identities, like the Word of God, are firmly fixed in the heavens. God has said who we are, and though we may rebel against him, we cannot change who humanity is or who we are. We may deny our creatureliness, but denial cannot undo the work of God. We may act as creatures of the wild, but we cannot become wild. The mark of God is immovable and on humanity; God has set his mark. Marc Cortez contributes helpfully here: "we need to view the *imago Dei* as a declaration that God intended to create human persons to be the physical means through which he would manifest his own divine presence in the world."[41]

The foregoing emphasizes the ontological nature of the image. The image in which we are made is a matter of our being, we might say. We represent God as his image-bearers. Of course, our ontological status does not in any way close us off from a rich understanding of the gifts God has given us as human persons, gifts of intellection and creativity, profoundly relational natures, distinctly moral existences, rich psychological lives, and personal freedoms, among others. Ontology does not stay still. It issues forth an active, purposeful, moral, volitional existence. We are not made to be doxological mannequins, static and staid in our

---

[41] Marc Cortez, *ReSourcing Theological Anthropology: A Constructive Account of Humanity in the Light of Christ* (Grand Rapids: Zondervan, 2017), 109.

otherworldly representation. We are made to be living displays of the intelligence and excellence and multifaceted capability of God. Clearly, this means ruling and subduing and multiplying, among other God-glorifying activities.

If the image should be understood in ontological terms, then—in terms of our very beings as humans—we cannot fail to link the image-bearing race with the imperatives of Gen 1:26–27 cited above. In denoting the various functions the image-bearing race may perform, we are not far from Hoekema's eclectic approach.[42] We surely are rational creatures, able to think and reason and know God mentally, as Calvin and Aquinas argued. We have the privilege of multiplying through marriage and living in relationship with a loved one, as Barth suggested. The significance of marriage in the metanarrative of the Bible reminds us of the priority accorded to it by the divine mind. The Bible begins with a human marriage and ends with a spiritual one. Our abilities, furthermore, to create and rule are front and center in meaningful human activity, particularly when performed with righteous and obedient hearts.

We may sum up the various God-pleasing functions of the human person with this phrase: *obedient worship*. Though the word *worship* does not occur in the first two chapters of Genesis, if we work from a canonical perspective that connects the Old Testament to the New, we recognize that the Scripture points

---

[42] See also Bruce A. Ware, "Male and Female Complementarity and the Image of God" in *Biblical Foundations for Manhood and Womanhood*, ed. Wayne Grudem (Wheaton, IL: Crossway Books, 2002), 76–79.

to worship as the very peak of human endeavor. Christ, we shall observe below, is nothing if not an obedient son, the true Son of God.[43] He is the image—the true image—of God (Col 1:15; 2 Cor 4:4). Jesus, we note, did not have to campaign to be the God-man. His obedience established him as who he was, but Jesus obeyed the Father because of who he was. In his very being, in his union of full humanity and full Godness, Jesus was and is the exact representation of the Father.[44] Nothing could change or diminish or alter his ontological identity. He was the true reflection of the divine, for he was and is divine.[45] We must press,

---

[43] On the importance of obedience in the life of Christ, see Brandon D. Crowe, *The Last Adam: A Theology of the Obedient Life of Jesus in the Gospels* (Grand Rapids: Baker Academic, 2017).

[44] Mankind is said to be the image of God in 1 Cor 11:7; we still do well to show sensitivity to the language of Genesis 1, and speak here of mankind being made in God's image. In the fullest biblical scope, man is the image of God per Paul, but Christ and Christ alone is the perfect image of God. Murray Harris captures this well in his comments on 2 Cor 4:4. "Given passages such as Phil. 2:6; Col. 1:19; 2:9, we may safely assume that for Paul εἰκών here, as in Col. 1:15, signifies that Christ is an exact representation *(Ebenbild)* as well as a visible expression of God. ἐστιν is a timeless present, indicating that Christ is eternally the perfect reflection of God or at least that in his glorified corporeality Christ remains forever God's visible expression." Murray J. Harris, *The Second Epistle to the Corinthians: A Commentary on the Greek Text*, New International Greek Testament Commentary (Grand Rapids: Eerdmans, 2005), 331.

[45] See F. F. Bruce's handling of Christ's imaging of God, which is very close to representative thinking regarding the nature of the image: "To say that Christ is the image of God is to say that in him the nature and being of God have been perfectly revealed—that in him the invisible

therefore, for an ontological (or representational) conception of both image (humanity) and true image (Jesus Christ).

Here as before, though, we must connect ontology with function. We do not blend these two philosophical categories in my view, but we do connect them because the Bible connects them. The image is an ontological reality, but the one who is made in the image of God will do certain things.[46] We think of how Jesus came to do the Father's will. He took on flesh, in other words, to give *embodied worship* to God. He does so by fulfilling the original mandate given to Adam: he rules the earth, and his physical rulership only points to his still-greater spiritual rulership. God clearly wants embodied worship, for he not only created humanity but sent his Son into the earth to do his works. We have strong reason, then, for drawing a line from obedience to worship; in Christ, the two concepts are virtually one. The God-man, John's Gospel shows, came to do the will of the Father (John 4:34; 6:38). Doing the will of the Father was not drudgery for the Son of God; such obedience was joyful, giving glory to the Father, and was without interruption. Jesus was the faithful Son who came to do what we will all do without interruption in the ages to come: he—a man with a God-given, God-created

---

has become visible." F. F. Bruce, *The Epistles to the Colossians, to Philemon, and to the Ephesians*, The New International Commentary on the New Testament (Grand Rapids: Eerdmans, 1984), 57–58.

[46] It is not the function that establishes the identity (ontology), although the function surely reinforces and even displays identity—the identity of the Son of God. Rather, the identity ensures that function will occur.

body—worshipped God in spirit and in truth. Every act he performed, every flicker of thought he had, and every word he said
were calibrated to obey and honor and reflect the splendor of the
one who sent him.

Worship is the end of humanity.[47] If we connect adoration
with obedience and service, we set ourselves up to understand
what eternity will involve. The theme of worship in the book
of Revelation is central and unmistakable. Worship is what the
twenty-four elders offer the crucified and resurrected Son at
all times (Rev 5:10). The last days bring about the fulfillment
of the Psalmist's promise, as the nations stream into the New
Jerusalem to worship the Lord (Ps 86:9; Rev 21:21–27). Jesus,
the true image, came to worship the Father through an obedient, dominion-taking life. He points us to the same: "The true
worshipers will worship the Father in Spirit and in truth. Yes, the
Father wants such people to worship him" (John 4:23).[48]

---

[47] G. K. Beale locates worship as that which Adam gave unto God
in his pre-fall state. In this paradigm, we are either worshipping self (and
Satan, ultimately), or God in Christ. We cannot help but worship; we
are worshipping creatures: "However, he not only exchanged worship of
God and proximity to God's demonstrated glory in the midst of Eden,
but he exchanged the actual divine glory that he personally reflected in
pristine manner. . . . On the other hand, those who have trusted in the
Lord . . . will not ultimately succumb to idolatry." Beale, *We Become What
We Worship*, 222–23.

[48] We experience the "fullness of God's gifts" through God, for our
access to God "is no longer mediated by all sorts of provisional and symbolic forms, but [is directed] by the Spirit of God himself," according to
Herman Ridderbos, *The Gospel of John: A Theological Commentary*, trans.
John Vriend (Grand Rapids: Eerdmans, 1997), 164.

We are made in the image of God. Christ is the "true" image, the obedient Son who came to embody the rule of God, and we are right to see ourselves as a living picture of the divine. As such, we live purposefully, having been given the original commission to rule the earth to the glory of God. But the Bible points us to a great and glorious reality as the text unfolds: all our ruling and subduing and procreating and dominion-taking express worship of the living God. This is what God most wants: obedient worshippers. The picture we gain of eternity to come shows the redeemed of God engaging in unceasing worship of God. Those made in God's image live (imperfectly) as the true image did in his incarnation: we obey as we worship, and we worship as we obey.

If we understand our image-bearing in these terms, we set ourselves up to live meaningful and joyful existences. Part of why many believers struggle to find grace in the ordinary workings of the day is they do not see their human existence as ordered around worshipful obedience. Worship, instead, seems to many an ecclesial activity. Worship takes place when the sound system is booming, the lights are off, and a praise band is playing. Accordingly, some people are "good" at worship, and some are not. Some are expressive and sing beautifully, and some do not. Some raise their hands high and are comfortable with public displays of emotion, and some are not. So it is with obedience: many believers have a truncated understanding of it and see it as drudgery, perhaps even hostile to the expressive self. Some allow (perhaps unwittingly) their doctrines of justification to overtake their doctrines of sanctification, and thus see obedience as that which Christ did, not what the Christ-follower does.

The human being was made to obey God. The human being was made for worship. All of us, even after the fall, retain our capacities for worship (though it is directed, as we shall see, to lesser and debased things). All of us are able by the restorative and redemptive grace of God to obey God with all our beings. Men and women are not robotic creatures by nature. We have been constituted by God, given minds and passionate hearts and bodies, and the Lord's good will for us is that we dedicate all our faculties and energies to living praise of him. This includes gathered worship, but it spills over into all our days, all our waking moments. Paul united these themes of worship and obedience elegantly in his letter to the Romans: "Therefore, brothers and sisters, in view of the mercies of God, I urge you to present your bodies as a living sacrifice, holy and pleasing to God; this is your true worship" (Rom 12:1). It is not explosive feeling that Paul identified as "true worship," but a life that is "holy and pleasing to God."[49] If we would worship God, we must be holy.[50] No other form of worship pleases the Lord.

---

[49] "The call to worship (λατρείαν) causes the theme of the letter to resurface, for the fundamental sin is the failure to worship . . . God. Those who worship God give their entire lives over to him so that he is honored and praised in everything they do." Thomas R. Schreiner, *Romans*, Baker Exegetical Commentary on the New Testament (Grand Rapids: Baker Academic, 1998), 646.

[50] "'Holy' is a regular description of sacrifices; it implies here that the offering of ourselves to God involves a being 'set apart' from the

The image, as we have said, does not reduce to a certain function, even a holy one. The image of God is an ontological reality. You are either in the image of God or not. A salamander is not; a rock is not; a waterfall, however beautiful, is not; a dog, though communicating real affection, is not. Only human beings are made in the image of God, and only Jesus Christ is the true image. Nothing we do can change these realities. But the image is not static. Those made in the image are made for action, for embodied worship through obedient rulership. Believers will live very different lives and will be called to very different means of God-glorification, but we may know that all of us are able, gifted, and responsible by the Spirit's power to live like the true *eikon*, Jesus Christ, and offer up a life of praise to God.

Comprehending the Spiritual
Element of the Christian Life

Mankind is spiritual and thus worshipful—for good or ill—by nature. Before we consider other aspects of human existence, we must nail this idea to the door: you can only understand man if you understand God. If you do not start with God, you will never comprehend man. If you do not begin with divine design, you can have no sure foundation for human dignity and human

---

profane and a dedication to the service of the Lord." Douglas J. Moo, *The Epistle to the Romans*, The New International Commentary on the New Testament (Grand Rapids: Eerdmans, 1996), 751.

uniqueness *at all*. There is no way to a sure and stable conception of the human race apart from the Bible. The Word of God alone tells us the truth on this and every matter it engages.

The Scriptures unlock our capacities for the worship of the living God by teaching us about the soul. The Bible does not expressly define the soul, but it speaks of it throughout the canon. When David and Jonathan reached the richest stage of friendship, they were so close as to be joined together: "The soul of Jonathan was knit to the soul of David, and Jonathan loved him as his own soul" (1 Sam 18:1 ESV). The soul is fitted for the strongest passions of existence—in this case, friendship of a transcendent kind. (Discussion of whether David and Jonathan had some kind of illicit relationship reveals just how enfeebled our conception of friendship is.) In Ps 103:1, the soul in its fullness praises the Lord: "My soul, bless the LORD, / and all that is within me, bless his holy name." The Virgin Mary voices similar joy in God upon learning the wondrous news that she will bear the Messiah:

> My soul praises the greatness of the Lord,
> and my spirit rejoices in God my Savior,
> because he has looked with favor
> on the humble condition of his servant. (Luke 1:46–48)

The fact that a humble young woman, untrained in theology, could nonetheless delight in God in her soul shows us that the soul is not a far-off matter. It is of vital importance to proper self-understanding. It is *us*.

We think here of the first and greatest commandment given us by Christ: "Love the Lord your God with all your heart, with all your soul, and with all your mind" (Matt 22:37). The Lord has given us the ability to know him through our affections, through our spiritual capacities, through our analytical abilities. We are beings, the text makes clear, whom God summons to knowledge and closeness. We are *spiritual* beings. As stated above, this need not entail any radical disjuncture between the body and the soul. We are embodied spiritual beings. The body, in fact, is very much incorporated into our worship of God. We *must* present our bodies to God as acceptable worship (Rom 12:1), worship that takes place every second of every day for the believer. But our bodies alone cannot grant us access to God. We are souls, and we have the distinct gift of a body. It is this unique constitution, formed and ordered by God himself, that enables us to worship the Lord in the fullness of our beings. The ensouled nature of humanity accounts for the spiritual character of our beings.

The stakes on this point are very high. Our ensouled natures require that we will exist eternally in either heaven or hell. Of course, we go astray (more on this in chapter 2), but all who are in Christ and redeemed by the blood of the Lamb must take stock of the conflict that is not only all around us, but zeroed in on us. The apostle Peter urges his readers "as strangers and exiles to abstain from sinful desires that wage war against the soul" (1 Pet 2:11). The soul, which often stands in for the whole human person in the biblical mind, is under attack. Shockingly the attack comes primarily from within, and the wages of gratifying fleshly desire are the loss of the battle: eternal damnation. Even after the body expires and wastes away, the soul endures. John sees this in his spectrascope vision of the apocalypse: "I also saw the souls of those who had been beheaded because of their testimony about Jesus and because of the word of God, who had not worshiped the beast or his image, and who had not accepted the mark on their foreheads or their hands" (Rev 20:4). The bodies of the martyrs suffered violence and decayed. Their souls, however, lived on. In time, God will put together what man has split asunder.

The breathtaking scenes found in texts such as Revelation 20 show us the high stakes of ensouled existence. This world, we learn, is definitively not all there is. We hear this refrain constantly today: we live, we die, we go into the ground. Everything fades to black. This common way of thinking conveniently excuses mankind from any call to transcendence, or even a basic ethical framework. Many people operate by a loose version of this theme, using it to forswear any greater personal accountability and to follow their basic desires without guilt. If you close off the external supernatural—denying the existence of a divine being in any form—and the internal supernatural—denying that the conscience points us to a higher authority—then you attempt to see existence in exclusively earthly terms. But this will not do; both Bible and conscience counter such thinking. Every life is lived between God and the devil. Every existence is spiritual, teleological, and eschatological—and this means everyone is headed somewhere.

Mankind is not merely corporeal. Mankind is made in the image of God. This is the first truth about humanity. You cannot understand mankind without it. The human person is a complex being, and spirituality—the capacity to know ultimate reality, that is, God—is at the core of the human essence. Our identities as human beings are constituted by God. We can commune with God because we are covenantal beings, made to be known, formed for relationship, and never intended for isolation and dissolution. When through divine grace we come to faith in Christ and enter covenant with Christ, our souls—we ourselves—have awakened. Previously, we did not care for our souls. Previously, we did not think of our bodies as vehicles for God-honoring worship. But now we are alive to God. Now all our being functions as God intended. Now we pray, we worship, we mourn, and we rejoice *in God*. Adam was made a living being when God breathed into him. We are made spiritually living beings—our souls turning to God for the first time—when the Spirit births repentance and faith in us.

When the Immanent Swallowed Transcendence

The Bible, when allowed to speak, produces a crystalline picture of the human person. In no other system or worldview does humanity have such luster, such promise, such dignity. Yet this enchanted vision has received fierce pushback in the West. In recent centuries, philosophers and theologians have staged an intellectual revolution against the nature of humanity. First, Western thinkers downplayed miracles. They reduced reality to that which can be empirically verified. Next, they assaulted supernaturalism itself. The idea that God was necessary to existence was challenged. This fit neatly with a reworked understanding of the cosmos. The creation lost its createdness as the Bible's historicity and accuracy came under serious fire, even in evangelical circles.[51]

In the latest phase of this long and systemic disenchantment, mankind is drained of meaning. The human race (building off of the foregoing ideas) has no inherent design. Anthropology bears no teleology. Humanity is a blank slate with no script for existence beyond mere impulse and desire. There is no ought, for there is no ought-giver. There is no *is*, in the stable sense. Humanity has become a fabrication, not a creature. Orientation and consent and self-construal remain to define us, and even these may change at a moment's notice.

This does not mean, however, that mankind no longer strives for greater significance to guide our lives. We still want our existences to matter, despite an ateleological natural realm that gives us no reason for such a desire. In times such as ours, man is

---

[51] These are major developments that would take considerable space to identify. For starters, consult A. N. Wilson, *Charles Darwin: Victorian Mythmaker* (New York: Harper, 2017); Philipp Blom, *A Wicked Company: The Forgotten Radicalism of the European Enlightenment* (New York: Basic, 2010). George Marsden has traced these shifts in the academy in *The Soul of the American University: From Protestant Establishment to Established Nonbelief* (Oxford: Oxford Univ. Press, 1994). See also George Marsden, *Twilight of the American Enlightenment: The 1950s and the Crisis of Liberal Belief* (New York: Basic Books, 2014).

the measure of all things. The so-called death of God does not mean the lights go out in the cosmos. The death of God means the ascendance of man, albeit detheologized man. We take the spiritual capacities and personal gifts endowed by the Creator for the worship of his holy name, and we turn them to self-glorification. We do not give up on spirituality (at least many of us do not); rather, we spiritualize ourselves, our lusts, our identities, our causes. What follows are, in brief, four modern cultural examples of such a shift.

One example is the spiritualizing of sexuality. Whether thinkers and influencers use religious language or not, they seek their own conceptions of this project. The movement to normalize and promote neopagan sexual identity and practices offers a fully realized anthropology and eschatology embedded within it. If we embrace our raw desires and reconceive our bodies according to our true identities, then we ourselves will be fulfilled. As Michel Foucault said, sex is "the explanation for everything," and "more important than our soul."[52] The implication of this teaching is that our culture must divorce itself from traditional inhibitions and realize a sexually enlightened, judgment-free society. The motivation, the quest for justice, bends toward sexualized wholeness; and those who do not join this quest win rejection of the sternest kind. In an age when man is the measure of all things, we enchant our lives by enlarging our desires and making them the very measure of our authentic existence.

---

[52] Michel Foucault, *The History of Sexuality*, vol. 1, *An Introduction*, trans. Robert Hurley (1978; New York: Vintage Books, 1990), 78, 156.

Others focus their spiritual attention on the made universe, in particular the earth. Naturalistic environmentalism replaces Christian theology. This worldview believes in eternal matter (instead of an eternal Maker), evolution (instead of divine will), and manmade obsolescence (instead of John's apocalypse). Despite the fact that this thinking allows no metaethics or metaphysics, adherents of this view seek the salvation of the physical earth and condemn in chiliastic terms those who do not join them. Saving the earth means awakening to the unity of all creation and sharing consciousness with every living being. Environmentalism is spirituality; spirituality is (in truth) environmentalism.[53]

There is even a Christianized version of the secular reenchantment heresy. According to prosperity theology—which does not so much deny standard biblical doctrines as reframe them—the story of history is really us.[54] The Bible is not fundamentally about God, at least in the way prosperity teachers preach. The Bible is fundamentally about us. The way to true happiness is reaping financial rewards and owning nice things—while also experiencing lasting "favor" and apprehending said niceties. We glimpse here the human instinct for greatness and transcendence. This project, to be clear, is not focused on the Lord. The *telos* (τέλος) of this school is our own happiness.

---

[53] See Matthew Fox, *Original Blessing: A Primer in Creation Spirituality* (1983; New York: Tarcher/Putnam, 2000), 15–16.

[54] The best-known (and best-selling) book of this ilk is Joel Osteen, *Your Best Life Now: 7 Steps to Living to Your Full Potential* (Nashville: FaithWords, 2004).

Such self-focused Judeo-Christian consumerism is not different from the self-driven spirituality of our age.[55] The province of traditional religion is in some form the following of God's will, which usually entails the subservience of the individual to the divine or a divine-like principle. But the typical Western person seeking "balance" or practicing self-realization through "the secret" or other such methods is not actually trying to serve God—or even the gods—in any focused way.[56] Though they disclaim belief in traditional religion driven by authorities embedded in crusty hierarchies, the spiritual seekers among us flock to teachers and guides, paying handsomely for the privilege of eating "clean" food and practicing yoga in a sweaty studio. Spirituality persists, but this is a spiritualized self-help, not the joyfulness of all-of-life Christianity.

Each of the previous views functions as a working belief system. These theologies, whether they center around the person of God or not, brand themselves as antiauthoritarian and bereft of the trappings of traditional religion; but all are in truth religious. In each worldview there is a goal and a purpose behind human existence, and gurus and teachers who will open the way to us. It is striking that we are all nonconformists now, happily following the leads of our chief contrarians. Perhaps (we cannot fail to

---

[55] For context, see Peter Jones, *The Gnostic Empire Strikes Back: An Old Heresy for the New Age* (Phillipsburg, NJ: P&R, 1992), 24–26.

[56] As one wildly popular example of such ideology, see Rhonda Byrne, *The Secret* (New York: Atria, 2006).

note) true rebellion and true self-realization come from recognizing our creatureliness, and not fighting against it.

None of the foregoing visions makes good on its promises. Nothing and no one can imbue our lives with hope and direct our days to a logical, sensible, truthful end. Nothing and no one on the earth can reenchant humanity. This only God can do. By this we mean that only God can show us just how noble human origins are, and just how lofty are the heights God would have us reach. But the pathway to this superlative end does not come in the way we might think, or in the manner we have been trained to expect. We cannot start with platitudes that inflate our self-esteem. In recapturing human worth and human dignity, we begin where the Bible begins: with mankind, made in the image of God, beholden to the holy Lord, who alone is transcendent and holy and great. Rediscovering God—who is in no way dead—enables us to rediscover the wondrous reality of worshipping the Lord in spirit and truth. We welcome the rediscovery of the soul, and we see ourselves embodied souls. We let our hearts savor divine creation, and we see God as the fountain of our gifting, the reason for our loving, and the purpose behind our doing.

Our purpose as human beings is not to exist for ourselves. Our purpose is to be living doxology, living glory to God. We think of the masterful theological reflection of Jonathan Edwards, the great pastor-theologian of the colonial period:

It appears that all that is ever spoken of in the Scripture as an ultimate end of God's works is included in that one phrase, *the glory of God*. . . . In the creature's knowing, esteeming, loving, rejoicing in, and praising God, the glory of God is both *exhibited* and *acknowledged*; his fullness is received and returned. Here is both the emanation and remanation. The refulgence shines upon and into the creature, and is reflected back to the luminary. The beams of glory come from God, are something of God, and are refunded back again to their original. So that the whole is of God and in God, and to God; and God is the beginning, middle, and end in this affair.[57]

In this fulsome and technical exposition, we glimpse the end for which God created us. We are not the end, we note; it is God who is the purpose of all things. We exist for his glory. We "receive" and "return" his glory through knowing and adoring our Maker and Redeemer. We live only by his allowance, and we love him only by his decree. So far from being a project of self-expression and internalized meaning, life is one grand affair of the godly kind. It is all from God, in God, and to God. It is not self-discovery that we seek; it is God-exaltation that we crave. In such an existence, we not only find the deepest happiness there is, but—if we may blend the wisdom of Calvin and Edwards momentarily—we find who we are and what we were intended to be.

Edwards sends us down the right path. It is not possible to repristinate humanity without respect to the biblical God. All

---

[57] Jonathan Edwards, "The End for Which God Created the World," in *The Works of Jonathan Edwards*, ed. Paul Ramsey, vol. 8, *Ethical Writings* (New Haven, CT: Yale Univ. Press, 1989), 529.

other attempts, however well-intentioned, will fail. All the world
has being and exists because of the Lord. There is no way back to
a shining, shimmering vision of humanity without God. There
is no way to understand humankind without God. There is no
secular bargain we can strike; there is no way to preach and agitate for human flourishing outside of a high vision of God. But
with God in proper perspective, we gain afresh a right-sized conception of his greatest creation: the human race. God has acted.
God has spoken. It is this speech, as Carl Henry understood,
that constitutes reality: "Judeo-Christian religion worships the
God who takes the initiative—who plans, creates, judges, reveals
and redeems—not some divinity, perhaps ultimately unknow-
able, that man is left to discern by his own ingenuity." It is "The
God of Abraham, Isaac and Jacob" who "is the active, speaking
God" who enables us to know ourselves even as we know him.
With divine revelation, we can know God's own mind. Without
divine revelation, we can know nothing.[58]

The Bible's first words about humanity tell us what we must
know, as a matter of first principles, about the human person:

So God created man
in his own image;
he created him in the image of God;
he created them male and female. (Gen 1:27)

[58] Carl F. H. Henry, *God, Revelation and Authority*, vol. 1, *God Who Speaks and Shows—Fifteen Theses* (1976; Wheaton, IL: Crossway Books, 1999), 62.

This is the first step toward the reenchantment of humanity. By rediscovering the theological nature of humanity in the biblical text, we prepare ourselves to rise from the primordial ooze. Mankind is not an accident; mankind is the special creation of almighty God. By recapturing the biblical account of human origins, we recapture human dignity, human worth, and our own identities.

CHAPTER 2

DEPRAVITY

From Mans effeminate slackness it begins,
Said th' Angel, who should better hold his place
By wisdome, and superiour gifts receav'd.
                              —John Milton, *Paradise Lost*

There is no tragedy like the tragedy of the historical fall of the
human race. Biblical Christianity brooks no rivals when it
comes to this momentous event. The fall of Adam and Eve following the creation of the world is symphonic in its terribleness.
Man throws himself from the highest peak, becoming a trans-
gressor in actuality and in nature by his disobedience.

We take the fall for granted in Christian circles, perhaps. Other worldviews and belief systems contain no such epic event. In evolutionary thought, for example, no such fall occurs; "nature has always run red in tooth and claw."[1] Things go awry because the gene is inherently selfish, as Richard Dawkins has argued.[2] Where instinct ends and morality begins is difficult to discern in such a framework. The Christian story of the world allows for no such murkiness. With a bang, the Bible introduces us to a

---

[1] Alfred, Lord Tennyson, *In Memoriam A. H. H.*, canto 56, st. 4. There is within Christian circles a lively discussion over whether God used evolution to achieve his purposes. The scientific discussion is a complex one; for sound material on the doctrinal challenges "theistic evolution" poses to traditional Christian doctrine, see Wayne Grudem, "Theistic Evolution Undermines Twelve Creation Events and Several Crucial Christian Doctrines" in *Theistic Evolution: A Scientific, Philosophical, and Theological Critique*, ed. J. P. Moreland, Stephen C. Meyer, Christopher Shaw, Ann K. Gauger, and Wayne Grudem (Wheaton, IL: Crossway, 2017), 783–837.

[2] Dawkins promotes the idea that the gene is a "survival machine." His framework for life is remarkably amoral and chilling to contemplate in terms of the conclusions to which it leads: "To a survival machine, another survival machine (which is not its own child or another close relative) is part of its environment, like a rock or a river or a lump of food. It is something that gets in the way, or something that can be exploited. It differs from a rock or a river in one important respect: it is inclined to hit back. This is because it too is a machine that holds its immortal genes in trust for the future, and it too will stop at nothing to preserve them. Natural selection favours genes that control their survival machines in such a way that they make the best use of their environment. This includes making the best use of other survival machines, both of the same and of different species." Richard Dawkins, *The Selfish Gene*, 30th anniv. ed. (Oxford: Oxford Univ. Press, 2006), 66.

serpent, a wavering couple, and a real and destructive fall of the human race.

The Christian vision of humanity is exalted. Never is the value of the human race more obvious than when we take stock of biblical anthropology. This is the recovery of the "enchanting" of humanity. This enchantment begins with the concept of the *imago Dei*, a true idea that is unsurpassed as a force for dignity and value. Scripture teaches us that human beings have intrinsic value granted us from on high. God made us; God made us in his image; God has a special relationship with the human race. We do not need to pursue extrinsic value—the granting of worth from outside forces, the quest that we naturally undertake in our fallen pursuit of dignity. All that we need, we have, though in Adam we have lost sight of this precious truth.

Here we arrive at an irony of biblical doctrine. The same Scripture that tells us we have infinite worth also tells us we have lost God. Christianity does not speak of only one side of mankind, affirming it as without blemish or failing. We build out a comprehensive doctrine of the human person from all of Scripture, and thus all of theology. This means that we must simultaneously savor the significance of man as the image of God even as we square with the sordid sorrowfulness of personal depravity. This may seem counterintuitive to some—surely, if we are to "reenchant" humanity, then we will speak only positively and offer affirmation of a needy race? Such wonderings depend upon a fiction. We cannot leave our terrible state by positivity alone. We must know the truth about ourselves. If we would rise from the ashes, then we must know why we are here and why we are so innately sinful and selfish, and thus position ourselves to marvel at the mercy of God in Christ. So we do now.

The Serpent's Antiwisdom

Genesis 3 gives us the true story of the fall of the human race. We examine this chapter now to understand what has gone wrong with mankind, a matter that requires careful attention if we are to grasp afresh how this benighted race may rise once more.

> Now the serpent was the most cunning of all the wild animals that the LORD God had made. He said to the woman, "Did God really say, 'You can't eat from any tree in the garden'?"
>
> The woman said to the serpent, "We may eat the fruit from the trees in the garden. But about the fruit of the tree in the middle of the garden, God said, 'You must not eat it or touch it, or you will die.'"
>
> "No! You will not die," the serpent said to the woman. "In fact, God knows that when you eat it your eyes will be opened and you will be like God, knowing good and evil." (Gen 3:1–5)

The account of the origin of human evil begins with the subversion of the created order.[3] In Gen 1:26 and 1:28, the man and

---

[3] "The fall of humanity . . . was engineered by a complete reversal of the divine design. Instead of God's authority being mediated from

woman are called to "rule . . . the creatures that crawl on the earth." The serpent, one of the wild animals made by God, was formed on the sixth day, just as humanity was. The Lord had taken pains to provide for such creatures, having given them "every green plant" for their sustenance (Gen 1:30).[4] The serpent was not made by God to stalk and devour fellow animals, but to enjoy the good gift of the Creator who revealed himself to be Sustainer as well. But this is just what the snake did on the day when Adam fell: he hunted the man who was made to rule over him.[5]

Adam to Eve to the rest of creation, the biblical fall narrative recounts how the Serpent (Satan) approached Eve, who took the initiative, with Adam following her lead, in breaking God's commandment." Andreas J. Köstenberger and Margaret E. Köstenberger, *God's Design for Man and Woman: A Biblical-Theological Survey* (Wheaton, IL: Crossway Books, 2014), 41.

[4] There is a lively debate among theologians over the possibility of animal death due to predation in the pre-fall creation. It is instructive, if not definitive, that the biblical text here speaks to the means of sustenance for even the animals. For the opposite view, see Ronald E. Osborn, *Death Before the Fall: Biblical Literalism and the Problem of Animal Suffering* (Downers Grove, IL: InterVarsity, 2014).

[5] Mathews calls attention to the numerous distortions and fabrications of the divine command offered by the serpent here: "First, the opponent does not controvert outright the saying of the Lord (2:16); rather, he questions God's motivation with the subtle addition 'really say.' Second, the serpent uses the name 'God' rather than the covenant name 'LORD' that has characterized the narrative of 2:4–25, where 'LORD God' appears. Third, the serpent reworks the wording of God's command slightly by (1) adding the negative 'not' at the head of the clause, which with 'any' expresses an absolute prohibition; (2) omitting the emphatic

Adam and Eve would not have been confused about God and his desires. The first words of the Lord spoken to humanity in Genesis 2 express God's moral law. Before the woman came into being, the Lord gave the man the following command and prohibition: "You are free to eat from any tree of the garden, but you must not eat from the tree of the knowledge of good and evil, for on the day you eat from it, you will certainly die" (Gen 2:16–17). The sentence structure is noteworthy here; it matters for discussions of the agency of the human person.[6] Adam first learns that he is "free" to consume food from any tree; the Lord's communication to him centers in the bounty spread before him.[7] With this boundless gifting noted, the Lord prohibited Adam

---

'freely'; (3) using the plural 'you' (hence bypassing the man) rather than the singular as in 2:16; and (4) placing the clause 'from any tree' at the end of the sentence rather than at the head as in 2:16, thereby robbing God's command of its nuance of liberality. All of this is to say that the divine injunction in the mouth of the serpent was refashioned for its own interests." Mathews, *Genesis 1–11:26*, 235 (see chap. 1, n. 20).

[6] "As God had given the natural world and all life-forms boundaries, human life too is instructed to live within prescribed boundaries." Mathews, 210.

[7] R. Kent Hughes captures the liberation given to the man: "God's word to him was first *permissive*: 'And the LORD God commanded the man, saying, "You may surely eat of every tree of the garden"' (v. 16). Adam was to partake of everything in the garden to his heart's content, which included the tree of life. This is lavish, extravagant abundance, and Adam could take from the tree of life if he wanted it. Everything was there for him—everything he could possibly want." R. Kent Hughes, *Genesis: Beginning and Blessing*, Preaching the Word (Wheaton, IL: Crossway Books, 2004), 54–55.

from eating the forbidden tree's fruit. It is clear that Yahweh did not fear Adam assuming a moral understanding of the world. His command and prohibition show that Adam is fundamentally a moral being, but Adam was not to seek knowledge that was not his right to possess.

Here, before the fall, is a sure sign of human contingency and dependency. The man was not an end to himself. He did not have all the rights and privileges that the Lord had. He lived in freedom, and his responsibility to obey the Lord was a real responsibility.[8] Still, we are right to speak of Adam's freedom as circumscribed.[9] Human freedom in the biblical mind does not consist of leaping all fences and demolishing all boundaries. It certainly does not mean separating oneself from any divine influence. Freedom in Genesis 2 looks like obedience (and thus humility).[10] Mankind at his freest does not volunteer his

---

[8] "Adam was like God in his person, an intellectual, moral, voluntary being different from beasts. Man was put at the culmination of the Creation, a self-conscious being, a spiritual self-governing and self-determining." This strong language from such a revered Calvinist theologian suggests that Warfield put real effort into capturing Adamic responsibility before the Lord. See Fred G. Zaspel, *The Theology of B. B. Warfield: A Systematic Summary* (Wheaton, IL: Crossway Books, 2010), 400.

[9] Mathews suggests that "freedom has no meaning without prohibition; the boundary for Adam is but one tree." This is sound. But this is no soft-edged prohibition; its form mirrors that used in the Ten Commandments. Mathews, *Genesis 1–11:26*, 212.

[10] Luther considers Adam's charge as that of continual "worship" before the Lord. There is a link here between the nature and charge of man as laid out in the previous chapter. "It is moreover very profitable

thoughts to God; he is silent before God, listening to the expression of the divine will, receiving from the Lord direction and guidance. Adam was not responsible for formulating his own morality, his own outlook on death. He was told, succinctly and straightforwardly, that if he transgressed God's law he would die. The man was free, but he did not even speak as he learned this. He was utterly dependent on divine sustenance and divine disclosure in his freedom.

There is much more to say on this score, but given how controverted discussions of human liberty are, we do well to ponder Genesis 3 anew. Before Adam sins, before we learn of God's foreknowledge, predestination, and election, we observe that the man is wholly subject to the terms God has laid out. He does not make his own destiny, in Eden or outside it. The idea that Adam was a free agent in spiritual terms before the fall is a myth, though he did truly face a moral test in Eden. Mankind is and always has been a contingent being; mankind is and always has

---

to consider from this text that God gave unto Adam a Word, a worship and a religion, the most simple, most pure and most disencumbered of all laborious forms and sumptuous appearance. For God did not command the sacrificing of oxen, nor the burning of incense, nor long and loud prayers, nor any other afflictions or wearyings of the body. All that he willed was, that Adam should praise him, should give him thanks, and should rejoice in him as the Lord his God; obeying him in this one great thing that he ate not the fruit of the forbidden tree." Martin Luther, *Genesis Commentary: Chapters 1–4*, trans. John Nicholas Lenker and Henry Cole (Aurora, CO: Everyone's Luther, 2017), 145. The point is plain: Adam was free in the garden, but we should understand this freedom as the freedom to obey the Lord.

been fully dependent on God for existence, for moral insight, and for knowledge itself.[11] Bonhoeffer says of the divine prohibition, "The limit is grace because it is the basis of creatureliness and freedom."[12] By this limit, this command, Adam knows a key part of his identity. So it will be with all divinely ordered "limits" to human identity.[13]

But mankind is not only a contingent being. The human person is a covenantal being. We are made, as introduced in chapter 1, for fellowship with the living God.[14] Adam's world is structured in covenantal terms: in the beginning, there are covenant partners: God and humanity. The Lord details his requirements, explaining what will follow from obeying or disobeying

---

[11] "Precisely as *natural* to humankind, the moral law was not an external authority imposed from without expressing abstract commands, but the expression of God's own personal character that he communicated, albeit analogically, to his image-bearer." Michael S. Horton, *Lord and Servant: A Covenant Christology* (Louisville: Westminster John Knox, 2005), 133.

[12] *The Bonhoeffer Reader*, ed. Clifford J. Green and Michael P. DeJonge (Minneapolis: Fortress, 2013), 233.

[13] This entire discussion assumes that Adam was a real historical person. For interaction with theologians who deny or question the historicity of Adam, see Henri Blocher, *Original Sin: Illuminating the Riddle*, New Studies in Biblical Theology (Downers Grove, IL: InterVarsity, 1997), 48–56. If we loosen the historicity of Adam, we cannot help but loosen the historicity of Christ, which in turn loosens the historicity of our Christic salvation.

[14] Barth homes in on the uniqueness of humanity when he notes that "the distinctiveness of this creature consists in the fact that it is for God." Barth, *Doctrine of Creation*, 1:70 (see chap. 1, n. 31).

his teaching. Adam clearly has a representative role relative to the human race and thus functions as a covenant head. It is important to identify the "covenant with creation" in terms of the biblical metanarrative and scriptural superstructure, for the historical Adam is one of two federal heads introduced in the Bible, the other being the (equally historical) Lord Jesus Christ.[15]

But the importance of affirming the covenantal nature of Adam's role and identity extends beyond to a proper conception of the nature of humanity. The human person is not constituted a lone ranger or a cosmic outlier. The Lord himself calls the man and the woman into relationship with him.[16] The fall, then, is not merely a finger in the eye of God. The fall is a

---

[15] There is significant and justifiable conversation among theologians over the "covenant with creation." For a short but potent justification for this reading of Adam's status before the Lord, see Thomas R. Schreiner, *Covenant and God's Purpose for the World*, Short Studies in Biblical Theology (Wheaton, IL: Crossway Books, 2018), 19–29. See also Peter J. Gentry and Stephen J. Wellum, *God's Kingdom through God's Covenants: A Concise Biblical Theology* (Wheaton, IL: Crossway Books, 2015), 257–63.

[16] John Frame elegantly frames the concept of covenantal knowledge: "God's lordship is a deeply personal and practical concept. God is not a vague abstract principle or force but a living person who fellowships with His people. He is the living and true God, as opposed to all the deaf and dumb idols of this world. Knowledge of Him, therefore, is also a person-to-person knowledge. God's presence is not something that we discover through refined theoretical intelligence. Rather, God is unavoidably close to His creation. We are involved with Him all the time." John M. Frame, *The Doctrine of the Knowledge of God: A Theology of Lordship* (Phillipsburg, NJ: P&R, 1987), 17.

rejection of the special connection mankind possessed through Adam with its Creator. Following the fall, we seek relationship in fallen ways, unable in ourselves to lay hold of the joy and satisfaction intended for us in living communion with the living Lord. What riches we forfeited in Adam. Instead of trusting the true covenant lord and living in what Michael Horton calls "genuine freedom and partnership," Adamic humanity sought a new authority, one who keeps no covenant.[17] From this choice comes the loss of a trustworthy and kind head, the living God, and a new and terrible obeisance to the anti-God, the serpent, who trades freedom for slavery and partnership for abuse.

We return to Gen 3:1–5. The serpent, we learn here, was "cunning."[18] Without any explanation or backstory, the evil animal speaks to the woman. The serpent's words matter, but so too does this conversation itself. The man is to lead his wife; she is made from his body, and he named her. But the man does not act here; he does not speak and rebuke the snake as he should have, summoning his strength and God-delegated authority to do so. The serpent, representing Satan, has already subverted the created order.[19] The man is the one God holds responsible for leadership of the earthly home, as the man and the woman

---

[17] Horton, *Lord and Servant*, 132.

[18] Victor Hamilton notes that the translation "crafty" would work well. The serpent does indeed show terrible craftiness in his ability to rework the Lord's command. Hamilton, *The Book of Genesis*, 187 (see chap. 1, n. 12).

[19] See Henri Blocher, *In the Beginning: The Opening Chapters of Genesis* (Downers Grove, IL: InterVarsity, 1984), 142–43.

together must rule over the creation. In the fall, however, the creation seeks rule over the woman, tempting her in turn to lead her husband, as she does. The fall of Adam and Eve is not merely the story of them biting into forbidden fruit. It is the unraveling of the good and gracious order of God.[20] It is the first instance of mankind voluntarily succumbing to the subversion of God's good purposes.

The serpent executes two attacks against God and man in this passage. He lies about the Lord's instructions to Adam, and Eve's response shows that she is already softening in her understanding of God's direction.[21] He then directly defies the testimony of the Creator, accusing the Lord of spreading falsehood and giving the woman a false vision of fruit-eating.[22] If the woman eats the fruit, she will not die but will become like God and possess the knowledge of good and evil that only God has. The serpent's words here suggest that God has bound and blinded the first couple. He has harmed them by giving them his moral will. The opposite, of course, is true; it is the serpent

---

[20] "Evil is not in the good that God has created, but in the rejection of the order that God has instituted for the enjoyment of the world." Blocher, 140.

[21] "The pathology of this dialogue of descent is so clear: Satan offers a question based on the perversion of God's word. Eve then begins to question it herself, as is evidenced by her revisions of God's word. And then Satan is free to declare God's word as wrong." Hughes, *Genesis*, 69.

[22] The Köstenbergers point out that the serpent also changes the name used to identify God—from Yahweh Elohim ("LORD God") to Elohim ("God"). This is important. Köstenberger and Köstenberger, *God's Design for Man and Woman*, 44.

who is slowly winding barbed wire around the woman, and the Lord who gave her protection through his decree.[23] The man and the woman were made for glory but not to be God himself, despite what the serpent intimates here. As Derek Kidner states, "This prospect of material, aesthetic and mental enrichment (6a) seemed to add up to life itself; the world still offers it (1 John 2:16). But man's lifeline is spiritual, namely God's word and the response of faith (Deut 8:3; Hab 2:4); to break it is death."[24]

This last observation matters for our broader interests. We must distinguish between a full-orbed doctrine of humanity grounded in Scripture and a counterfeit doctrine of human exaltation anchored in unbounded affirmation and the sure prospect of limitlessness. The text of Genesis 3 is communicating clearly that mankind is not made to become God, and thus has heights he cannot reach.[25] In different versions of cultural teaching, we

---

[23] Doubt of God fuels and drives the sin of the man and woman: "It was by doubting God and by desiring in a wrong way something good in creation that the first couple sinned." Lest we think that doubt leads to knowledge, Blocher continues, "If doubt exists, then ungodly sin has already entered on the scene. . . . The woman in Eden had no reason to doubt God, and every reason to trust him." So it is with us. Blocher, *In the Beginning*, 141, 148.

[24] Derek Kidner, *Genesis*, Tyndale Old Testament Commentaries (Carol Stream, IL: Tyndale, 1967; Downers Grove, IL: InterVarsity, 2016), 73. Citation refers to the InterVarsity edition.

[25] This point matters greatly: there is no sign in the Genesis account that Adam was to function as Christ. Even if the fall had not occurred, one could argue that we would still need the God-man, the one who never sinned and would perfectly obey the will of the Father in the fullest sense.

hear the serpent's suggestion. Whether stated directly or indirectly, we are encouraged to believe that we are the measure of all things and that we can transcend our ordinary boundaries and limitations.[26] We can become "like God," transforming into quasi-deified figures, crossing the normal borders of biology, psychology, and consciousness.[27]

We hear this promise not only in the garden of Eden but also the valley of Silicon. Technologists have been pursuing an enhanced humanity for decades, and many today speak of an overhauled future for the human race. The best-selling book *Homo Deus* predicts the following: "*Homo sapiens* is likely to upgrade itself step by step, merging with robots and computers in the process, until our descendants will look back and realise they are no longer the kind of animal that wrote the Bible, built the Great Wall of China and laughed at Charlie Chaplin's antics."[28]

---

[26] Humanity is never more like a lord than when obeying God and never more like a slave than when seemingly liberated. This formulation is similar to Luther's famous dictum about Christian freedom: "A Christian is a perfectly free lord of all, subject to none. A Christian is a perfectly dutiful servant of all, subject to all." Martin Luther, "The Freedom of a Christian," in *Three Treatises*, trans. W. A. Lambert, 2nd rev. ed. (Minneapolis: Fortress, 1970), 277.

[27] "We are all part of the *Wirküngsgeschichte* (effective history) of the curse and the pervasive effects of the fall. The past is present not only among us but within us." Horton, *Lord and Servant*, 136. The technological vision of man attempts, at the very least, to forget the past that is "within us." But this we cannot do, whether in the shape of our faces, the colors of our hair, or the Adamic trajectory of our spiritual conditions.

[28] Yuval Noah Harari, *Homo Deus: A Brief History of Tomorrow* (New York: HarperCollins, 2017), 49.

Yuval Noah Harari makes his claims carefully, but alert readers can spot the presuppositions behind his predictions. Mankind is a "kind of animal"; we are constantly evolving, and evolving upward, so that we will one day be robot-human hybrids; we will soon—in perhaps a few centuries—look back at the Bible as an artifact of essentially prehistoric times, as the average person today views a stone club. This is a revolution in thought in the subtlest of terms. By mixing the physical—the Great Wall—with the theological—the Bible—Harari reveals his true beliefs: the Scripture is outdated, unneeded, and will be discarded in the future.

Biblical wisdom is not all *Homo deus* will discard. Evolved humankind will put an end to death itself. In an interview, Harari framed theological truth as a thing of the past: "If traditionally death was the specialty of priests and theologians, now the engineers are taking over," Harari said. He continued, "My position is that humankind has the potential to overcome old age and death, but it will probably take a few centuries rather than a few decades."[29] A close read of Harari's seemingly gentle prophecy shows that he is not neutral on the matter of theology and its eclipse. He is cheering for the "engineers" who will close the door on "old age and death." This may be a long-term project, but it is achievable.

---

[29] Yuval Noah Harari, quoted in Dan Falk, "Godlike 'Homo Deus' Could Replace Humans as Tech Evolves," *NBC Mach*, May 31, 2017, https://www.nbcnews.com/mach/technology/Godlike-homo-deus-could -replace-humans-tech-evolves-n757971.

Mankind hungers for secularized immortality. We have no issues with those who would upgrade us without spiritual change; in the twenty-first century, we greet our scientistic world changers with open arms, granting them carte blanche to reengineer us. It is surely true, as we shall see, that technology brings us many blessings. God is the original Creator, the very first Maker. But the programmatic language of scientific development may mask chillingly secular beliefs. "You shall not die" is not a new statement. It is an ancient promise with a blood-curdling provenance. Except for the Lord himself, we should fundamentally distrust those who utter it.

The Historical Fall of Humanity

The human race has always craved immortality without the divine. We want greatness—even godness—without God. So it was that Eve obeyed the serpent and ate the forbidden fruit:

> The woman saw that the tree was good for food and delightful to look at, and that it was desirable for obtaining wisdom. So she took some of its fruit and ate it; she also gave some to her husband, who was with her, and he ate it. Then the eyes of both of them were opened, and they knew they were naked; so they sewed fig leaves together and made coverings for themselves.
>
> Then the man and his wife heard the sound of the LORD God walking in the garden at the time of the evening breeze, and they hid from the LORD God among

the trees of the garden. So the LORD God called out to the man and said to him, "Where are you?"

And he said, "I heard you in the garden, and I was afraid because I was naked, so I hid."

Then he asked, "Who told you that you were naked? Did you eat from the tree that I commanded you not to eat from?"

The man replied, "The woman you gave to be with me—she gave me some fruit from the tree, and I ate."

So the LORD God asked the woman, "What is this you have done?"

And the woman said, "The serpent deceived me, and I ate." (Gen 3:6–13)

The tree and its fruit were not ugly or off-putting. Made by Yahweh, the tree's branches teemed with delicious and appealing food. The gifts of God will not seem gross to us even as we partake of them—in truth, misuse them—in a sinful way. Up to the moment we consume them, they will delight us, dazzle us, even intoxicate us. We must learn from this text, and mark it carefully for our own spiritual battles, our own encounters with temptation. The tree of the knowledge of good and evil was not evil itself. It did not have a discomfiting smell or a disgusting appearance. It was sensorily appealing and aesthetically stimulating. But enjoying its fruit was evil—the very height of evil.

The woman took the tree's food, ironically, to gain wisdom. But she had rejected wisdom itself in making this decision. Wisdom, for those who wish to rebel against God, seems injurious, while rebellion seems enlivening. We think we will reach our potential and come fully alive when we transgress authority and ignore wisdom. Those who warn us and seek to guide us in fact seek to oppress us, we convince ourselves. They do not have our best interests at heart. Eve believed this lie. So did Adam, who should have rebuked it in the strongest terms. Instead, the woman led the man, reversing the rightful order of the marital relationship.[30] The man, we learn in verse six, was not far off from this interaction; he had not been cultivating a tough patch of brush, and then come upon his wife seeking a little snack. He was "with her," and she gave him the food.[31] Playing a passive role, the man did nothing in the face of pure evil at the dawn of wickedness. He acquiesced.[32] He put up no fight. The one created to "rule" the serpent was thoroughly ruled by the serpent. He obeyed Satan rather than his Creator. He did

---

[30] "Indeed, it was not only for the sake of complying with the wishes of his wife, that he transgressed the law laid down for him; but being drawn by her into fatal ambition, he became partaker of the same defection with her." John Calvin, *Commentaries of the First Book of Moses called Genesis*, vol. 1, ed. Anthony Uyl, trans. John King (Ontario: Devoted, 2018), 60.

[31] John Hartley points out that the woman speaks in the plural; in other words, she is speaking for Adam, too: "This is visible in her use of plural forms in speaking with the serpent, showing that she was speaking for both of them." Hartley, *Genesis*, 67–68 (see chap. 1, n. 21).

[32] "Although 'with her' does not in itself demand that he is present since the serpent speaks 'to the woman,' nevertheless, the action of the verse implies that Adam is a witness to the dialogue. 'You' at each place in 3:1–5 is plural and thus suggests his presence." Mathews, *Genesis 1–11:26*, 238 (see chap. 1, n. 20).

the anti-God's bidding. Here is John Milton's charge of "effemi-nate" failure in full bloom.

This last sentence bears further comment. If we are merely tracking the technical play-by-play of the fall, we could miss the profoundly realized vision of human flourishing that the serpent has offered Adam and Eve. With nary a syllable of introduction, he has set himself up as an authority. The sheer panache of the evil one startles us; he feels no need to justify his presence or his overweening challenge to God's rulership. He questions this rulership, as we have already noted, and in doing so gives a countervision of human happiness. Seen from the eyes of faith, the serpent is not only a competitor to God, but a severely misplaced one. The serpent is the anti-God. He speaks antiwisdom. Following his directions breeds antijoy. His is a worldview, too, but it is a corruption of the true one, containing only perversions of divine decretals. Satan does not have his own full-fledged system of belief and practice; the anti-God has a full-fledged anti-system made up of antibeliefs and antipractices. It is a system, to be sure, but it is neither original nor unique. It is corruption and desiccation. We shall return to this observation in due course, for the antisystem offers itself afresh to the world today.

Following antiwisdom brings immediate consequences for the first couple. Their eyes "were opened" and they gained sudden awareness of their nakedness; before this, they had dwelt together in purity and perfect innocence. This does not mean that they felt no desire for one another, for it seems the man fairly shrieked with delight when he got his first glimpse of the God-made woman. Following the eating of the fruit, however, they see their bodies with shame. They wish to hide. They cover themselves. What was beautiful, formed by the Lord himself, now appears grotesque.

It is remarkable that the spiritual fall leads to the first instance of shame and despair over physical appearance. This, too, is a pattern that recurs unendingly in human history, and is a regular part of the post-fall human experience. We are ensouled creatures, but most people worry far more about their appearance than their souls. Here in Gen 3:7 is the fountain of all ungodly thinking regarding the body. Here is the beginning of all gender dysphoria, of feeling as if our bodies do not fit our true identities. Here is the starting point of all insecurity over our imperfections and weaknesses and shapes. The fall of man unleashed a perpetually breaking wave of bodily dissatisfaction, one that has manifold and often punishing consequences for men and women. Aside from seeing our bodies wrongly or caring about them too much, we also express in our bodies the dissolution we feel in our souls. Truly, we are children of Adam and Eve, engaging in debilitating struggles with our bodies that play out decades after they began, whether wanted or unwanted. We are creatures who war *in* our bodies *against* our bodies. The tableau of our depraved spirituality plays on the physical tablet of our persons.

The man and the woman undertake physical means to cover up their spiritual wickedness. The text clearly reveals just how fruitless this endeavor is. The first couple wears fig leaves, hastily sown together, a sight that may well have bordered on the ridiculous. Mathews finds a helpful linkage in the text to the covering God will provide: "Their efforts to hide their shame are as puny as their efforts to hide from God since their man-made coverings are ineffective (v. 21). 'Made' (ʿāśâ, Heb. עשה) and 'coverings' (ḥăgōrōt, Heb. חֲגֹרֹת) anticipate v. 21, where God 'made' durable 'garments' (kotĕnôt, Heb. כָּתְנוֹת) from animal skins for their needed apparel."[33] This fruitless human effort is the natural response of people to their sins. Humanity often seeks a mask, a lavish presentation, an avant-garde appearance, to hide its heart of darkness. But there is no hiding from God. Before they could see him, they heard him, so they sheltered among the trees. (It was a tree that undid them, and no tree except one can save them now.) Three times the Hebrew uses the kingly term for the Lord, identifying him as "the LORD God," indicating not his creational ability but his ethical fiat. The one who was the overjoyed Maker now presents himself as the iron judge. He comes for answers, and it is answers that he will have.

The Lord does not, surprisingly, address the woman. She has dominated the human side of the account thus far. Instead, the Lord God zeroes in on the man, asking him where he is (Gen 3:9).[34] The Lord knows where the man is; he is not confused. His question—"Where are you?"—is intended to draw the man out literally and figuratively, and the man cites his fear upon learning of the Lord's visitation (Gen 3:10). The Lord does not address the fear the man mentions; he responds by asking who told him he was naked and whether he ate of the forbidden tree.

---

[33] Mathews, 239–40.

[34] "God, by addressing man, woman and serpent in that order, has shown how he regards their degrees of responsibility." Kidner, *Genesis*, 75.

The man sinks even further into the mire of shame. He puts his own responsibility at the end of his response, first blaming the woman and then the Lord himself for his iniquity (Gen 3:12).[35]

This exchange tells us a great deal about the Lord's expectations for the man. Though the man was not the protagonist in this act of disobedience, the Lord addressed him directly. He gave the man no opportunity to wiggle out of his position; although the man had avoided the primary role in the eating of the fruit, the Lord still held him responsible for the fall. Adam was made by God to lead his wife and protect his wife (see Gen. 2:15), but he had failed miserably in his tasks. Ortlund says it well: "As the God-appointed head, Adam bore the primary responsibility to lead their partnership in a God-glorifying direction."[36] His sin did not, however, signal the termination of his domestic authority or his God-given leadership. Here is the first-ever instance of sin, but not only of sin—of a man acting like a coward, neglecting his mandate, and then doing verbal damage to his wife. This one act is the poisoned wellspring of countless broken, defeated, wounded marriages.

---

[35] "By postponing his own involvement until the last word in the verse, Adam attempts to minimize his part in this sin." Hamilton, *The Book of Genesis*, 194 (see chap. 1, n. 12).

[36] Raymond Ortlund, "Male-Female Equality and Male Headship," in *Recovering Biblical Manhood and Womanhood: A Response to Evangelical Feminism*, ed. John Piper and Wayne Grudem (Wheaton, IL: Crossway, 2006), 108.

The fall is not only a conscious choosing of evil and a sampling of prohibited goods. It is a thorough breakdown of creational order and divine design. To fill out the picture sketched
above, Satan has instituted by his cunning a reverse portrait of the
home. He has sold the man and woman an antimarriage based
on the inversion of biblical roles. He has effectively convinced
the man to be an anti-man and the woman to be an anti-woman.
These creatures were made to glorify the Lord in distinct ways,
but they rejected God's good blueprint and embraced Satan's
perverted, upside-down vision of marriage and the family. We
cannot isolate the fall as only the first sin, the moment when
darkness fell on once-shining humanity. The fall cannot be
understood outside of God's design for the man and the woman,
the first family, and the home. Many of us are familiar with such
a stripped-down, detail-evacuated conception of the fall, but in
the Bible, this historic denouement is not gender-neutral. It proceeds according to the rejection of God's wisdom for men and
women.

The woman, for her part, focuses on the serpent's agency in
this transaction: as the man did, she places someone else before
herself in accounting for her actions (Gen 3:13). The serpent
deceived her, she says, and she ate. The woman does not blame
the man, but neither does she own her actions in full. What a
sign this is of human pride. We sometimes hear, and perhaps
even think, that if we could deal with God directly, our lives
would be simpler and better. We would trust the Lord more;
we would keep shorter accounts. But the behavior of the man

and the woman instructs us. Even when faced with Almighty God himself, mankind exercises a slippery yet fierce capacity for blame-shifting. We learn something about ourselves here: without any coaching or depravity-based training from the cradle, we are experts at self-justification.[37] Even when God himself demands a reason for our wickedness, we will not necessarily tell the truth.

Such dissembling may allow us to escape justice on this soil, but there is no ducking the God of heaven and earth. After the fall comes the curse. The curse, though, is not only a death sentence. It is a mix of just condemnation, certain foretelling, and holistic self-mapping of those involved in this awful scene. We

---

[37] D. A. Carson connects our propensity for self-justification to the garden: "That sin goes back to the Garden, where Adam blames Eve and Eve blames Satan himself. It is difficult to think of any sin we commit that does not include a dollop of self-justification. Jesus tells the parable of the Good Samaritan to a lawyer who asked a question because he 'wanted to justify himself' [Luke 10:29]. Elsewhere he condemns the Pharisees because, he says, 'You are the ones who justify yourselves in the eyes of others, but God knows your hearts. What people value highly is detestable in God's sight' [Luke 16:14–15]. The difference between the Pharisee and the tax collector lay in the fact that only one of the two was confident in his own righteousness [Luke 18:9]. In other words, self-justification wears many faces. . . . The common ingredient, self-justification, similarly lurks behind so many of our sins of pride, inverted or otherwise." D. A. Carson, "The Trials of Biblical Studies," in *The Trials of Theology: Becoming a 'Proven Worker' in a Dangerous Business*, ed. Andrew J. B. Cameron and Brian S. Rosner (Fearn, UK: Christian Focus, 2010), 120–21.

are not to understand the curse as positive in any sense (save one); we are to see in the Lord's sentencing the future dynamics of both the spiritual conflict humanity now faces and the relations between the sexes. In what follows, we will briefly examine three of these effects, though we will reserve substantial comment on the fall's effect on men and women for the next few chapters.

So the Lord God said to the serpent:

> Because you have done this,
> you are cursed more than any livestock
> and more than any wild animal.
> You will move on your belly
> and eat dust all the days of your life.
> I will put hostility between you and the woman,
> and between your offspring and her offspring.
> He will strike your head,
> and you will strike his heel.

He said to the woman:

> I will intensify your labor pains;
> you will bear children with painful effort.
> Your desire will be for your husband,
> yet he will rule over you.

And he said to the man, "Because you listened to your wife and ate from the tree about which I commanded you, 'Do not eat from it':

> The ground is cursed because of you.
> You will eat from it by means of painful labor
> all the days of your life.
> It will produce thorns and thistles for you,
> and you will eat the plants of the field.
> You will eat bread by the sweat of your brow
> until you return to the ground,
> since you were taken from it.
> For you are dust,
> and you will return to dust." (Gen 3:14–19)

First, the serpent is cursed such that he will face "hostility" from the woman's offspring. Initially it seems the conflict may be between the serpent and the woman, but in verse 15 the focus of this epic struggle shifts to the woman's seed: "He will strike your head, and you will strike his heel." We have no greater explanation of this violent pairing, but we have learned the essential thrust of the rest of the biblical story.[38] Satan will lash out at humanity over and over again, acting in extreme and undiluted "hostility"

---

[38] "Once admitted that the serpent symbolizes sin, death, and the power of evil, it becomes much more likely that the curse envisages a long struggle between good and evil, with mankind eventually triumphing." Wenham, *Genesis 1–15*, 80–81.

to the human race. He will have "seed" that carry out this mission for him just as the woman's offspring will battle against his demonic power. The rendition of the spiritual conflict promised by God does not, however, focus on the perpetual battle but on two decisive blows: the head-crushing and the heel-striking. The war of the seeds terminates in a terrible flurry of blood and death. The implication is obvious: to undo the serpent's calamity, an awful and unprecedented price must be paid. We do not learn in early biblical history what this precise outcome will be, but we learn here the essential narrative of Scripture and world history: all-out war is to come.[39]

We shall explore the dynamics of post-fall marriage in pages to come. For our purposes here, it is enough to note that the Lord brings judgment upon the union of the man and the woman.[40] The woman will seek mastery of her husband and will try to rule him, but he will not take this (Gen 3:16). Instead, he will "rule over" her. In neither instance should we see this in happy terms. The text exudes not glee over this fractured relationship but pain. The woman was made by God to be cared for by the

---

[39] I concur that this promise, the *protoevangelion*, "drives the entire storyline of the Bible." Gentry and Wellum, *God's Kingdom through God's Covenants*, 258.

[40] The Köstenbergers note that while the Lord curses the serpent and the ground, he does not directly curse the man and the woman, though he does "pronounce judgments" on them. Köstenberger and Köstenberger, *God's Design for Man and Woman*, 47. See also John H. Walton, *Genesis*, NIV Application Commentary (Grand Rapids: Zondervan, 2001), 236–39.

man's loving leadership; now, she will not receive his authority happily, and he will not exercise it benevolently.

All this is because the man listened to his wife when he should have rejected her invitation to eat the tree's food and seized control of the serpentine situation (Gen 3:17). Both the man and the woman now experience serious pain: the woman in maternal labor and childbearing, the man in material labor and earth-cultivating. The one created from the dust and given the ability to rise far above it will now return to it (Gen 3:19). Rejection of divine design and divine decree has led to sin; sin has led to the cursing of the created order; the created order must now decay and die.

The Fourfold Death of Adam

We have lingered on the historical narrative of the fall of Adam because original sin is the father of our own sins. But Adam is not only the first to transgress God's law; he is the first to die. He is the dark angel who leads all people into the valley of death. This is not only a corporeal undoing; it has multiple effects.

First, Adam dies judicially. The Edenic paradise was a kind of outdoor courtroom, and Adam's sin left him condemned before his Creator. By his sin, he dies judicially. He has no way to remove this sentence. He has forensically sinned against the Lord and disobeyed divine teaching. He is not vaguely broken; he is legally guilty, and he cannot do otherwise. Guilt in biblical terms is not a psychological sensation that a pharmacist or therapist can erase. Guilt in biblical terms owes to the performance of evil. Murray says it eloquently: "The sin of Adam was what all sin is, transgression of the law of God. As such it was pravity and perversity; it was *culpa* without mitigation."[41] It stems from actual wrong, wrong that the Lord reckons to the account of every person. Adam is our representative in Eden.[42] His sin—and ours—receives redress only through one who can take on this guilt and justly clear our guilt.[43] Until this happens and is

---

[41] John Murray, *The Imputation of Adam's Sin* (1959; Phillipsburg, NJ: P&R, 1977), 91.

[42] Schreiner states that "The sway of death over all of humanity can be traced to Adam's sin. Whether human beings like it or not, we are one community. The fountainhead of the human race affects all who come after him." Thomas R. Schreiner, *New Testament Theology: Magnifying God in Christ* (Grand Rapids: Baker Academic, 2008), 538.

[43] This is a crucial matter, for the concepts of federal headship and imputation are challenged today. There is much that needs elaboration here, but in the interest of space, we may point out that if one reckons Christ as the head of the blood-bought people of God, one can scarcely avoid seeing Adam as the first representative of the human race. The two concepts stand or fall together. Murray says it well: "And since the analogy instituted between Adam and Christ is so conspicuous, it is surely necessary to assume that the kind of relationship which Adam sustains to men is after the pattern of the relationship which Christ sustains to men. To put the case conversely, surely the kind of relationship that Christ sustains to men is after the pattern which Adam sustains to men (cf. Rom. 5:14). But if all that we posit in the case of Adam is simply his natural headship or parenthood, we do not have the kind of relationship that would provide the pattern for the headship of Christ." Murray, "Imputation of Adam's Sin–II," *Westminster Theological Journal* 19, no. 1 (November 1956): 42–43.

made efficacious in the sinner, this crime against the infinite carries an infinite sentence: death to the full.[44]

Second, Adam dies spiritually. He has not only consented
to evildoing, but he has welcomed the virus of wickedness into
his soul and his being. Previously, he suffered no infection and
knew no iniquitous pollution or contamination. Now, his whole
person suffers the effects of the fall.[45] Made a spiritual being,
Adam cannot commune with God by his nature.[46] He does not
know the Lord, and he is sealed off from the divine. Adam and
his children remain fundamentally spiritual beings and still are
image-bearers, but they cannot know the Lord in spiritual terms.
Because Adam dies, he and all his progeny lose the love and care
of God. They no longer fellowship with him. They are not separated from God by a little distance, like a sick patient whom the
doctors quarantine in another room. The sinner is now separated
from God by an infinite distance, a gap uncloseable by human
means. Horton says it well: "Instead of being eschatologically
oriented toward Sabbath life with God, each other, and the

---

[44] This section is a development and expansion of the argument
of Robert Reymond on the effects of the fall. See Robert L. Reymond,
A New Systematic Theology of the Christian Faith, 2nd ed. (Nashville:
Thomas Nelson, 1998), 446–49.

[45] Culver summarizes by saying, "the whole of man, the very center
of being is defiled," a defilement that includes body, speech, spirit, mind,
and conscience. Robert Duncan Culver, *Systematic Theology: Biblical and
Historical* (Fearn, UK: Mentor, 2005), 413.

[46] On this point see Louis Berkhof, *Systematic Theology*, new combined ed. (Grand Rapids: Eerdmans, 1996), 215–43.

whole creation, we grow increasingly aware that we are 'being toward death' (Heidegger)."[47]

Third, Adam dies physically. His body, made for health and vibrancy, must now suffer destruction. As we have seen, Adam had a direct connection with the earth. God made him from the dust of the ground, connecting him forever with the made world. But the Lord did not intend for his prized creation to crumble back into dust; he wished him to conquer the earth and live forever in communion with God. He wanted the man and the woman to enjoy the fullest health and glorify him through unblinking, undimmed physical vitality. Blessing came through the God-made physical realm, but so did cursing. The Lord provided for Adam in abundance, filling the garden with nourishment, but Adam chose to eat the one physical product banned for consumption. He took the handiwork of God—a physical thing, food—and used it in ways God had not intended. Spiritual disobedience came through physical compromise and brought physical destruction. Now, our sinful race must suffer the effects of Adam's choice and die Adam's death. So says Culver: "Because of sins the circle of activity which constitutes life on this planet, originally intended to be blessed and the source of true pleasures, has always overtones of regret, pain, boredom, ennui: finally exhaustion and death."[48]

---

[47] Michael Horton, *The Christian Faith: A Systematic Theology for Pilgrims on the Way* (Grand Rapids: Zondervan, 2011), 413.

[48] Culver, *Systematic Theology*, 416.

Fourth, Adam dies eternally. There is a close linkage between his spiritual death and this last point, but this aspect of Adam's fall deserves further comment. As noted above, Adam's sin is not finite, for it does not offend a finite person. It offends and wrongs a holy God, a being of infinitude. The stakes and consequences are impossibly high on this count. It is here that we delve into the darkest element of the fall: it is not fundamentally about Adam's sentencing and just suffering, but about God. It was God who was wronged. It was God whose moral will Adam and Eve transgressed. It was God whose wisdom—loving wisdom—the man and the woman rejected in favor of the serpent's antiwisdom.

The fall represents holistic personal rejection of God by Adam and Eve. It is a demolitional moment, a spiritual extinction-level event. It is occasioned by trusting the devil over the divine. God is offended, wronged, and rejected in the fall. It is not merely his command that is set aside; it is God himself. To disobey the moral will and the stated law of the Lord is to disobey God. Disobeying God is full-out rebellion against him and denial of him. The man and the woman, in other words, are choosing Satan's vision of the world in eating the tree's food, and they are also operating as if God does not exist and his declared will is irrelevant.

The man and the woman are the first God-deniers. They allow themselves to forget that God is real and operate accordingly. They choose to lay their stock behind a divinized natural order in which a talking animal is trustworthy, not Almighty God. But they do not actually want to follow the serpent; that is not what the serpent sold them. Acting as if God does not exist and following the devil, they quest for God's own throne. They may be denying the Lord, but they are monotheistic nonetheless, for they believe in their own right to rule. The first couple simultaneously does not believe in God and does believe in themselves. Guided by the serpent, they are what matter. God and his word have no meaning for them. They do not want God; they want to be gods. They do not wish to follow the Lord; they wish to follow their hearts, a choice underwritten by the devil's own forked tongue.

In this broader scope, we understand why mankind must die eternally. The man and the woman did not make a momentarily bad choice; they sought the overthrow of God himself from his rightful throne. Satan seduced them into making the very move he had previously attempted when he sought the rulership of the cosmos and was thrown from the celestial realm. This kind of God-denying action merits a sentence of the strongest kind. Eternal death alone suffices as the just punishment of the first couple.[49] To deny the divine is to reap divine vengeance. God put eternity in the heart of man, and it is thus into eternity that man goes after Adam's fall (Eccl 3:11). But it is not neutral eternity that we speak of; it is hell, the place of eternal condemnation and torment (Matt 25:46; Rev 20:10).

---

[49] Thus sin brings to a horrible conclusion the original work of the serpent. See Berkhof on eternal death: "The restraints of the present fall away, and the corruption of sin has its perfect work. The full weight of the wrath of God descends on the condemned. . . . And the smoke of their torment goeth up for ever and ever." Berkhof, *Systematic Theology*, 261.

The Ruined State of Mankind Following the Fall

The sin of Adam is the sin of all humanity. The death of Adam is the death of all humanity. The terrible effects of the fall show themselves plainly in the Old Testament, but it is the New Testament that offers fuller explanation and unpacking of these effects. In 1 Corinthians, the apostle Paul connects Adam to all people: "For since death came through a man, the resurrection of the dead also comes through a man. For just as in Adam all die, so also in Christ all will be made alive" (1 Cor 15:21–22). The apostle refers not to a myth or a spiritual archetype, but a man. Through Adam, all die—all without exception. Paul's letter to the Romans teaches just the same: "Therefore, just as sin entered the world through one man, and death through sin, in this way death spread to all people, because all sinned. In fact, sin was in the world before the law, but sin is not charged to a person's account when there is no law" (Rom 5:12–13). Paul reinforces his point in three other places in this passage. In verse 17, "the one man's trespass" leads to death's reign; in verse 18, "one trespass" brings "condemnation for everyone"; in verse 19, "one man's disobedience" made many "sinners." Adam's sin was real, occurring in history; it was representative, leading to the inherited corruption of all the human race; it was destructive, occasioning the death of every person.

Paul's teaching helps us understand what has gone wrong with the human race. Mankind perennially asks this question, but takes great pains to ignore the plain teaching of the Word of God. According to the Scripture, original sin explains human suffering and global breakdown. Our problem is not first environmental but personal. Sin takes root in our very beings; it is present from birth and corrupts us thoroughly. We inherit sin. When speaking of the fall of Adam, we could call it "hereditary sin" rather than "original sin." This entails that we affirm both the federal headship of Adam and the historicity of his transgression. Adam acted on behalf of the entire human race, just as Christ died in place of his bride (Eph 5:25). Adam cannot be a fictional character any more than Christ can. Adam's actual fall explains our own present darkness.

This is not to argue that our own actions do not matter in divine record-keeping. We all fell in Adam; we became sinful as a race in Adam; we died in Adam. Our lostness did not become a possibility in Eden but an actuality. It is also true, though, that we act out our sins in time and space. We make good on the sinful nature gained through Adam's fall. This union with Adam is not fundamentally natural or genetic, though we are formed and birthed through the agency of sinful parents. This union with Adam is representative and federal.[50] Such concepts occur throughout the Bible; kings, for example, represent their nations, as do commoners. Achan's sin in Joshua 7 brings judgment on the people of Israel and leads to widespread destruction. The priest makes atonement for the Israelite community in Leviticus 16; one man's levitical fidelity symbolically represents the people collectively confessing and repenting of their sins. Sin is inherited through corporate solidarity with Adam. But our own actions

---

[50] And, to cite Horton once more, this union is "covenantal." See Horton, *Christian Faith*, 423–31.

matter, and though we might like to think otherwise, they will only ensure that we heap up the wrath for ourselves that is the just response of God to our actual sins.

The overarching term for man's spiritual condition is this: *total depravity*. In this historic Protestant formulation of biblical teaching, sin reaches into every aspect of the human person. We have corrupt natures and are guilty of sin due to Adam's fall. Evil has reached into every corner of our beings, and we are pervasively corrupted as a result. Our minds, hearts, souls, bodies, and entire beings are oriented toward wickedness; we are not as bad as we could be, left without any moral intuition or instinct whatsoever, but we are totally ruined by sin, and as such are comprehensively evil.

The Bible portrays the human heart as "desperately wicked" in the words of Jer 17:9 (KJV). So it is. "The Lord looks down from heaven" in pursuit of one who innately seeks God, but the pursuit comes up empty. "All have turned away; / all alike have become corrupt. / There is no one who does good, / not even one" (Ps 14:2–3). To make the picture even plainer, Isaiah testifies that even our good works garner no salvific favor with the Lord: "All of us have become like something unclean, / and all our righteous acts are like a polluted garment; / all of us wither like a leaf, / and our iniquities carry us away like the wind" (Isa 64:6). The letter to the Ephesians brings these threads together into a convulsive summation of human depravity:

And you were dead in your trespasses and sins in which you previously lived according to the ways of this world, according to the ruler of the power of the air, the spirit now working in the disobedient. We too all previously lived among them in our fleshly desires, carrying out the inclinations of our flesh and thoughts, and we were by nature children under wrath as the others were also. (Eph 2:1–3)

What a head-spinning rebuke of human pride. We are not inherently righteous; instead, we lived according to our trespasses and sins that left us dead, we followed the wicked ruler in disobedience, we held and exercised evil desires natural to us, we obeyed our fallen inclinations and thoughts, and our natures demand and deserve wrath. All this Paul packs into just three verses.

Our optimistic, sin-eliding age might encourage us to fundamentally affirm ourselves as good and beautiful and perfect, but the Bible communicates the opposite. We are inestimably valuable as those made by God, but in Adam we have plunged into death and sin and evil. We cannot come to God; we cannot of ourselves know the Lord. We cannot please the Lord: "A good tree can't produce bad fruit; neither can a bad tree produce good fruit" (Matt 7:18). We neither want nor follow God's will. In our fallenness, we can't even understand the things of God: "The natural person does not accept the things of the Spirit of God, for they are folly to him, and he is not able to understand them because they are spiritually discerned" (1 Cor 2:14 ESV). We are totally depraved and thus totally unable to come to God.[51]

---

[51] In other words, we cannot earn the approval of God, and we cannot do any spiritual good. See Berkhof, *Systematic Theology*, 247.

Where does all this dark energy go? Our natures are neither quiet nor dormant. Though humanity typically defines the sinful as those who make headlines for their crimes—murderers, rapists, abusers—in truth every person has both the capacity and the natural drive to commit sin, and to do so on a perpetual basis. We act in ways that are right and even good, this is true; but the Bible speaks honestly and with multidimensional accuracy about our sinfulness. What follows are six different types of sin we engage in according to the Scripture.[52]

First, we commit the sin of ignorance. Ignorance in the sinful reckoning gets one off the hook. "I didn't know that was wrong," we say. But the Bible presents ignorance of God and his will quite differently. The high priest of Israel offered sacrifices "for the sins the people had committed in ignorance" (Heb 9:7). Unbelievers, Paul says, are "darkened in their understanding, excluded from the life of God, because of the ignorance that is in them and because of the hardness of their hearts" (Eph 4:18). Paul pairs ignorance—lack of awareness of God and the life he offers—with the human heart's spiritual obstinacy. This two-headed force that comes from within—it is "in them"—leaves the sinner without understanding or spiritual vitality. Put more simply, the fallen sinner lives in ignorance of God's will and wants to do so. We do not naturally yearn to obey God in a true sense; we want to wander far from him, and so we do, blithely shielding ourselves from the fact that the paradise of

---

[52] See Erickson, *Christian Theology*, 583–600 (see chap. 1, n. 28).

our imagining, our carefully cultivated habitat absent the divine presence and holy mandate, is on fire.

Second, we make errors. We go astray and make mistakes. Here we run straight into our era's most common excuse for wrongdoing, when it is admitted at all: "I messed up. I made a mistake." It is true that such statements contain a modicum of admission of infelicitous outcomes. But the Bible does not merely label mistaken behavior as unfortunate; it treats it as transgression against God.[53] It is human to err, but this does not excuse error, for God is a holy being. Any action that is outside his will, whether motivated by a foul motive or not, wrongs and dishonors the Lord and necessitates confession and repentance. If an Israelite ate the food set aside for the priests, then he drew a fine—this was an error, a *shogag* (שְׁגָגָה) in the Hebrew—and demanded restitution.

In similar terms, if people act "hastily" without proper forethought for their actions (Prov 19:2), they miss the way and must repent. We see in similar terms in the New Testament that pastors and church members alike must exercise discernment and submit only to the truth and those who teach it. As Jesus taught his closest disciples, "Watch out that no one deceives you. Many will come in my name, saying, 'I am he,' and they will deceive many" (Mark 13:5–6). Peter issued several such warnings, commanding

---

[53] In most cases, what the Bible terms error refers to behavior that "ought not to have occurred," for the person "should have known better, and was responsible to so inform oneself." Erickson, 585. This is quite right and needs to be recovered and believed in modern-day life.

the people of God to reject false teachers and their false teaching. No one has an excuse for following deception; every believer, Spirit-gifted and Spirit-led, has the full ability to turn away from deceivers. We can sharpen the point: every believer must turn away from deceivers or else face eternal jeopardy. Being deceived is itself wrong because Jesus warns against it.

The preceding passages show us that God does not judge us according to our behavior. He judges us according to his standard. His standard is perfect. It is absolute holiness at all times and in all situations. God is perfectly, unerringly holy; "Holy, holy, holy," cry the angels in Isa 6:3. The Lord who brings his people into covenant with him in no way relaxes his righteousness due to his relational love. His relational love, by contrast, activates a holistic urgency on the part of the covenant people to obey the Lord without fail. We confess our conscious sins, those we have premeditated; we also confess our unknown failings, our missed marks in so many areas of life, knowing that we are such profoundly limited creatures that we do not even know ourselves— and our flaws—aright. Even our confession depends upon the Lord; even our repentance fails his righteous regulations.

Third, we may grow inattentive to God's wisdom. We may either fail to listen to God, or we may listen uncarefully and thus act and think incorrectly, failing to glorify the Lord. The Shema of the Old Testament called the people of God first to "Hear" (Deut 6:4 ESV). One could make a convincing case that the very essence of Christian faith is listening to God and the Word of God. So many wish to hear the voice of God; so few read the Bible, his declared revelation. If we want to hear the Lord's voice, then we need to open the pages of Scripture and listen. Doing so, of course, requires focus: "we must pay attention all the more to what we have heard, so that we will not drift away" (Heb 2:1). It is not only a father or mother, it seems, who must urge concentration. The very writers of holy writ sought to compel their audiences to sit at the feet of Holy Scripture and do nothing other than listen. Pay attention. Submit. Follow. Don't flag or drift. Stay the course.

Fourth, we sin when we rebel against God. All sin is rebellion, but some sin involves a direct rejection of the Lord and his holy will. The fall of Adam and Eve fits several categories but is chiefly characterized by rebellion, by turning away. Gentry and Wellum suggest that it is this outcome that is the worst of all the results of the fall: "human beings, who were made to know, love, and serve God, are now enemies of God, living under his judgment and wrath and no longer in a living relationship with him . . . to live apart from him is death."[54] There is nothing worse than identifying humanity as an enemy of God, a state that is the opposite of the creational intent of the Almighty.

Itching against one's God-ordained boundaries is ancient. Throwing off the rule of God and turning to one's own wisdom or the counsel of ungodly figures is the original problem with the cosmos. Small wonder that Paul warns Timothy of the propensity of professing Christians to wander: "[they] will multiply

---

[54] Peter J. Gentry and Stephen J. Wellum, *Kingdom through Covenant: A Biblical-Theological Understanding of the Covenants*, 2nd ed. (Wheaton, IL: Crossway Books, 2012), 261.

teachers for themselves because they have an itch to hear what they want to hear. They will turn away from hearing the truth and will turn aside to myths" (2 Tim 4:3–4). We follow false teachers because, at some level, we want them; we do not want the sturdy substance of divine truth. We itch for affirmation. We are not confused by myths; we want them.

Fifth, we sin due to a lack of integrity, or what we call *iniquity*. We deviate from what is right and become perverse in our actions.[55] We do not act according to clear and fair guidelines. Speaking of the covenant with Levi, the Lord says in Mal 2:6 that "True instruction was in his mouth, and nothing wrong was found on his lips. He walked with me in peace and integrity and turned many from iniquity." Iniquity, represented in Hebrew by the word *avon* (עָוֹן), speaks to the perverse nature of our depravity; when we act as iniquitous beings, we bend and distort the goodness of God. Several of the most wicked perversions of God's design earn the *toebah* (תּוֹעֵבָה) designation, meaning "abomination," sin that is especially evil in God's eyes. This includes evils such as idolatry (Deut 7), homosexuality (Lev 18:22), cross-dressing (Deut 22:5), and witchcraft (Deut 18). Erickson suggests that "these sins are not simply something that God peevishly objects to, but that produces revulsion in him."[56]

Of several of these sins we shall say more in pages to come. At this point, it is important to note that one sin of any kind

---

[55] Erickson, *Christian Theology*, 590.

[56] Erickson, 593. For helpful commentary on pagan practices, see also Merrill, *Everlasting Dominion*, 333–36 (see chap. 1, n. 26).

separates a person infinitely from an infinitely holy God. The foregoing discussion of the complexity of human sinfulness must not obscure this reality, and it must not lead any sinner to think he is superior to any other wrongdoer. There is equality of iniquity before the feet of God. Yet in doing justice to the texture of the biblical text, we must note that some sins particularly offend the Lord and go against his nature and will. People who partake of such depravity do not lose their humanity irrevocably; they do, however, fall into terrible patterns of sin, and they may well find their identities in their sins, and turn their wickedness into righteousness in their own eyes.

There are no happy limits to what Adam has wrought. We are all in a desperate condition before the Lord, and we all have only one hope: God graciously intervening in our self-inflicted ruin to rescue us.

Conclusion

The modern project to reenchant humanity may falter when, in conversation with unbelieving and skeptical friends, we introduce the concept of Adam's fall and our subsequent depravity. We must know that from every angle—intellectual, ethical, personal, and otherwise—mankind is straining to shut its eyes to the reality of indwelling sin. Whether we undertake elaborate academic work to recast human nature, join a spiritual enlightenment class to receive affirmation without critique, or merely shut out the well-intentioned exhortations of family members to amend our ways, our spirits are wired to reject the truth, silence conviction of sin, and embrace in a self-justifying way our depravity. No one trains us in such defensiveness; no one need coach us in such habits. We may come from a home torn asunder by evil, or we may hail from the most respectable family in the community. It matters not. People do, say, think, and hunger after bad things because they have inherited a corrupt nature in Adam and are totally depraved. We are not merely misaligned; we are not confused; we are not uninformed; we are not fundamentally victims, whatever we may have suffered; we are evil to the core. We are dead in our sins and transgressions.

How, then, does this knowledge revivify humanity? It does so in two ways: first, it helps us see how fallen we are, and second, it drives us back to the Lord, from whom our help and our worth come. Facing the plain truth of our inherent badness reminds us what potential God has given us, and what a mess we have all made of it. We could have lived for the Lord; instead, in one form or another, we have lived for ourselves. But we are not hopeless, no matter how troubled we may be. We may act as respectable citizens, or we may live on the wild side of the tracks; it matters not. There is one problem before humanity: sin. There is one hope for sinful humanity: Christ.

To own this truth, however, we must square with our sins. To reenchant humanity is no airy, ethereal exercise; it is gritty and difficult, and we enter the kingdom only after much travail.

CHAPTER 3

$$\boxed{\textbf{WORK}}$$

A servant with this clause
Makes drudgerie divine:
Who sweeps a room, as for thy laws,
Makes that and th' action fine.

—George Herbert, "The Elixir"

Christian theology treats numerous doctrines because the Bible necessitates such engagement. Here is the curious thing: depending on how we structure our material, we theologians may spend much of our careers avoiding the subjects that occupy most of our daily time. Work, rest, and entertainment do not rank as classical subjects for students of biblical doctrine; these matters may seem subacademic, below the gaze of the high-flown academician, but work, rest, and entertainment fill the majority of our time as human beings. This is true for most healthy, well-functioning individuals; we commonly spend our limited hours on this globe either laboring, taking time off from our labors, or exercising our avocations. I suspect the intellectual climate of the guild militates against a careful study of such time pursuits; we feel as if talking about our minute-by-minute activities somehow detracts from our studies of higher things. Perhaps we are prone to an incipient gnosticism, in which the mind ranks and the body rankles.

If we fall prey to such a trap, it is not the fault of Scripture. As we shall see in this chapter, our minutes matter to the Most High. We seek here not a step-by-step ethics for on-the-ground involvement, but a richly biblical and thus theological understanding of our vocations and avocations. If our lives matter to God, then we may rest assured that our work, rest, and play matter to God; if the Bible treats these subjects throughout the canonical narrative, we do well to pay attention to its treatment and shape our faith accordingly.

How the Bible Stirs Our Interest in Work

The Bible calls us to worship God, work a lot, rest easily, and play some. In a fallen world, we do not always calibrate our lives as God would have them. This is true of our modern culture. As sinners, we do not order our lives according to righteous standards. With work, we may either worship our daily labors or despise them. With rest, we may either ignore the need to recharge or indulge in it. With entertainment and recreation, we struggle not to lose ourselves in these pursuits, particularly in a consumptive, wealthy climate such as the twenty-first-century West.[1] These matters are related; those who do not worship God find something with which to replace him. Perennial candidates include one's career, one's bank account, one's rest, and one's pastimes. Many around us work and live and play selfishly, with no thought of God. In so doing, we come to worship ourselves.

But we may just as easily err on the other side. Some people must overcome workaholism; others must conquer addictions to triviality. One temptation today is to take serious things unseriously, and unserious things seriously. We now have TV channels, for example, dedicated twenty-four hours a day to sports coverage, and to cooking delicious food, and to minor political goings-on. Neither sports nor food nor politics deserve rancor. God in his common grace has given us the blessings of fun exercise and tasty sustenance and good governance.[2] But we may, if we are not

---

[1] One thinks here of the classic text by Neil Postman, *Amusing Ourselves to Death: Public Discourse in the Age of Show Business* (London: Methuen, 1985). To understate things, Postman's critique of a "show business" approach to life only matters all the more in our performatist age (more than forty years after his book debuted).

[2] Kuyper defines "common grace" helpfully: "God is glorified in the total development toward which human life and power over nature gradually march on under the guardianship of 'common grace.' It is his created order, his work, that unfold here. It was he who seeded the field of humanity with all these powers. Without common grace the seed

careful, bestow upon the good gifts of God a status they do not deserve. We may even lose our souls questing after things, mere earthly pleasures, a self-enacted destruction that is as foolish as it is needless.

Scripture helps us recover properly balanced visions of our daily lives. It begins, as we have seen, with a working God. The deity of the Bible is no abstract being. The God of Scripture introduces himself not with a lengthy theological prologue, a catalogue of his traits, or a disquisition of sovereignty and human agency, but with an action shot of creation ex nihilo. The Lord is a *worker*. He works for six days making something from nothing. The Lord is the original entrepreneur, introduced to the reader as the Creator. He needs no assistance, he desires no guidance, and he finds evident satisfaction in the world he makes. Mirroring his own nature, it is a "very good" creation that he brings into being.[3]

That the Lord is a purposive being who voluntarily works means a great deal for our theology of vocation. In learning the Bible's first truth, that God created all things, we learn a second:

---

which lay hidden in that field would never have come up and blossomed. Thanks to common grace it germinated, burgeoned, shot up high and will one day be in full flower, to reward not man but the heavenly Farmer. . . . A finished world will glorify God as Builder and supreme Craftsman. What paradise was in bud will then be in full bloom." Abraham Kuyper, "Common Grace," in *Abraham Kuyper: A Centennial Reader*, ed. James D. Bratt (Grand Rapids: Eerdmans, 1998), 180.

[3] See "The Nature of Good," in *The Works of Saint Augustine: A Translation for the 21st Century*, vol. 19, *The Manichean Debate*, ed. Boniface Ramsey, trans. Roland J. Teske (Brooklyn: New City Press, 2006), 1.

that God loves work. He does not love idleness and nothingness; he desires a world that exists for his glory. The rest of history and the future that awaits the people of God consist of just this activity: glorifying God. We do so not as passive, do-nothing creatures, but as those who celebrate the Lord consciously and image him purposefully. He is a worker; he is pursuing the completion of his plan and the fruition of his will; he is a God of never-ceasing interest in his glory who is always working to manifest it in all the earth.[4]

The human race is like its maker a working race. Before the fall, Adam is placed in the garden by God to work in it. He must steward it, take dominion of it, and rule it. No evil exists to push against Adam's efforts, but regardless he has genuine duties to perform and responsibilities to discharge. He is not made to lie around, plucking grapes from a vine. He is made for action, formed for a mission that pulses with purpose and meaning. Mankind does not *have* to work in the Edenic scheme; mankind *gets* to work. We do what our Creator does.[5] We use

---

[4] "It seems to be a thing in itself fit and desirable, that the glorious perfections of God should be known, and the operations and expressions of them seen by other beings besides himself. . . . As God's perfections are things in themselves excellent, so the expression of them in their proper acts and fruits is excellent; and the knowledge of these excellent perfections, and of these glorious expressions of them, is an excellent thing, the existence of which is in itself valuable and desirable." Edwards, "The End for Which God Created the World," 430–32 (see chap. 1, n. 57).

[5] Wayne Grudem argues that since "the entirety of Genesis 1 describes God's work of creation" we may see "our work [as] a faint

our minds to handle matters, troubleshoot challenges, overcome difficulties, and create new systems. We use the full force of our bodies and our minds in doing so, and if blessed (and mature), find our hearts and souls thrilled by the labor God gives us to do. Work is not a curse in the biblical portrait; work is a blessing.[6] We do all our work, further, in the created world that is itself a kind of sanctuary-garden—a place of unreserved worship of the living God.[7] We are, as Richard Middleton has suggested, "priests of creation" as human beings.[8]

The fall muddies the story in literal terms. Now, work involves pain, long toil, and earthly resistance. The farmer must

---

imitation of God's own activity of creative work (see John 5:17)." Wayne Grudem, *Christian Ethics: An Introduction to Biblical Moral Reasoning* (Wheaton, IL: Crossway Books, 2018), 922.

[6] Work is not, therefore, that which man must do as a result of the curse. God, as we have noted, is the original worker. We work in light of his work; Adam stewarded the earth in productive activity before he fell from God. Con. Umberto Cassuto, *A Commentary on the Book of Genesis*, part 1, *From Adam to Noah*, trans. Israel Abrahams, Perry Foundation for Biblical Research in the Hebrew University of Jerusalem (1961; Jerusalem: Magnes Press, 2009): 22–23, 102; see also John H. Sailhamer, *Genesis*, The Expositor's Bible Commentary, rev. ed (Grand Rapids: Zondervan, 2008), 40–41, 45; Derrick McCarson, *Origins: An In-Depth Study of Genesis 1–11* (Bloomington, IN: Crossbooks, 2012), 110–38. For a helpful refutation of the argument that work is a part of the curse, see Andrew J. Spencer, "The Inherent Value of Work," *Journal of Biblical and Theological Studies* 2, no. 1 (2017): 52–65.

[7] See Richard Middleton on the theme of "creation as a cosmic sanctuary." J. Richard Middleton, *The Liberating Image: The Imago Dei in Genesis 1* (Grand Rapids: Brazos, 2005), 81–90.

[8] Middleton, 90.

effectively fight the ground for produce. The woman must bear children in jolts of agony. The old covenant priest finds the people of God resisting his liturgical leadership. The warrior must earn his keep by risking the blade and putting his life in danger. Fast forward a bit, and the office worker must navigate internal politics and the ever-shifting realities of spreadsheets and file uploads. The governmental employee seeking needed change runs headlong into the stasis of a system that rewards lassitude. On and on the story goes. No one escapes the Lord's curse on work. All must feel these effects in some way.

When TV shows present work as drudgery, Christians cannot agree. We know well the effects of the fall, and we sympathize with those who feel them. Our theology, however, will not allow us to abandon labor. We too would love more time in the Caribbean, but we know that the work-for-the-weekend mentality does not hold up under biblical scrutiny. In Christian doctrine, personal fulfillment comes not from escaping work, but from finding the right work driven by the right cause.[9] In this sense, every believer shares the same cause: the magnification of God by every moment of our existence. Paul urges the Colossian church to grasp this in his teaching on everyday Christianity:

---

[9] "Work did not come in after a golden age of leisure. It was part of God's perfect design for human life, because we were made in God's image, and part of his glory and happiness . . . Work is as much a basic human need as food, beauty, rest, friendship, prayer, and sexuality; it is not simply medicine but food for our soul." Timothy Keller and Katherine Leary Alsdorf, *Every Good Endeavor: Connecting Your Work to God's Work* (New York: Dutton, 2012), 36–37.

"Whatever you do, do it from the heart, as something done for the Lord and not for people, knowing that you will receive the reward of an inheritance from the Lord. You serve the Lord Christ" (Col 3:23–24).[10]

While modern individuals spend a great deal of time trying to find just the right career, the commitment that will justify and call forth their maximal best, the apostle trains his eye on the "heart." He wants the family of Christ to work for God. He wants them to see that the sovereignty of God matters hugely for our daily tasks. God sees them all. Nothing falls outside his sight. He will give "the reward of an inheritance" to all who faithfully labor in his name.[11] This inheritance is personal. It comes directly from God. Few things more threaten to obscure the omnipresence of God and the special joy of ongoing union with our savior Christ than the shower of tasks that confront

[10] We cannot forget, as Douglas Moo reminds us, that this passage addressed the work of slaves, not free people. Paul is here teaching that "slaves should do their work 'with the constant realization' that they are working for the Lord Christ and not just for human master." This is a remarkable point: the slaves, doing work that is considered the lowest of the low in human terms, should *constantly remember* that the menial work they perform is *coram deo* work, work that is "unto God." Douglas J. Moo, *The Letters to the Colossians and to Philemon*, The Pillar New Testament Commentary (Grand Rapids: Eerdmans, 2008), 311–12.

[11] N. T. Wright suggests that Paul is using irony here: "One should properly read '*the* inheritance'; the reference is clearly to the life of the age to come. This is ironic, since in earthly terms slaves could not inherit property." N. T. Wright, *Colossians and Philemon: An Introduction and Commentary*, vol. 12, Tyndale New Testament Commentaries (1986; Downers Grove, IL: InterVarsity, 2008), 153–54.

us each day. We all feel as though the waters will overflow our banks, and it is often the simple, small things that push us to our limits—the never-satisfied email inbox, the meetings that sap our energy and do not come to clear conclusions, the people who trade on our goodwill and do not show gratitude for our investments. Yet in these and countless other smaller trials, the Lord sees us. He watches us. He waits to see if we will work "from the heart." He promises to reward all who work in his name. Behind the anonymity and the burden of daily labor stands the Lord God. Bruce makes the point nicely: "Christian slaves—or Christian employees today—have the highest of all motives for faithful and conscientious performance of duty; they are above all else servants of Christ, and will work first and foremost so as to please him."[12]

Work is thus a crucial part of a properly God-centered existence. Work matters to the Lord. C. S. Lewis said it well: "Most men must glorify God by doing to His glory something which is not *per se* an act of glorifying but which becomes so by being offered. If, as I now hope, cultural activities are innocent and even useful, then they also (like the sweeping of the room in Herbert's poem) can be done to the Lord. The work of a charwoman and the work of a poet become spiritual in the same way and on the same condition."[13] We do not teach

---

[12] F. F. Bruce, *The Epistles to the Colossians, to Philemon, and to the Ephesians*, 168–69 (see chap. 1, n. 44).

[13] C. S. Lewis, *Christian Reflections*, ed. Walter Hooper (1967; Grand Rapids: Eerdmans, 2014), 29.

a sacerdotal Christianity, where only full-time ministers give God glory. All believers "serve the Lord Christ" every day they have on the earth.

There are no exceptions here. Noting this may sound simple, even trite, but it is not. The Christian, whatever his or her calling, works in a completely different way than the unbeliever. The Christian serves God, not man; the Christian values man in working and does not see his fellow man as a means to an end; the Christian views all labor as teleological, oriented to the renown of God and driven by the reward of God. Whether a house cleaner or a doctor, a painter or a CEO, these biblical teachings supercharge our daily efforts, imbuing them with unerasable importance and undeniable purpose.[14]

Scripture has little to say about the "perfect career." Our modern era conditions us to seek out the perfect in all things, and ends up pitting the good against the very good, and the very good against the ideal. Without a strong theological perspective on life, we may easily lose our bearings. We cease worshipping the one who is perfect, and whose perfections promise to captivate us for all eternity, and transfer our quest for the God who

---

[14] Martin Luther argues of Christian men and women that "even their seemingly secular works are a worship of God and an obedience well pleasing to God." This is true of daily labor around the home, for example, which may have "no appearance of sanctity . . . and yet these very works in connection with the household are more desirable than all the works of all the monks and nuns, be they ever so laborious and impressive." Martin Luther, *Luther's Works*, vol. 2, *Lectures on Genesis, Chapters 6–14*, ed. Jaroslav Pelikan (St. Louis: Concordia, 1960), 349.

is perfection to a world flooded with imperfection. We miss the one who is ideal and begin searching for the ideal in the world of things, but we will not find the ideal without returning to the Lord. This does not derail our hunts for meaningful jobs; it does correct our utopian presumptions.[15]

The Bible takes us aback with its advice on "calling." In 1 Corinthians 7, for example, the apostle Paul gives this church some rather surprising advice, encouraging the congregants to stay where they are: "Let each of you remain in the situation in which he was called. Were you called while a slave? Don't let it concern you. But if you can become free, by all means take the opportunity" (1 Cor 7:20–21). In general, the Christian should bloom where he is planted.[16] In this verse Paul does not label

---

[15] The efficiency guru Cal Newport has an alternate take on this conversation. He urges people not to follow their passion, but to train themselves for skilled work that is highly desired. See Cal Newport, *So Good They Can't Ignore You: Why Skills Trump Passion in the Quest for Work You Love* (New York: Grand Central, 2012); also, Cal Newport, *Deep Work: Rules for Focused Success in a Distracted World* (New York: Grand Central, 2016). Though this advice is not distinctly Christian, one could argue that it resonates with the Christian mentality outlined in this chapter. My thanks to historian Thomas Kidd for the initial recommendation to read Newport.

[16] Part of remaining in a job may mean doing that which we prefer not to do. Summing up Luther's doctrine of vocation, Gustaf Wingren observes that "a Christian finds himself called to drab and lowly tasks, which seem less remarkable than monastic life, mortifications, and other distractions from our vocations. For him who heeds his vocation, sanctification is hidden in offensively ordinary tasks, with the result that it is hardly noticed at all that he is a Christian." Wingren, *Luther*

leaving one's workplace—in this case, servitude—sinful behavior. But he does seem to privilege stability. We Christians have freedom to tweak our situations, yes, but generally speaking we should err on the side of stability and solidity.

Our doctrine of work is ringingly eschatological.[17] Work *will* be perfect; we will find our ideal callings. This will happen in the age to come. The issue of the return of the Son of God makes all the difference here. We cannot taste the absolute best now; we can only lay hold of it in the age to come. Knowing this helps us avoid a theology of salvation by vocation. Many around us buy such theology and follow such poor thinking. They ask their jobs to function as their saviors; they think that if they just sacrifice a little more, climb the ladder a little higher, and see their family a little less, then they will attain their goals. In some form, though, God will always frustrate such plans. We may make major gains in our labors, and we may enjoy God's blessing on our endeavors. But those who ask work to be their purpose will never be fulfilled. There is no perfect job; there is only a perfect God. [18]

---

on Vocation, trans. Carl C. Rasmussen (1957; Eugene, OR: Wipf and Stock, 2004), 73.

[17] It is only in what Keller and Alsdorf call the "gospel worldview" that work truly matters and is truly contributing to something eternal. See Keller and Alsdorf, *Every Good Endeavor*, 160–63.

[18] Instead of a search for "perfect work," we do well to search for productive work. On this point and the benefits of such labor, see Grudem, *Christian Ethics*, 926–29.

So far from dampening our conception of vocation, the foregoing truths free us. This freedom involves and draws out the full measure of our unique gifting. Too often, believers approach work from what is nearly a utilitarian vantage point. The work does not really count, we might think, but the godly attitude and gospel testimony do. Scripture corrects such thinking, showing us that the application of God-given skill honors our skillful Creator. The one who does all things well would have his children do all things well. We think here of the craftsmanship displayed in the Old Testament temple. Francis Schaeffer captures well the artistry that beautified this holy building:

[I]n verses 16 and 17 [of 2 Chronicles 3] we read, "And he made chains in the oracle, and put them on the tops of the pillars; and he made a hundred pomegranates, and put them on the chains. And he set up the pillars before the temple, one on the right hand, and the other on the left." Here are two free-standing columns. *They supported no architectural weight and had no utilitarian engineering significance.* They were there only because God said they should be there as a thing of beauty. Upon the capitals of those columns were pomegranates fastened upon chains. Art work upon art work. If we understand what we are reading here, it simply takes our breath away. This is something overwhelmingly beautiful.[19]

---

[19] Francis Schaeffer, *Art and the Bible* (1973; Downers Grove, IL: InterVarsity, 2009), 27.

Schaeffer's argument informs our conceptions of work. The text tells us that Solomon managed the building, but we know he tapped craftsmen for this project. The subsuming of individual laborers into the king's design actually expands our appreciation of the temple's beauty. It reveals to us both that the king cared about these fine details and that he had artisans who could enflesh his aesthetics. Love of beauty, of artistic performance, and of labor that produces such performance are not new. They stretch back thousands of years to God himself. The race made beautiful by the special creation of God—the one who is beauty[20]—has the privilege of making beautiful things, both in an intrinsic and theocentric sense.[21]

Our work to glorify God is not limited. We work because God works and has given us the chance to emulate him. Doxology is in the details.[22] We glorify God when we start honest businesses and grow them to produce much value for many

---

[20] On the beauty of God, see Owen Strachan and Douglas Sweeney, *The Essential Jonathan Edwards: An Introduction to the Life and Teaching of America's Greatest Theologian* (Chicago: Moody, 2018), 115–30.

[21] We have the opportunity, in other words, to create things that are beautiful, even as our work in God's name is itself a thing of beauty.

[22] Reflecting on the goodness of work leads us far beyond our own feeble efforts. Martin Luther says it well: "When you mention and pray for daily bread, you pray for everything that is necessary in order to have and enjoy daily bread . . . You must open wide and extend your thoughts not only to the oven or the flour-bin but to the distant field and the entire land, which bears and brings to us daily bread and every sort of sustenance." Martin Luther, *The Large Catechism*, trans. F. Bente and W. H. T. Dau in *Triglot Concordia: The Symbolical Books of the Ev. Lutheran Church* (St. Louis: Concordia, 1921), accessed January 20, 2019,

people, creating jobs and wealth and value where none previously existed. We glorify God when we train for years in a specific field to acquire elite skills that may have no mass-market effect, but will serve us well in a profession. We glorify God when we teach and love children, doing all we can to build into them; this, too, is work, deep work, though our culture may not recognize it as such. We glorify God when we serve in menial jobs that others may despise, and our coworkers may groan about, but that we approach from a God-centered perspective. Every moment we live, and work, is a moment to remanate his divine excellency, as Jonathan Edwards argued.[23] It is not constraint that characterizes the God-entranced laborer; it is freedom and a zest for doxology and purpose. We work *coram deo*, and we taste the enchantment of this world in doing so.[24]

We do well to remember that our work glorifies one figure above all. Christians believe that the promotion of Jesus Christ in all the earth is the highest privilege known to man. Whether we do so directly by teaching and preaching Christ, or more indirectly as evangelical witnesses in our God-given vocations, we

---

http://www.iclnet.org/pub/resources/text/wittenberg/luther/catechism/web/cat-12.html.

[23] Edwards, "The End for Which God Created the World," 530–32 (see chap. 1, n. 57). On the importance of pursuing excellence in all areas of life, see Andreas Köstenberger, *Excellence: The Character of God and the Pursuit of Scholarly Virtue* (Wheaton, IL: Crossway Books, 2011).

[24] For more on this brand of vocation, see Gene Edward Veith Jr., *God at Work: Your Christian Vocation in All of Life*, Focal Point (Wheaton, IL: Crossway Books, 2011).

find no greater calling than this. We must have ministry workers, or else the church of Christ cannot know health; this is a high calling, and we do well to prioritize it. Yet we must have witnesses unto God in manifold vocations, or else unbelievers will never encounter the truth. The believer gives honor to God by working unto the Lord and applying skill to daily tasks, but the believer also honors God by taking Christ everywhere he goes. There is no tension between theistically meaningful work and Christocentric witness. The two go hand in hand. Ideally, unbelievers will see the unique ethic and skill of believers and wonder aloud as to the genesis of such efforts. Ideally, believers will witness unto God in such moments, not only pointing to Genesis and the Creator God, but also drawing attention to the Christ who came, worked hard, and always transacted his Father's business. He is the emblem of our work; he is the *telos* (τέλος) of our work. Kuyper makes the point eloquently:

> Wherever man may stand, whatever he may do, to whatever he may apply his hand, in agriculture, in commerce, and in industry, or his mind, in the world of art, and science, he is, in whatsoever it may be, constantly standing before the face of his God, he is employed in the service of his God, he has strictly to obey his God, and above all, he has to aim at the glory of his God.[25]

---

[25] Abraham Kuyper, "Calvinism and Religion," lecture, Princeton Univ., October 11, 1898, Princeton, NJ, in *Lectures on Calvinism* (1931; repr., Grand Rapids: Eerdmans, 2000), 53.

The believer who labors well experiences many dimensions of divine blessing. The satisfaction of work done well and consecrated to the Lord rates highest. We do not labor for wages alone; we find reward in the work itself. The Father does not withhold good gifts from his children, and so the believer fundamentally sees God as a God of plenty, not miserliness. We approach work and provision from the standpoint of abundance, not scarcity.[26] Western society has negotiated several waves of alarmism over the last few years; we have heard that humanity dangled on the precipice of extinction, and that the race as a whole needed to drastically alter its habits—and in some cases, cull its herd—in order to survive.[27] Though this secular eschatology has found a strong audience, these prophecies in the paranoid style have not borne out. We would not expect this in theological terms; we should not abide such doomsaying in civilizational terms, for though we must always steward this realm, humanity has seen its life expectancy, standard of living, and average household income skyrocket in recent generations.[28]

---

[26] For more on a mentality of abundance funded by doctrinal thinking, see Wayne Grudem and Barry Asmus, *The Poverty of Nations: A Sustainable Solution* (Wheaton, IL: Crossway, 2013).

[27] See Thomas Robert Malthus, *An Essay on the Principle of Population* (London: J. Johnson, 1798). For a helpful approach to this concept and related ideas—scarcity of resources among them—see Jay W. Richards, *Money, Greed, and God: Why Capitalism Is the Solution and Not the Problem* (San Francisco: HarperOne, 2011).

[28] See the notable statistical work by Hans Rosling on this matter. Hans Rosling, "The Best Stats You've Ever Seen," (lecture, TED2006, Monterey, CA, February 23, 2006), https://www.ted.com/talks/hans

Christians love abundance. We do not despise it. But we do exercise caution when it comes. We know that the sinful human heart, eager for an object of worship, may easily fall under the spell of money and of self-driven consumption. To state it bluntly, we would be fools not to exercise vigilance over our interest in money. The Old Testament commends such carefulness: "Give me neither poverty nor wealth; / feed me with the food I need" (Prov 30:8). Instead of over-mastering consumptiveness, the wise Christian quests after sustenance. If we have what we need, we should give thanks to God.[29] We should not make the mistake of sanctifying poverty, for the Bible does not, but neither should we endanger our souls to live comfortably. Paul concurs in 1 Tim 6:17–19, where he counsels the rich:

> Instruct those who are rich in the present age not to be arrogant or to set their hope on the uncertainty of wealth, but on God, who richly provides us with all things to enjoy. Instruct them to do what is good, to be rich in good works, to be generous and willing to share, storing up treasure for themselves as a good foundation

---

_rosling_shows_the_best_stats_you_ve_ever_seen. Life expectancy has, on average, doubled over the last two hundred years: Hans Rosling, "How does Income Relate to Life Expectancy? Short Answer: Rich People Live Longer," n.d., Gapminder, video, 01:45, accessed January 21, 2019, https://www.gapminder.org/answers/how-does-income-relate -to-life-expectancy.

[29] For a biblical-theological perspective on finances and possessions, see Grudem, *Christian Ethics*, 1012–43.

for the coming age, so that they may take hold of what is truly life.

Paul does not indict rich Christians in this passage. He does not condemn them for having wealth, even great wealth. Wall and Steele dive to the heart of Paul's directives: "Christianity does not demonize money or possessions, but only a preoccupation with and privatization of them."[30] The apostle offers no censure of their financial largesse but exhorts them to view their God-given money in theistic terms. The rich person will be tempted to "set their hope" on their material blessings, but only God can bear such expectations.[31] Money is an uncertain proposition; God is a surety. Money may come and go; God's love endures in all seasons. For the curse of the love of money, an affliction that crosses all barriers and eras, Paul proposes one cure: God.

Believers grounded in the knowledge of God seek a proper outlook on their finances. They resist the desire to find their identities in their money; they simultaneously resist the desire to gain true and lasting security by getting just a little bit more. They do not despise what they have; they do not evince a world-hating mentality in the sense that they reject all nonspiritual

---

[30] Robert W. Wall and Richard B. Steele, *1 and 2 Timothy and Titus*, The Two Horizons New Testament Commentary (Grand Rapids: Eerdmans, 2012), 149.

[31] Living in this way is deeply ironic: it is trusting in that which is fundamentally untrustable. See I. Howard Marshall and Philip H. Towner, *A Critical and Exegetical Commentary on the Pastoral Epistles*, International Critical Commentary (New York: T&T Clark, 2004), 671.

gifts. They exude a simpler, happier faith than this. They remember the provider behind all providence. God "richly provides" us with many good things, things that bring real delight (6:17). The implication is clear: if we view the Lord as miserly, and if we receive whatever good comes our way with sour twists of our mouths, then we dishonor the divine. He has seen fit to harvest the world for us, and when the harvest comes in full, we should rejoice and enjoy it.[32]

A proper theology of money has a healthy place, too, for dispersal. The blessed Christian gives freely and cheerfully. Instead of storing up earthly "treasure," we store up heavenly treasures through good works (1 Tim 6:18–19). Letting go means taking hold in the economy of grace. If we regularly release our money in order to show generosity, we reveal that our hearts no longer grasp at this world, but yearn for another. The Christian is already freed from the love of money by the power of Christ's cross; now we put this liberation into everyday practice. Many around us of varying income levels are ensnared by the pursuit and love of wealth. The Christian, whether rich or poor, abounds in good deeds and images the one who gives every good gift.[33]

---

[32] Treating the larger issue of wealth, Joe Rigney observes that "In the Bible, wealth is a sign of blessing" even as "prosperity and abundance are gifts from God" per Deut 28:11–12, Prov 14:24, and the text cited above. Joe Rigney, *The Things of Earth: Treasuring God by Enjoying His Gifts* (Wheaton, IL: Crossway, 2015), 186.

[33] Commenting on this text, Randy Alcorn sums up the appropriate posture of the rich: "The rich are not told they must take a vow of poverty. They are told essentially to take a vow of generosity. They

The Bible teaches neither poverty theology nor prosperity theology.[34] It bids us work hard, earn as much as we can, and give richly to the work of God. If God chooses that we know material abundance, so be it. If God designs that we know hardship, so be it. The Christian avoids mistakes on either end. We cannot condemn the rich by means of an unbiblical take on wealth; neither, however, can we baptize the ferocious quest for more goods for their own sake. Our work, done out of love for the Lord, glorifies him. Our wealth, stewarded with divine generosity squarely in view, also glorifies him. It is this doctrine, and this doctrine alone, that releases the human heart from a malnourished approach to our daily tasks. The Christian avoids nihilism, for our daily undertakings matter to God; the Christian steers clear of consumerism, for God is our chief delight and not any earthly thing; the Christian cuts the cords of miserliness, for giving provides its own release, a release that only generosity actuates. In all this, we experience the goodness of God, remembering that all this is prelude, and that the best things—the best life—lie ahead.

---

are to be rich in good deeds, quick to share, and quick to part with their assets for kingdom causes. In doing so, they will lay up treasures in heaven." Alcorn, *Money, Possessions and Eternity*, 2nd ed. (Carol Stream, IL: Tyndale, 2003), 291.

[34] See Craig Blomberg, *Neither Poverty nor Riches: A Biblical Theology of Possessions*, New Studies in Biblical Theology (Downers Grove, IL: InterVarsity, 2015). For a practical take, see Owen Strachan, *Risky Gospel: Abandon Fear and Build Something Awesome* (Nashville: Thomas Nelson, 2013), 115–34.

A Biblical Consideration of
Rest and Entertainment

We are freed in Christ to work; we are freed in Christ to rest. The preceding has laid out the duty, and joy-laden duty at that, of working as a Christian for God's glory. The Scripture calls us to steward our finances well from generous hearts. In similar terms, the Bible does not condemn resting. As we shall see, the Bible gives us a gracious framework from which to gain physical and especially spiritual refreshment.

As with the handling of money, we see divergent, even polarized, perspectives on rest today. Some view it as an evil, an impediment to what gives life meaning—the discharge of one's calling and the padding of one's bank account. In this outlook, rest represents an intrusion, an invasion. Sleep is a bad idea; time with family gets in the way of meaningful productivity. Workers of various kinds may practice such a mind-set; I recall various Silicon Valley celebrities talking in one breath about "work-life balance," while in another describing how as soon as the kids are tucked into bed they lock in for several more hours of email time.[35] The same technology that ostensibly frees us—and definitely eases the debilitating physical load borne by most laborers

---

[35] As one of many such examples, see Drake Baer, "The 5 Secrets to Sheryl Sandberg's Super Powers," *Fast Company*, November 4, 2013, https://www.fastcompany.com/3021002/the-5-secrets-to-sheryl-sandbergs-super-powers.

in human history—also lashes us to our devices, robbing us of quiet, sleep, and peace.[36]

On the other hand, we may despise work and unhealthily esteem rest. Instead of recognizing the goodness of vocation and the fulfillment inherent in daily labor, we may try to evade hard work and "live for the weekend." In such a view, retirement looms over all as the grand goal; the summer is when living really happens; the weekend brings true happiness, while the rest of the week serves a merely utilitarian function—the getting of money. To a surprising degree, modern educational culture prepares the young for this kind of decrepit lifestyle. One's classes and studies have little actual import; it is the parties, the sporting events, the time wasted with peers that gives real substance to one's high school and college experiences.[37] But this is a reversal of the case. For the Christian, learning and maturity have paramount importance; embracing a pseudo-Dionysian existence does not enhance life, as is promised, but ironically makes having fun a matter of work.[38]

---

[36] Consider the disturbing testimony of CEO Arianna Huffington, who reported that she became so exhausted from a frenetic schedule of travel, advocacy, and digital engagement that she passed out and broke her cheekbone. Arianna Huffington, *The Sleep Revolution: Transforming Your Life, One Night at a Time* (New York: Harmony, 2016), 7.

[37] Consider on-the-ground reports from elite universities that speak to this sorry state. See William Deresiewicz, *Excellent Sheep: The Miseducation of the American Elite and the Way to a Meaningful Life* (Tampa: Free Press, 2014).

[38] The blistering but accurate portrait of college life sketched by Tom Wolfe stands as the best modern critique of the devolution of what

The Christian doctrine of rest stems from proper theology. God, we read with wonderment, rested on the seventh day: "On the seventh day God had completed his work that he had done, and he rested on the seventh day from all his work that he had done. God blessed the seventh day and declared it holy, for on it he rested from all his work of creation" (Gen 2:2–3). The Lord did not need physical rest.[39] He had not grown tired from his creative labors. Instead, rest signals security and satisfaction on God's part. He had accomplished his tasks; he had carried out his holy will. From nothing, something glorious emerged. This occasioned divine celebration. The Lord did not simply sit back, as it were, on the seventh day. He made this day "holy," setting it apart as a picture of work done well, of the blessing that accrues when the will of God comes to full fruition.[40] Rest in biblical

---

is sometimes called "higher education." See Tom Wolfe, *I Am Charlotte Simmons: A Novel* (New York: Picador, 2004).

[39] "This 'rest' is not the rest of one who is exhausted (Exod. 5:5; Matt. 11:28), although that may be included. Creation rest describes the rest of one who is satisfied, one who looks at the world saying, *Behold, it is very good.* Karl Barth reminds us that to talk about God at rest is to talk about a loving God (1958: 215). Never ceasing, never satisfied, never finding time for any creature does not characterize a loving God." Eugene F. Roop, *Genesis*, Believers Church Bible Commentary (Scottdale, PA: Herald, 1987), 32–33.

[40] "By the commemoration of 'Sabbath,' God and his creatures share in the celebration of the good creation, and God's people are enjoined to enter into the rhythm of work and joyful rest. Embracing God's sabbath rest meant experiencing the sense of completeness and well being God had accomplished at creation in behalf of all human life." Mathews, *Genesis 1–11:26*, 180 (see chap. 1, n. 20).

orientation is not a curse. It does not interrupt good activities
that must continue without stopping. Biblical rest is charged
with the holy satisfaction and resulting joy of God.[41]

According to the law given to Moses, the people of God
emulated their Creator by resting. The Ten Commandments
carved the Sabbath day into stone: "Remember the Sabbath day,
to keep it holy: You are to labor six days and do all your work,
but the seventh day is a Sabbath to the LORD your God. You
must not do any work—you, your son or daughter, your male or
female servant, your livestock, or the resident alien who is within
your city gates" (Exod 20:8–10). We should not view this commandment from God as a killjoy. The nation celebrated their
dependence on the Lord once per week.[42] The Israelites enjoyed

[41] "God's finished task is sealed in the words *he rested* (2, 3; literally
'ceased'; from *šābat* (שָׁבַת), the root of 'sabbath'). It is the rest of achievement, not inactivity, for he nurtures what he creates; we may compare
the symbolism of Jesus 'seated' after his finished redemption (Heb. 8:1;
10:12), to dispense its benefits." Kidner, *Genesis*, 57 (see chap. 2, n. 24).

[42] John Walton suggests the uniqueness of the Israelite calendar in
the ancient Near East: "The hallowing of the seventh day—even the use
of a seven-day week—was unique in Israel within the broader ancient
Near Eastern world. Calendars and most measurements of time were
based on the lunar or the solar cycle; the seven-day week is based on neither. Still, a period of seven days seems to have had special significance."
Walton rightly calls attention to the gracious nature of God's directive:
"While the law in Exodus also carries religious overtones, it includes a
humanitarian component, allowing rest for everyone at all levels of society." Walton, *Genesis, Exodus, Leviticus, Numbers, Deuteronomy*, 232–33
(see chap. 1, n. 22).

freedom from their work, but theirs was a theocentric freedom.[43] Their "time off" was not dedicated to a lazy Sunday brunch and the indulgence of creature comforts. The Sabbath was set apart for worship of the living God. Pharaoh offered no rest; the Lord offered his own rest.[44]

This does not only mean that we must perform our duties. It meant for the Israelites that they had to rest. They could not allow their labors to dominate their lives. They were people just like modern people; they had tasks that needed handling, fences that needed repairing, ambitions they wished to enflesh. Yet the Lord barred his covenant people from drowning in work. Though the Lord wants his people to take dominion of the earth, we never cross over to self-sufficiency. We must always

---

[43] "The Sabbath is not portrayed as a day of recuperation from those too weak to keep working day after day without rest. It is portrayed rather as a stoppage good for everyone, for the purpose of refocusing on holiness (all concerns that stem from *belonging to God*, which is what holiness is) in order to enjoy God's blessings of that day and its potential ('Therefore the LORD blessed the Sabbath day and made it holy')." Douglas K. Stuart, *Exodus*, The New American Commentary, vol. 2 (Nashville: B&H, 2006), 460.

[44] "Yahweh's conferring of this gift on his people establishes them as his new moral, ethical, religious people as much as his gift and renewal of his moral, ethical, and religious commands. Without this sharing and recognition of the Sabbath, they could not be his true people. After their birth (creation) at the Reed Sea, Yahweh created a new Sabbath for them. Pharaoh had refused to give them any rest in Egypt (Exod 5:5); their new Master gives them a regular time of rest." Eugene Carpenter, *Exodus 19–40*, Evangelical Exegetical Commentary (Bellingham, WA: Lexham, 2017), 45–46.

fight to find our identity in the Lord. We should labor well in this life, but the God-fearer labors differently than the God-denier. We do not work to justify ourselves. We do not work to lord our skills over others. We work for God, and then we rest for God. Rest of the theological kind renders us a living testimony. We effectively confess this: Some may get ahead of me in my workplace by clocking punishing hours, but I will rest and accept the consequences. God is my portion.

The Christian can sleep and sleep well. It is not always easy to do so; we are frail creatures, easily tossed about and beset at any given moment with numerous difficulties. But we seek the goodness of sleep nonetheless. "I will both lie down and sleep in peace," says the Psalmist, "for you alone, Lord, make me live in safety" (Ps 4:8). Here, as in so many dimensions of biblical anthropology, we find God at the center of the matter, the heart of the issue. We sleep well not through mastering breathing techniques, or perfuming the air with just the right floral notes, or even straining to shut out the stresses that crowd in upon us. These things may help. But we sleep well—or at least pray to sleep well—by fundamentally reclaiming reality, that is, by remembering that God gives us safety and health so we may rest, and rest completely.[45] He guards us at night. He gives us

---

[45] Much as we may struggle to drift off, the unbeliever in view in this passage cannot rest in this way (Ps 4:7): "This is in direct contrast to the opponents who are to tremble 'when you are on your beds.' Thus, Yahweh's people may enjoy security *in the midst of* distress." Craig C. Broyles, *Psalms*, Understanding the Bible Commentary Series (Grand Rapids: Baker Books, 2012), 54–55.

peace that overcomes the flesh. He quiets what nothing else—not food, not drink, not medication, not techniques—can.

The Christian knows he is a creature. We are not God, and we cannot live as God. We do not combat our creatureliness; in appropriate terms, we welcome it. We walk through the valley of the shadow of death with foes all around us, but the Lord leads us beside quiet waters (Ps 23:2). This Psalm speaks of a stillness that transcends our surroundings. Here in the Old Testament, we have the stirrings of the greater rest that Christ gives in the New. "Come to me," he tells us, a battle-scarred people, "all of you who are weary and burdened, and I will give you rest" (Matt 11:28). Jesus, we note, does not do a great deal of resting in the Gospels. He does help the believer find physical rest, but that physical rest points to the rest of the matter: the rest of the soul. Sinners, desperate and burdened, thrashed and flailed, try to find peace. They cannot. Jesus, we learn, is the giver of peace. Jesus is peace. To know him is to rest.[46]

Rest is not a collection of minutes and hours. Rest is a person. This person is Christ. The Son of God shows us that he is the greater David, and he is the one who gives a greater rest. This rest is full. It awaits eschatological completion, to be sure, but we cannot miss the freight of this phrase: to know Christ by faith is

---

[46] "Astonishingly Jesus calls people in the first instance *to himself* and only subsequently to the yoke of discipleship. It is moreover he, rather than God, who gives rest. Jesus stands not only in the place of Wisdom and truth but even in the place of Yahweh. ἀναπαύσω, "I will give you rest," connotes here a refreshing and a fulfillment, and thus anticipates messianic or eschatological blessing." Donald A. Hagner, *Matthew 1–13*, Word Biblical Commentary, vol. 33A (Dallas: Word, 1993), 323.

to enter his rest. The dawn of salvation means there is no longer any work for the believer.[47] The repentant sinner rests "from his own works" (Heb 4:10). Joshua could not eventuate this peace; David could not actualize this release; only Jesus brings the exhausted laborer to unending spiritual quiet. Christ has overwhelmed our total depravity and our total insufficiency with his total righteousness. We thus live in a state of total restfulness.

Believers struggle mightily to comprehend the Sabbath. The actual position of many Christians on the Sabbath is a kind of halfway Sabbatarianism, combining in unfortunate terms both a confused strictness and a willful antinomianism. Our muddled theology fails to make good on the newness of the new covenant. Christ is our law, not the words of Moses, holy as they are. The old covenant law teaches us much about the will and ways of God, but it no longer binds us. Christ is our law, the law of love (John 13:34). He has not swept away the old covenant law as if it never existed and never mattered. Instead, he has fulfilled the old covenant law, which is the foundation of the new covenant law.[48] The teaching of Christ, expounded by the apostles and New Testament authors, now regulates, rules, and directs the life

[47] See Robert H. Mounce, *Matthew*, Understanding the Bible Commentary Series (Grand Rapids: Baker Books, 2011), 108.

[48] There is no more insightful concise treatment of this vexing matter—over which Christian scholars disagree—than Thomas R. Schreiner, "Good-Bye and Hello: The Sabbath Command for New Covenant Believers" in *Progressive Covenantalism: Charting a Course Between Dispensational and Covenant Theologies*, ed. Stephen J. Wellum and Brent E. Parker (Nashville: B&H Academic, 2016), 159–88.

of the Christian. Jesus is our law; Jesus is our righteousness; Jesus is our Sabbath. We are no longer bound by the old covenant command to take the Lord's Day off from work; instead, we live in the fullness of new covenant rest. The Sabbath is *now*, for Christ has fulfilled it. Schreiner concludes the point nicely: "the Sabbath has passed away with the coming of Jesus Christ and the ratification of the new covenant."[49] Jesus is our rest.

We do await, as stated, the final phase of this rest. The whole earth will soon bend and become the Lord's footstool. He will remake the cosmos, and the kings of the earth will stream into the New Jerusalem to offer him worship (Revelation 21). Then, we will know rest in the fullest possible dimension. We will not only know that our works cannot save us; there will be no self-righteousness budding in our hearts, no guilt complexes nipping at our heels, no struggles for proper identities ricocheting through our minds. There will be no battle, period. We will all have faces then. We will cease our frustrated striving. Our struggles will resolve. We will rest completely and finally, and in our rest serve the Lord our God and exult in him beyond the wildest reverie of our spiritual imaginations.

We will not only rest from our striving. We will also bid farewell to our boredom. Boredom is a common malady of earthly life, and one way we fight it off is through entertainment. It may seem strange to surface such a subject in a serious theological text. We must reiterate, however, our commitment not merely to theoretical anthropology, but to lived anthropology. The doctrine

---

[49] Schreiner, 180.

of humanity goes many curious places and introduces numerous fascinating questions, but to be biblical in the richest sense—and therefore truly theological—we must deal with humanity in the shape it actually takes.

We find ourselves in the age of unserious things. More than ever before, millions upon millions of people in the West have time and personal space in which to dedicate themselves to their favorite pastimes. Our avocations may morph into our vocations, for good and for ill. For most people in most eras of history, entertainment was a rarity. Today, entertainment sits just beyond our fingertips like a pet sitting at our feet, tail wagging, hungry for attention. We may queue up thousands upon thousands of movies, songs, and books on portable devices, watching media whenever we want and wherever we want with very little cost. We can go to any number of concerts, shows, attractions, and festivals for less than a day's wages. We may spend hours dissecting our leisure interests, and then listen to hundreds of hours of podcast content featuring the same. It is the same for our children, many of whom may approach entertainment like work, so plenteous are the possibilities before them.

We have to put a doctrine of leisure together with care. Beyond Sabbath, the biblical event that helps us carve out a doctrine of leisure is celebration. In the Old Testament, the community kept the fiftieth year as a year of Jubilee.[50] In this year, called

---

[50] For more on the Jubilee, see *Holman Illustrated Bible Dictionary*, ed. Chad Brand, Charles Draper, and Archie England (Nashville: Holman Reference, 2003), s.v. "festival."

the "year of liberty," the people did not work. They took the year off, forgave the debts of their debtors, and spent time with their loved ones (Lev 25:8–12). This should not be confused with a boisterous, unending party in the non-Christian sense. It does, however, show us that the Israelites observed this relaxed year by the directive of the divine. God himself wanted his people to cease their striving; God wanted them to enjoy time with one another in this holy year.[51]

Feasting and celebration recur in the Bible.[52] Isaiah pictures the king who conquers all Israel's enemies as himself throwing a grand feast. From atop a mountain, "the LORD of Armies will prepare for all the peoples a feast of choice meat, / a feast with aged wine, prime cuts of choice meat, fine vintage wine" (Isa 25:6). In contrast to the starving Gentiles of Isa 21:13–17—a related passage—the Lord invites his people to a banquet table overflowing with provision and goodness.[53] The Lord does not grimly celebrate his end-times routing of his foes. He celebrates this conquest with a feast for the ages, using delicious provision as the sign that the hard times have come and gone. The Lord has fought for his people; justice has dawned in the land. Those

---

[51] The believer, we recognize, lives fully in the unending "year of liberty" through the finished work of Christ. Every year, we could say, is a Jubilee year.

[52] See Rigney, *Things of Earth*, 124–25.

[53] J. Alec Motyer, *The Prophecy of Isaiah: An Introduction and Commentary* (Downers Grove, IL: InterVarsity, 1993), 209.

who love God cannot mark this occasion with mumbled thanks, but with nearly delirious joy.[54]

We find a similar scene in the New Testament. When the prodigal son returns in the parable Jesus tells about this once-woebegone man, his father immediately initiates a feast. Luke portrays a delightful event driven by deep thankfulness:

> The son said to him, "Father, I have sinned against heaven and in your sight. I'm no longer worthy to be called your son."
> But the father told his slaves, "Quick! Bring out the best robe and put it on him; put a ring on his finger and sandals on his feet. Then bring the fattened calf and slaughter it, and let's celebrate with a feast, because this son of mine was dead and is alive again; he was lost and is found!" So they began to celebrate.
> Now his older son was in the field; as he came near the house, he heard music and dancing. (Luke 15:21–25)

As in the Isaianic passage, the end of a difficult time brings great happiness. The father cannot restrain himself from celebrating the miracle of his younger son's return. Though his reaction might seem over-the-top, the father takes no care about his appearance. He clothes his son in finery, has the best food prepared, and

---

[54] "[O]n the true Zion (*cf.* Heb. 12:22–24) there is no element of representation; all come, all participate." The feast, in other words, has reached its eschatological apex. Motyer, 209.

begins a party that features music and dancing.[55] Luke's account paints this festal awakening as the natural response to the return of a sinner to God; it enlarges our appreciations, and our capacities, for the expression of theocentric delight. It is not wrong to give praise to God and do so in a time of celebration; it is in fact wrong to do the opposite and squelch joy when it rightly arises.[56]

If we pay attention to the scriptural witness, we glean an appreciation for celebration. The Christian does not feel indifferent to joy or the full range of human emotions. The Christian knows joy above all others on this earth, but a deeper joy than the natural man can imagine.[57] This joy is fundamentally God-centered and rooted in the kindness of the Lord, but it is by no means closed off from the good creational gifts of our sovereign.

We consider the words of Paul to the Corinthians (surrounded as they were by non-Christian pleasure seekers): "'Everything is permissible,' but not everything is beneficial. 'Everything is

---

[55] The food prepared here—the fattened calf—mirrors that offered on the Day of Atonement, but this death, is "for a celebration." Darrell L. Bock, *Luke*, vol. 2, *9:51–24:53*, Baker Exegetical Commentary on the New Testament (Grand Rapids: Baker Academic, 1996), 1315.

[56] Leon Morris's commentary informs our understanding of the uniquely compassionate and celebratory nature of divine love as expressed in the Christian life: "The old man's overflowing joy finds expression in his memorable opposition of *dead* to *alive again* and of *lost* to *found*. In the feast where *they began to make merry* perhaps the son found some of the solid pleasure he had looked for in vain in the far country." Leon Morris, *Luke: An Introduction and Commentary*, Tyndale New Testament Commentaries (Downers Grove, IL: InterVarsity, 1988), 260.

[57] See the classic work by John Piper, *Desiring God*, 25th anniv. ed. (Colorado Springs: Multnomah, 2011).

permissible,' but not everything builds up. No one is to seek his own good, but the good of the other person" (1 Cor 10:23–24). This guidance helps frame our approach to entertainment and leisure. The apostle Paul comprehends that this world contains many goods and avocations and even foods in which Christians may engage or not. He does not simply say do whatever one wishes; if the action in question is not immoral, then the Christian asks the question, "Is this helpful to others?" If no offense attaches to the action in question, then the believer possesses full freedom of conscience on the matter. The "earth is the Lord's," and so believers may enjoy the common-grace goodness of this earth. We do not wall ourselves off from our cultures and our neighbors. We have theological grounds for doing the opposite and for savoring the kind providence of God so abundantly found in this realm.

When it comes to entertainment and leisure, the Christian must do theological application. Our authoritative source does not tell us how much media to consume, what movies to watch, or whether our favorite hobby honors the Lord. Further, while we modern people have more options for our spare time than we can count, we have little direct commentary on how we should spend our time. The Christian does well to scrutinize daily habits, shaping them according to biblical priorities. Paul tells us, "When I was a child, I spoke like a child, I thought like a child, I reasoned like a child. When I became a man, I put aside childish things" (1 Cor 13:11). As one outworking of this teaching, though the apostle Paul does not answer whether we should play kids' games, he does encourage us to follow his example and "put aside childish things." Our entertainment culture accomplishes nothing if not this: it encourages us to see ourselves as children and to occupy our time with childish things. Childish things, we note, are not necessarily sinful, but serious believers will find their interests in such things lessening as they grow in godliness. The kingdom of God, after all, is at hand.

Conclusion

Such an approach to leisure, entertainment, and culture rests within a broader spirituality. The believer, whether we eat or drink, does all things to the glory of God (1 Cor 10:31). Our existence is a doxological one, and irreducibly spiritual. The believer approaches all of life as an adventurous, thrilling enterprise, a doxological undertaking. We seek to give God glory in our work, and not merely pass the time at our jobs. We seek to rest well, and avoid the traps of workaholism or passivity. We receive God's good gifts as what they are—gifts—and feel no guilt for enjoying this world.

We do all of these things as Christians. Our approach is distinct on these matters. We do not work as the pagans work, rest as the pagans rest, or play as the pagans play. God is our focus; God is the key; God is our greatest gift. Christians who see these truths free themselves from the prison of drudgery, the insubstantiality of lassitude, and the counsel of lawlessness. We are not free to sin against God, but we are freed from our iniquities and sent sprinting into a purposeful life oriented around the Lord. The question before the believer is not, *Is there joy to be found here?* but, *How am I going to harvest all this happiness with the time I have?*

CHAPTER 4

SEXUALITY

Do not forget that the fundamental contrast has always
been, is still, and will be until the end: Christianity and
Paganism, the idols or the living God.
—Abraham Kuyper, *Lectures on Calvinism*

There may be no more controversial statement today than this:
there are men, and there are women.[1] The Christian voices

---

[1] Consider the controversy, as one example, surrounding the ideas
promoted by University of Toronto professor Jordan Peterson. Peterson's
program deserves engagement on numerous issues, including his lack of
belief in the person of God. We cannot miss that a good portion of the
visceral pushback against Peterson has come because of his approach

this conviction not primarily because of psychological evidence, social observation, or emotional difference. The Christian bases this claim in the Word of God. Scholars can refute studies; skeptics can challenge opinions; individual stories can counter experience. The Word of God, however, cannot be silenced. What God makes cannot be undone. What God does cannot be overturned. What God opens no man can shut; what God shuts no man can open.

God's revelation and action—his revelatory action, not infrequently—create actual reality. That which we see with our eyes reflects exactly what the Bible trains us to expect. The Scripture tells us there are men and women, and this is what we see in the world before us. Manhood and womanhood explain so much of life in this sphere; our bodily structure, emotional tendencies, personal interests, and much more often reflect our God-given sex. This sounds controversial in our context, but it is the merest dose of wisdom. We live our lives as men or as women. Try as we might, we cannot do otherwise.

In the pages that follow, we will study the man and woman as initially created by God. In these foundations, we gain much wisdom for our own twenty-first-century lives. We then consider

---

to manhood and womanhood. Peterson treats these concepts as if they are actual realities. See Nellie Bowles, "Jordan Peterson: Custodian of the Patriarchy," *New York Times*, May 18, 2018, https://www.nytimes.com/2018/05/18/style/jordan-peterson-12-rules-for-life.html; Pankaj Mishra, "Jordan Peterson and Fascist Mysticism," *New York Review of Books*, March 19, 2018, https://www.nybooks.com/daily/2018/03/19/jordan-peterson-and-fascist-mysticism.

God's plan for men and women in marriage, looking afresh at the gift of children and the calling of singleness. We then contrast biblical sexuality with fallen sexuality, understanding as we do so that our quest to reenchant humanity—to see the human race through divine eyes—collides with a neopagan perspective on the human person.

God's Original Design of the Sexes

The first truth of manhood is that God made it. Manhood in the biblical system does not owe to impersonal processes or chaotic sorting. The waters of the seas churned, but the Lord—as we have seen—brought order from the wildness and made a human being, a man, with a distinct body. The man was formed first and made from the ground's dust (Gen 2:7). The man did not have life in himself; the Lord breathed into him, and so the man came fully to life.

The man had duties from the beginning. By both divine mandate and geographic placement, he had a tremendous charge from his Maker. A garden, bursting with vitality, beckoned to him. The first man had a home, and he inhabited a definite place (Gen 2:8). Adam had much to do—the Lord called him to both "work" and "watch over" the garden (Gen 2:15).[2] Coded into the

---

[2] Raymond Ortlund translates "watch over" as "guard," reminding us that even before the fall, the Lord was setting up a defense against evil. Ortlund, "Male-Female Equality and Male Headship," 100 (see chap. 2, n. 36).

man's mind was the expectation that he would work in Eden; God had not placed him there to whittle away the time. He had both a provisional role—in seed form, if you will—and a protective role.[3] The text here does not articulate what exactly Adam would need to watch for, but we find out soon enough.

The first man lived under authority, and though possessing considerable agency, he could not have understood himself as an automaton.[4] His divine Father gave him high-definition instructions about his conduct, separating right from wrong, as we have discussed at some length (16–17). The man had no part in laying out the terms of the arrangement; he dealt with a totally sovereign being, and he is not quoted in the text while the Lord outlines his holy duties. Ortlund sums it up nicely: "For the man to . . . attempt an autonomous existence, freed from God, would be his ruin."[5]

The man is not autonomous in two senses. First, he lives under the lordship of God, and second, he is made for marriage. Genesis 2:18 introduces the need for woman by identifying the man's aloneness as "not good." He needs a "helper" fit for him,

---

[3] Tragically, even before eating the forbidden fruit, Adam will fail in this protective role. It is thus appropriate to see a chain of disobedience and sin leading up to the climactic moment when the woman and man partake of the tree's produce. See Beale, *Temple and the Church's Mission*, 87 (see chap. 1, n. 34).

[4] Hamilton observes that Adam has "ample permission" to labor in the garden. Hamilton, *The Book of Genesis*, 172 (see chap. 1, n. 12).

[5] Ortlund, "Male-Female Equality and Male Headship," 100 (see chap. 2, n. 36).

one who would partner with Adam to obey the Lord and carry out his heavenly commission. The woman's identity, that of *ezer* (helper), stands out, for the text nowhere identifies the man as such.[6] The woman is called to see herself as her husband's helper.[7] The Lord makes the woman in order to bless the man and serve him. She is formed second and corresponds to him; he already has been given the initiative to glorify the Lord. She does not receive her own set of instructions from God; she helps the man fulfill the charge already handed down from the Creator.

As the Lord forms new living beings, he has Adam name them (Gen 2:19). This indicates Adam's leadership over the animal kingdom. He has significant responsibility in the God-made world, but he has no "helper." The animals do not "correspond to him"; nothing from the fields, the skies, or the seas can fit with Adam to populate the earth. This only the woman can do. So the Lord sends Adam into deep slumber, and he makes the woman from the man's rib (21–22). The woman owes her very life in physical terms to the man; she is dependent upon his body and strength for her existence. Bruce Ware comments, "In the

---

[6] "The woman was created to meet the man's need for companionship and to assist him and partner with him in subduing the earth, particularly through procreation." Köstenberger and Köstenberger, *God's Design for Man and Woman*, 39.

[7] So far from indicating the inferiority of the woman, this term connotes dignity and unique abilities. It "is applied several times throughout the Old Testament to none other than God himself." See Exod 18:4, Pss 20:2; 33:20; 146:5, among other texts. Köstenberger and Köstenberger, 36.

very formation of the woman, it was to be clear that her life, her constitution, her nature, was rooted in and derived from the life, constitution, and nature of the man."[8] In other words, that which Ephesians 5 and 1 Corinthians 11 call headship is already present seminally in Genesis 2.

The man exults when he sees the woman for the first time, and just as he has done for all living creatures, he names her—*ishah* (אִשָּׁה), "woman" (Gen 2:23). The man's song of praise speaks to both literal and spiritual realities: the woman does derive from his body, but she is the one who fits him, who delights him, who greeted him in what must have seemed like a waking dream.[9] She is bone of his bone physically; she is bone of his bone spiritually, for they are united by God himself. If ever there was a holy moment filled with innocence and joy and thankfulness, it was

---

[8] "Her very human nature is constituted, not in parallel fashion to his with both formed from the same earth, but as *derived from his own nature*, so showing a God-chosen dependence upon him for her origination." Ware, "Male and Female Complementarity and the Image of God," 83 (see chap. 1, n. 41).

[9] "It is the beauty of loftiness that the man embodies, even as the beauty of comeliness is the possession of the woman. . . . To the man belongs the strength of physical prowess, the wide chest, the commanding eye, the full beard, the powerful voice; to the woman belongs a delicate shape, sensitive skin, full bosom, round shape, soft voice, long hair, elegant carriage, and supple movement. He engenders respect, she engenders tenderness." Herman Bavinck, *The Christian Family*, trans. Nelson D. Kloosterman (Grand Rapids: Christian's Library, 2012), 69. Bavinck does not communicate here that every man looks exactly alike, nor that every woman does. Rather, he focuses attention on the God-given design of the manly and womanly body.

this one. The Lord's design of the man and the woman is good; the Lord's design of marriage, the union of one man and one woman, is good.

Genesis 2 further underlines the man's leadership role in verse 24 (ESV). The man is called to depart from "his father and mother" and "hold fast" to his wife. In doing so, they "become one flesh." The man must set the tone in marriage; he must embrace adulthood and leave the care and nurture of his home in order to form a new family. As he launches out and takes a wife, the Lord holds him responsible for the sustenance and endurance of the marriage. Though our modern culture ascribes such duties to the woman, the Bible summons men to encircle their families with cords of love that do not break.[10] The man pursues his wife, reverences her as Adam does Eve, and glorifies the Lord in this "one flesh" relationship. The two become one not in the sense that they lose their distinctiveness, but by becoming one family. Their God-honoring sexual union unites them in a powerful way, and it bears no inherent shame.[11] Nakedness in the context of holy matrimony is no evil thing; it is a gift of God (25).

---

[10] In doing so, the man is acting as a Christlike "head" of his wife. Christ does not ask the church, his bride, to hold fast to him; rather, he holds fast to her, as is clear in the language directed at husbands in Eph 5:25–33. For this connection, see George W. Knight III, "Husbands and Wives as Analogues of Christ and the Church: Ephesians 5:21–33 and Colossians 3:18–19," in *Recovering Biblical Manhood and Womanhood: A Response to Evangelical Feminism*, ed. John Piper and Wayne Grudem (Wheaton, IL: Crossway, 2006),170–71.

[11] "One-flesh union is deeper than sexual union" though it includes it. Schreiner, *New Testament Theology*, 777 (see chap. 2, n. 42).

The Lord has done a great deal in Genesis 2. The rest of the Old Testament builds off this creational activity. Though the man and the woman fall from the Lord, God does not destroy marriage or the family. He pronounces a curse upon the very bodies and relational dynamics that he has created. The woman will bear her children in pain and will vie to lead her home, a role that is not given her by God (Gen 3:16).[12] The man will correspondingly abuse his authority in the home, and will not treat women as he should.[13] Now, he will work the ground in pain (17–19). As we have seen, the subversion of God's good plan leads to untold marital and familial suffering; the man and the woman harm no one more than themselves by sinning against the Lord in Eden.

But none of this means that manhood and womanhood vanish into the ether. To the contrary, the Bible gives us many glimpses of what redeemed men and redeemed women can do in the name of the Lord. In the context of the people of God, the Lord continues

---

[12] The language of Gen 3:16 is strikingly similar to the language of Gen 4:7. In both instances, we read of "desire for" something. Sin's desire in 4:7 is clearly to master and rule over Cain; in 3:16, a woman will seek to master and rule over her husband, reversing God's design. See Ortlund, "Male-Female Equality," 108–9; Susan T. Foh, "What Is the Woman's Desire," *Westminster Theological Journal* 37 (1975): 376–83.

[13] This can mean *either* sinful passivity or sinful authoritarianism. Husbands of the Adamic kind will sometimes opt out of their God-given duties as in the garden or else "harshly dominate" their wives. Either sin deeply dishonors the Lord. The ideal role that is filled by the regenerate husband is thus neither soft nor angry, but rock-solid, righteous, confident, assertive, gracious, and loving leadership. See Köstenberger and Köstenberger, *God's Design for Man and Woman*, 47–49.

to call men to leadership and righteous authority. Men serve as the key figures in the nation of Israel, filling the roles of king, priest, and prophet, and they hold one another to a high standard. We think, for example, of David's deathbed words to his son Solomon:

> When David's time to die drew near, he commanded Solomon his son, saying, "I am about to go the way of all the earth. Be strong, and show yourself a man, and keep the charge of the LORD your God, walking in his ways and keeping his statutes, his commandments, his rules, and his testimonies, as it is written in the Law of Moses, that you may prosper in all that you do and wherever you turn, that the LORD may establish his word that he spoke concerning me, saying, 'If your sons pay close attention to their way, to walk before me in faithfulness with all their heart and with all their soul, you shall not lack a man on the throne of Israel.'" (1 Kgs 2:1–4 ESV)

The phrase "show yourself a man" stands out here. The modern equivalent, "be a man," usually signifies the need to exhibit toughness and assertiveness in the face of difficulty. To be weak means to compromise the nature of manliness. David does not disagree. In fact, his charge points to the performative nature of this God-given calling; Solomon must not fail to act out this vision of masculine strength. He has to show this. He has to be strong. Failure to show strength means a failure of manhood.

But what precisely does God-honoring strength look like? David says little here about feats of strength or grand displays of daring. While his conception of manhood surely includes physical fortitude and bravery, he sees manliness as spiritual in nature and grounded in sound doctrine. Solomon must obey God, following the divine will and keeping the Mosaic Law. The fourfold breakdown of the law here makes clear that Solomon must be strong to obey, rejecting sinful weakness and the weakness of sinfulness. A man is never less strong than when he rejects God's moral will and succumbs to sin. He may feel strong in such a moment, he may think he is bristling with power, but he is in truth picking himself apart piece by piece. David knew of such self-caused dissolution; he knew what it was like to crash into the dust in a hurricane of personal ruin. With the backdrop of his own failures in his mind, he called his son to a better way, to true strength grounded in the truth and righteousness of God.

The ancient man of God had no separate call. He had to lead, to protect, to provide, to teach, and to love his family. He trained his children wherever he went, and he had to instruct them in divine truth (Deut 6:6–9). When danger came, he was called to go to war and risk his life for his loved ones and his nation. If the people of God were called to battle, then they were called to fight with fearlessness. Among the "mighty men" of David, for example, Josheb-basshebeth killed eight hundred men with his spear (2 Sam 23:8). The biblical text celebrates, and in no way condemns, such courageous soldiering.[14]

---

[14] Soldiers, in fact, serve in both the old and new covenants as a model for manhood. We find examples in texts such as Exod 15:3 and 2 Tim 4:7. Exodus identifies the Lord himself as a warrior. As a culture

Men had to be ready to fight and die. Life in the ancient Near East was no picnic for either men or women. In addition to fending off attacks and threats, the man had the duty of keeping his family fed. What Exod 21:10 made explicit, various men in the Old Testament demonstrated. Few figures in the Bible better demonstrate godly manhood than Boaz, who cared for Ruth, helped her even outside of marriage, and then took her as his wife. In the book of Hosea, the prophet's wayward wife leaves his care and keeps company with foreign lovers. She later returns to him and his provision, as he abundantly meets her needs (Hos 2:5–9). So it is in God's own union with his covenant bride; he loves and blesses Jerusalem, his rescued people, with metaphorical clothing, adornments, and "fine flour, honey, and oil" (Ezek 16:13). A godly Hebrew man was a leader, protector, and provider.

The godly women of the Old Testament show the distinct beauty of womanhood. This beauty is not in high cheekbones or flowing locks, but in the fear of God. The Proverbs 31 woman presents us with a woman who does not live her life gripped by

---

moves away from any sense of a biblical conception of manhood (however imperfect), it moves away from an explicitly martial outlook and loses sight of martial virtues (even as it will practice a perverted form of them through passive-aggression or unrestrained violence). For a profitable if veiled philosophical discussion of these, see Harvey C. Mansfield, *Manliness* (New Haven, CT: Yale Univ., 2006), 86–90. In his discussion of William James's understanding of the martial virtues, Mansfield identifies them as "intrepidity, contempt of softness, surrender of private interest, obedience to command" (88).

the expectations of mere men. She lives for God (Prov 31:30). She is a vivid picture of the God-centered "helper," for her husband "trusts in her" even as he sits with the elders at the city gates (31:11, 23). He has the call to go and lead the people; while he is not home, he knows that she is producing a veritable harvest of good for them and their children. This righteous woman's burden is her family and home. She strengthens it through economic activity (31:13, 16, 24), cooking for her household (31:15), clothing her loved ones (31:21), and speaking truth and wisdom (31:25). The care and nurture of her family and her home occupy her attention constantly (v. 27).

The family is not a tiny corporation for the godly woman. The family is a living being. It is greater than a numerical collection of individuals. The family is alive, and alive in a way that mirrors the Trinity's own familial life. The family literally lives together; we hear this phrase commonly, so it has little punch, but this does not diminish the uniquely shared nature of the family. The family has a life and love unto itself as members spend time together and laugh and mourn and play and work and talk. Whatever one's role in the family, one participates in something greater than oneself. A godly wife and mother has the joy, according to Scripture, of making her home a happy dwelling for the family. The home is not an instrumental good for the godly woman. The home is the nest of the family, a haven, a refuge.

There are many skills a godly woman may learn with regard to the family, but in all her work, she is more creating art than

doing science. Edith Schaeffer captures the aesthetic dimension of family life when she speaks of the significance of a meal.
"Being challenged by what a difference her cooking and her way
of serving is going to make in the family life gives a woman
an opportunity to approach this with the feeling of painting a
picture or writing a symphony."[15] Serving her family by making
a home represents the masterwork of many Christian women.
This work is not lesser than wage-driven labor. In many respects,
it is greater. The Bible calls attention to the beauty and importance of such investment (Titus 2:5). Where Schaeffer captures
the aesthetic dimension of this labor, Elisabeth Elliot identifies
its spiritual nature:

> The routines of housework and of mothering may be
> seen as a kind of death, and it is appropriate that they
> should be, for they offer the chance, day after day, to lay
> down one's life for others. Then they are no longer rou-
> tines. By being done with love and offered up to God
> with praise, they are thereby hallowed as the vessels of
> the tabernacle were hallowed—not because they were
> different from other vessels in quality or function, but
> because they were offered to God. A mother's part in
> sustaining the life of her children and making it pleasant
> and comfortable is no triviality. It calls for self-sacrifice

---

[15] Edith Schaeffer, *The Hidden Art of Homemaking: Creative Ideas for Enriching Everyday Life* (Carol Stream, IL: Tyndale, 1985), 124.

and humility, but it is the route, as was the humiliation of Jesus, to glory.[16]

The viewpoint critiqued above both implicitly and explicitly by Schaeffer and Elliot was that of feminism. Feminism was the first of the four major modern sexual ideologies to challenge the church; it went hand in hand with "free love" and the severing of heterosexual sex (the second of the four major modern sexual ideologies, which we cover below) from marriage. Feminists argued that womanhood should not be tied to the roles of child raising and homemaking, but that women should feel free to embrace traditional masculine duties and vocations. Feminism was in truth a deeply theological movement from the outset, though few have paid attention to this reality. The theological vision of womanhood constructed in this section contrasts with modern feminism.[17]

This kind of life is theologically driven and empowered by God. If we consider the famous archetypal woman of Proverbs 31, we see that she is a woman of strength. Hers is a uniquely feminine strength, and it is grounded in God's design and God's

---

[16] Elisabeth Elliot, *Love Has a Price Tag: Inspiring Stories That Will Open Your Heart to Life's Little Miracles* (Ventura, CA: Regal Books, 2005), 209–10.

[17] Helpful resources offering a thorough engagement with feminism include Mary A. Kassian, *The Feminist Mistake: The Radical Impact of Feminism on Church and Culture* (Wheaton, IL: Crossway Books, 2005); Margaret Elizabeth Köstenberger, *Jesus and the Feminists: Who Do They Say That He Is?* (Wheaton, IL: Crossway Books, 2008).

righteous call. She draws on it regularly and uses it in many ways for the good of people all around her (Prov 31:17). Her arms are strong, and she does not give off the air of a defeated, listless, directionless laborer. She exercises dominion over her environment. But here again, she does so as a woman. She does not have the same body as the man; they are both human and both image-bearers, but they have different bodies, and their bodies have the shapes they do because of the plan of God for the sexes, for marriage, and for the family. God made the woman's body for the bearing and feeding of children, while the man has neither capacity.[18] God made the man stronger and faster and more aggressive in order to drive him into his duties; he has on average 1,000 percent more testosterone than women, one of the more startling realities of human biology.[19]

---

[18] "Women can and ought to be judged by the criteria of femininity, for it is in their femininity that they participate in the human race. And femininity has its limitations. So has masculinity. That is what we've been talking about. To do this is not to do that. To be this is not to be that. To be a woman is not to be a man." Elisabeth Elliot, *Let Me Be a Woman: Notes to My Daughter on the Meaning of Womanhood* (1976; repr., Wheaton, IL: Tyndale, 2013), 65.

[19] Anne and Bill Moir, *Why Men Don't Iron: The Fascinating and Unalterable Differences Between Men and Women* (New York: Citadel, 1999), 221. Anne Moir is an Oxford-trained geneticist with a PhD in the field. This data compares favorably to unbiased scientific research from the Mayo Clinic: "Testosterone, Total, Bioavailable, and Free, Serum," Mayo Clinic Laboratories, accessed January 21, 2019, https://www.mayomedicallaboratories.com/test-catalog/Clinical+and+Interpretive/83686. One resource, reading the data from the Mayo Clinic, lists the average male-female testosterone ratios as follows: average level for an

Godly women defy the devil and live for the Lord. They present themselves as women, and they do not try to rule men or deny the differences between the sexes. Yet they exercise faith no less energetically than men.[20] We think of righteous Hannah, who desired the gift of children and who prayed tenaciously during her barrenness and persecution at the hands of Peninnah (1 Samuel 1–2). We consider Esther, who obeyed her uncle Mordecai's prompting and used her unique position in the Persian kingdom—and her unique beauty, a gift of God not to be despised—to save the Jewish people (Esther 4). We remember the steely courage of Deborah and Jael. Deborah tried to rouse the manly instincts of Barak; though some see Deborah as an ambitious warrior-prophetess, the shoe and the helmet do not fit (Judges 4–5).[21] Deborah saw Barak's wavering, she challenged him to fight in the name of God (citing the Lord's promise of deliverance), but Barak would not go up alone (Judg 4:6–8).

---

adult male, 270–1070 (ng/dl); average level for an adult female, 15–70. See Alexia Severson, R. Sam Barclay, and Joy Bailey, "Testosterone Levels by Age," *Healthline*, accessed January 21, 2019, https://www .healthline.com/health/low-testosterone/testosterone-levels-by-age. Various behaviors are affected by these differing levels: sex drive, aggression, interest in physical violence, and more.

[20] See Mark Chanski, *Womanly Dominion: More Than a Gentle and Quiet Spirit* (Amityville, NY: Calvary, 2008).

[21] Schreiner has it right: in all this scene, "Deborah is not asserting leadership for herself; she gives priority to a man." Thomas R. Schreiner, "The Ministries of Women in the Context of Male Leadership," in *Recovering Biblical Manhood and Womanhood: A Response to Evangelical Feminism*, ed. John Piper and Wayne Grudem (Wheaton, IL: Crossway, 2006), 216.

Here again in the biblical narrative manly passivity—self-chosen weakness—reveals itself.

Deborah wanted Barak to lead God's people into battle. He would not, so she went, but not without a warning: "'I will gladly go with you,' she said, 'but you will receive no honor on the road you are about to take, because the LORD will sell Sisera to a woman.' So Deborah got up and went with Barak to Kedesh" (Judg 4:9). This is no happy moment for Israel; Deborah laments the weakness of a supposed man of God. John Piper and Wayne Grudem do justice to the passage when they denote Deborah as "a living indictment of the weakness of Barak and other men in Israel who should have been more courageous leaders."[22] For her part, Jael had no time for lament; when the evil commander Sisera fell into her hands, the righteous Jael "took a tent peg, grabbed a hammer, and went silently to Sisera. She hammered the peg into his temple and drove it into the ground, and he died" (4:21). Jael's faith led her to an unquiet, but definitely courageous, moment.[23]

The Lord did not design men and women to fight with one another. His plan in the Old Testament is for men and women to love one another. His overarching plan is that a man take a wife and, if possible, the couple bear children, thus growing the family per the blessing of God (Psalms 127; 139). He wishes for the man

---

[22] John Piper and Wayne Grudem, "An Overview of Central Concerns: Questions and Answers," in *Recovering Biblical Manhood and Womanhood: A Response to Evangelical Feminism*, ed. John Piper and Wayne Grudem (Wheaton, IL: Crossway, 2006), 72.

[23] Köstenberger and Köstenberger, *God's Design*, 67–69.

to lead the family, protect it, provide for it, and love it. In so doing, the husband and father images the God who takes a covenant people for himself and reveals himself as their familial head. The earthly husband sees no threat to his value in a gifted, godly wife; rather, like the husband of Proverbs 31, this man thrills to find such a woman and praises her to all he encounters. For her part, this woman delights to serve her husband and follow him; she loves the God-given duties of submission, procreation, nurture, familial care, and homemaking (1 Tim 2:9–15; Titus 2:3–5).

The couple together find delight in God's gift of marriage. Their love takes on joyful physical expression, as in the Song of Songs, but subsists of more than this. Their love is spiritual. It is body to body, but beyond this, soul to soul.[24] The couple faithful to Scripture is doing something more than making a day-to-day life; they are obeying God in one-flesh union.

God's Vision for Marriage in the New Testament

As we would expect, the New Testament builds off the Old Testament's visions of manhood, womanhood, marriage, and family. In the Bible's deepest look at the nature of marriage, the apostle Paul addresses the problematized dynamic of covenant marriage in Ephesians 5. The difficulties of post-fall union meet their match in the gospel:

---

[24] "The essence of marriage lies in the full and complete communion of husband and wife, with body and soul together, for all of life." Bavinck, *The Christian Family*, 85.

148

Wives, submit to your husbands as to the Lord, because the husband is the head of the wife as Christ is the head of the church. He is the Savior of the body. Now as the church submits to Christ, so also wives are to submit to their husbands in everything. Husbands, love your wives, just as Christ loved the church and gave himself for her to make her holy, cleansing her with the washing of water by the word. He did this to present the church to himself in splendor, without spot or wrinkle or anything like that, but holy and blameless. In the same way, husbands are to love their wives as their own bodies. He who loves his wife loves himself (Eph 5:22–28).

These verses, and those that follow, represent the New Testament answer to the Old Testament quagmire. The apostle Paul's picture of what marriage can be in Christ overturns Satan's attack on covenantal love. Satan wants husbands and wives to battle. He wishes for couples to engage in maximal marital conflict, to snipe at one another, and to pull apart. He wants wives to usurp their husbands and husbands to lord their authority over their wives. He wants every marriage to crumble because marriage is not only the means by which God's creation is populated, but it is also the visible sign of Christ's love for his church, as Paul teaches in this passage.

Satan especially wants the unions of Christian couples to crumble. Christians, after all, image consciously what unbelievers do without knowledge. Thankfully, the apostle Paul gives the Ephesian church the antidote to Satan's schemes: it is the

Christ-church picture, a picture realized by the power of grace that dawns in the believing heart. A man and woman may practice headship and submission in some way without spiritual renewal, but only the redeemed husband and wife may fully bring God's vision of marriage to life. We see here that God, unlike Satan, loves marriage. He gives it as a good gift to most believers.[25] So it is that, through the gospel of grace, Ephesians 5 overcomes Genesis 3 as the husband lovingly leads his wife and the wife submits, graciously and gladly, to her husband. Her husband, of course, is not her "source"; he is her *kephale* (head, Gk κεφαλή), her authority.[26] Just as Christ leads the church, so the man leads his wife. He does not do so perfectly, of course, and unlike Christ he will have to repent regularly of sin before his wife. But he is constituted a Christlike "head" by God himself and cannot shirk this role, this identity.[27]

---

[25] "Paul shows himself to be a 'philogamist,' regarding matrimony as the norm for the majority of Christians and commending it as a way of life sanctified by God (1 Cor. 7:3–14)." Bruce, *The Epistles to the Colossians, to Philemon, and to the Ephesians*, 386 (see chap. 1, n. 44).

[26] See the weight of evidence for this contention in Wayne Grudem, "The Meaning of *Kephale*: A Response to Recent Studies," in *Recovering Biblical Manhood and Womanhood: A Response to Evangelical Feminism*, ed. John Piper and Wayne Grudem (Wheaton, IL: Crossway, 2006), 425–68. For the opposite view, see Ronald W. Pierce, Rebecca Merrill Groothuis, and Gordon D. Fee, eds., *Discovering Biblical Equality: Complementarity without Hierarchy* (Downers Grove, IL: InterVarsity, 2004).

[27] This passage and its teaching depend upon the divine order created by God. See Arthur G. Patzia, *Ephesians, Colossians, Philemon*, Understanding the Bible Commentary Series (1984; Grand Rapids:

Marital headship is an all-of-life reality. Marital submission is an all-of-life reality. A man does not pick certain moments to imitate Christ in his marriage and his home; he is, whether he wants to be or not, the Christlike leader of his family. A woman does not embrace submission at certain points; she submits to her husband "in everything" (Eph 5:24).[28] Paul would not have in mind following one's husband into sin; outside of sinfulness, however, the Christian wife answers a high call in respectfully following her husband. The picture here is not of a husband holding an eleventh-hour trump card that he uses to get his will whenever he wants. The picture is of a husband who loves to love his wife, and of a wife who loves to trust and follow her husband

---

Baker Books, 2011), 268. This helps us understand Eph 5:21, which Paul does not contradict in the verses that follow; rather, Paul is teaching in verse 21 that the order he is laying out in the verses that follow is right. We should not speak of "mutual submission" in marriage, but should teach that verse 21 is an introductory word calling Christians to the authority-submission dynamics that follow. This order obtains not only between husband and wife, but all the way up, between the Father and the Son (1 Cor 11:3).

[28] "'In everything' (ἐν παντί) indicates that this should be the normal disposition of the wife toward her husband. It means that a wife should cultivate an attitude of affirming, supporting, and respecting her husband's leadership in the marriage without holding back certain areas where she wants to assert or maintain control." He rightly points out that it is inappropriate "that a wife should receive orders from her husband, be forced to engage in any kind of sinful activities or behaviors, or be victimized by abuse." Clinton E. Arnold, *Ephesians*, Zondervan Exegetical Commentary on the New Testament (Grand Rapids: Zondervan, 2010), 383.

(5:24–25). The man does not earn submission, for this is commanded of wives, but he does seek on a continual basis to emulate Jesus by giving himself for her. His strength, his energy, and his focus he directs toward his marriage; he lives with his wife on his mind, striving to bless her and sacrificing his own interests to express love for her.[29]

Men need a challenge to come fully alive. Paul's teaching to the Ephesian church represents a startlingly grand challenge for Christian men. "In the same way" that Christ loves his bride, and laid down his life for her, men of God must love their wives (5:28).[30] He cannot atone for her sins, for only Christ can accomplish such work, but the godly husband seeks his wife's growth in grace "by the word" (5:26). He acts as his wife's spiritual buttress; he cares for her in the most important way: pursuing her spiritual good. He does so not in a paternal way, but in a uniquely husbandly way, and always as a fellow sinner in need of the grace

---

[29] Arnold, 383.

[30] Frank Thielman captures the expansive nature of the love shared by a husband and wife: "In 5:23 Paul has said that Christ is the Savior of the church, and here he explains how he has become the church's Savior: he 'gave himself for her.' This has happened as a demonstration of his love, and this is the kind of love, Paul says, that husbands should have for their wives. The sweeping nature of the demand placed on the wife (ἐν παντί, en panti, in everything; v. 23) is therefore matched by an equally sweeping demand on the husband. Like Christ, the husband is to love (ἀγαπάω, agapaō) his wife by the sacrifice of his own life on his wife's behalf (cf. 1:7; 2:13–16; 5:2)." Frank Thielman, *Ephesians*, Baker Exegetical Commentary on the New Testament (Grand Rapids: Baker Academic, 2010), 381.

of God. No man, we must note, succeeds perfectly here; every Christian husband has regular occasion to repent of his failings in these ways. Nonetheless we strive toward the upward call and lean on God for fresh strength to cut new paths where weeds have choked our marital health.

In terms similar to Genesis 3, Ephesians 5 addresses husbands in the bulk of this passage. A healthy marriage will not simply happen, and a doxological marriage will not result without a man who owns his God-given role. He cannot hate his "own flesh," his spouse. He "provides and cares" for her, just as Christ does with his blood-bought bride (Eph 5:29–30). Paul does not define *provision and care* here, but we may assume he intends the widest possible application on the part of husbands. In a spousal manner, a man assumes full responsibility for his wife and by extension his children.[31] He does all he possibly can to love his wife, his own body. He provides for her physically, spiritually, and every way he can. He does not limit his care for her to one supportive remark a day; he pours out blessing on this woman, making her his treasure.

This teaching stands out in a secular culture. Though it seems controversial today, such biblical doctrine did not keep women in the early church era from embracing Christianity. It drove women to the church. The Christian call to men to love

---

[31] John Piper, "A Vision of Biblical Complementarity: Manhood and Womanhood Defined According to the Bible," in *Recovering Biblical Manhood and Womanhood: A Response to Evangelical Feminism*, ed. John Piper and Wayne Grudem (Wheaton, IL: Crossway, 2006), 42–43.

their wives in a genuine and self-sacrificial way had a tremendous effect two millennia ago. In contrast to the pagan Romans, the church offered women much agency and hope, as Rodney Stark has observed: "The Christian woman enjoyed far greater marital security and equality than did her pagan neighbor." The church did not force women to marry, or to do so at young ages without any real agency, while "pagan women frequently were forced into prepubertal, consummated marriages," as Stark notes. Surveying the unique Christian ethic, Stark concludes this: "Christianity was unusually appealing because within the Christian subculture women enjoyed far higher status than did women in the Greco-Roman world at large."[32]

The beauty of a Christian theology of marriage is veiled in a culture that attacks gender roles of most any kind. Yet this beauty is not hidden in the biblical text or in a God-honoring Christian marriage. The Scripture speaks with one voice to the goodness of wedded union, yet our grasp of the significance of this institution expands to nearly impossible scope in the New Testament. The plan of God for couples found in Gen 2:24 comes to fruition and fulfillment in the Ephesians 5 marriage (even as final fulfillment awaits in the age to come). When a young man leaves father and mother and holds fast to one wife, the two become one flesh, enfleshing a "mystery" that makes sense only in covenantal and eschatological terms (Eph 5:31–32). Earthly marriage points forward to the consummation of the betrothal already enacted,

---

[32] Rodney Stark, *The Rise of Christianity: A Sociologist Reconsiders History* (Princeton: Princeton Univ. Press, 1996), 95, 105.

the love of Christ for his people, the church. Earthly marriage is a wonder and a mystery in its own terms, as the union of one man and one woman already demands considerable alchemy to work, but it grows to cosmic proportions in light of Paul's teaching. Ephesians 5 not only overcomes the problems of Genesis 3, but it reframes marriage in light of the teleological purpose of the Creator God. Marriage was not made for man; man, redeemed humanity, was made for marriage—the marriage of Christ and his church at the end of all time.

God does not call every believer to marriage. Singleness unto God is an honorable state and even a vocation, a way of life, according to Paul (1 Corinthians 7). Jesus Christ, the Lord of the church, never married an earthly wife. His example shows us that sex need not define us, and that we need not marry or have a family to give God profound glory with our fleeting days. The church has a different conception of singleness than any other institution. We view it as a calling from God, an honorable way of life that allows the believer to devote himself to the people and purposes of God. The "gift" of God enables sinners and even former sexual libertines to serve him with happiness and contentment (1 Cor 7:7).[33]

This last point bears further comment. In a self-driven, pleasure-consumed era, single men and women have a marvelous

---

[33] Paul's focus here is not meritorious self-control, but rather grace-driven discipline. "The power to control oneself comes from God, not from oneself (so also Wis. 8:21)." David E. Garland, *1 Corinthians*, Baker Exegetical Commentary on the New Testament (Grand Rapids: Baker Academic, 2003), 272.

chance to point their peers to a much greater joy than anything this world knows: God himself. Spirituality is our identity, not sexuality. I do not mean, though, that the single Christian will always feel happy. He may not. She may struggle, frankly, to remain contentedly unmarried. But they may know that God is their portion, that they have all they need for life and godliness in Christ and his Word, that the local church is truly their family, and that in the age to come, they will not experience a single second of forlornness. In the new heavens and new earth, Jesus himself will welcome them home and bestow upon them a peace and love that will never ebb.

Fathers and Mothers for God's Glory

This kind of marriage functions as a little factory of praise to God. But in God's design, marriage is not normally the end of the equation. Throughout Scripture, childbirth is a blessing given by God, and barrenness a cross to be borne with God's own gracious care and kindness. The Bible, in other words, overturns modern cultural mores regarding children—where barrenness, or childlessness, is seen by some as a blessing and conception a curse.[34] Jesus himself models love for "the little children," bid-

---

[34] Children today are often seen as a curse, not a blessing. It is preferable, we hear, to avoid having children. See Lauren Sandler, "Having It All Without Having Children," *Time*, August 12, 2013, http://content. time.com/time/subscriber/article/0%2C33009%2C2148636%2C00 .html. As if to make the point sharp as a razor, the cover features a sunbathing couple splayed out on the beach.

ding them come to him (Matt 19:14; Luke 18:16). Paul goes
on in his writing to the Ephesian church to instruct fathers not
to "stir up anger" in their children, but to "bring them up in the
training and instruction of the Lord" (Eph 6:4). Proven mothers,
Paul teaches in his letter to Titus, must train younger mothers:

> In the same way, older women are to be reverent in
> behavior, not slanderers, not slaves to excessive drink-
> ing. They are to teach what is good, so that they may
> encourage the young women to love their husbands and
> to love their children, to be self-controlled, pure, workers
> at home, kind, and in submission to their husbands, so
> that God's word will not be slandered. (Titus 2:3–5)

Godly women prioritize their homes and their children.[35] They
love their husbands (2:4). As the Lord builds a strong marriage,
the trial-tested woman is called "to teach what is good," a teaching
ministry anchored in godly character and focused on day-to-day

---

[35] Paul's portrait of blessed domesticity endures across the ages:
"Contemporary protests against this portrait of an ideal woman are misplaced if their motive is to decanonize this passage as hopelessly irrelevant for today's Christian women. The text defines female competence
in terms of the Greco-Roman household; other prospects for women are
not demonized but perhaps thought irrelevant at that time. Moreover,
this ideal need not be demonized as making a woman of today a victim
of patriarchal society when in fact the opposite may be true: ambitions
shaped by a preference to be like males have left women even more
disaffected and unfulfilled." Wall and Steele, *1 and 2 Timothy and Titus*,
350 (see chap. 3, n. 30).

discipleship. Paul does not raise up a kind of second eldership among the women of the church, laying upon older women the burden to teach sound doctrine and ward off the wolves. This burden he gives to the elders of the church, sound men who preach sound words and live sound lives. His focus in Titus 2 is on training that yields a love for God's word, submissive practice, homemaking (he coins a term, *oikourgous* [οἰκουργούς], to communicate this priority), and loving one's husband and children.[36]

Every second of such a life matters to God. Doxology is in the details: a woman who sacrifices her own free time, her serious intellectual and vocational interests, and her goals to care for little children, make healthy and tasty meals for her loved ones, organize, manage, and clean a home, express support and love for her husband as he works hard to provide, and teach her progeny the word of God in all its fullness. Such an existence is more than a job conducted within the confines of a home; it is a vocation. It involves the full measure of a woman's gifts, abilities, and talents, and it is not a lesser call than a prestigious out-of-the-home career. In fact, such labor is in general terms far more demanding than paycheck-driven work, for the work of child raising and homemaking means the direct shaping of lives and even eternal

---

[36] In a chaotic world, the apostle Paul sets forth divinely orchestrated order: "Home management was the sphere of a woman's singular influence, where her virtue could have its most telling result. The exegete must not lose sight of the organizing conception of divine providence in these letters, which supposes that the Creator's way of ordering reality insinuates certain social patterns on human existence." Wall and Steele, 349.

destinies. The work involved is minute-by-minute, and it calls forth considerable and ongoing sacrifice. Elisabeth Elliot captures the substance of such vocational investment nicely:

> When women—sometimes well-meaning, earnest, truth-seeking ones—say "Get out of the house and do something *creative*, find something *meaningful*, something with more direct access to *reality*," it is a dead giveaway that they have missed the deepest definition of creation, of meaning, of reality. And when you start seeing the world as opaque, that is, as an end in itself instead of as transparent, when you ignore the Other World where this one ultimately finds its meaning, of course housekeeping (and any other kind of work if you do it long enough) becomes tedious and empty. But this is what we so easily forget. We have meekly agreed that the kitchen sink is an obstacle instead of an altar, and we have obediently carried on our shoulders the chips these reductionists have told us to carry.[37]

The kitchen sink, in Elliot's memorable phrase, does not represent an abnegation. It represents an altar.[38] The home and the family matter greatly.

---

[37] Elliot, *Love Has a Price Tag*, 206, 208.

[38] We remember here the words of Luther about the doxological nature of daily life in the home: "A wife too should regard her duties in the same light, as she suckles the child, rocks and bathes it, and cares for it in other ways; and as she busies herself with other duties and renders

Being Men and Women of God at All Times

The Bible, as we have seen, calls men to be leaders, protectors, and providers. It calls women—particularly within the covenant of marriage—to follow a godly husband, to nurture life, and to care for the home. The New Testament outlines these duties within the context of marriage, but we cannot miss that one does not become a biblical man or a biblical woman when a wedding takes place. The biblical ideal involves training children to grow into godly manhood and godly womanhood. The Israelites had the holy responsibility of shepherding their children at all times and in all places (Deut 6:4–9).[39] There was no off-the-clock time

---

help and obedience to her husband. These are truly golden and noble works. . . . Now you tell me, when a father goes ahead and washes diapers or performs some other mean task for his child, and someone ridicules him as an effeminate fool, though that father is acting in the spirit just described and in Christian faith, my dear fellow you tell me, which of the two is most keenly ridiculing the other? God, with all his angels and creatures, is smiling, not because that father is washing diapers, but because he is doing so in Christian faith." Martin Luther, "The Estate of Marriage, 1522," in *Luther's Works*, ed. Helmut T. Lehmann, vol. 45, *Christian in Society II*, ed. Walther I. Brandt (Minneapolis: Fortress, 1962), 39–40.

[39] Allan Harman explains how this teaching took practical form: "The Lord's words, in addition to being the driving force in the life of the individual, had also to be a living reality in family life. Whether at home or outside, in whatever activities were taking place, God required his words to be discussed. Clearly in such situations the discussion would be provoked by children's questions, such as Moses envisaged them asking at the time of the Passover (Exod. 12:26ff. 'When your children ask you . . .')." Allan Harman, *Deuteronomy: The Commands of a*

for fathers and mothers.[40] So it is for us today. We do not spring the need to have a "gentle and quiet" spirit upon our daughters after they bear rings on their fingers; in similar terms, we do not ambush our sons with the need to provide for a wife once the matrimonial festivities have concluded (1 Pet 3:4).

We train our children, and indeed the whole church, in biblical manhood and womanhood all the time. It is vital to underscore this point: marriage does not make us godly men or godly women. Indeed, a single man or single woman is called to biblical manhood or womanhood just as a married person is. Even as we never cease to prioritize and honor marriage—"let marriage be held in honor among all" (Heb 13:4 ESV)—so we encourage the unmarried among us to build a vocation (see chapter 6), to use all their gifts in service to God, church, and neighbor, and to do so as a godly man or a godly woman, in keeping with the pattern of biblical teaching on the distinctiveness of the sexes. Such a life is not a lesser life; it is a life lived in the glorious freedom of the gospel, a life abounding with possibilities that is marked by ongoing service to God (1 Cor 7:32–35).

This is true of single men and single women; it is also true of married men and women in the pre-child years in particular. When children come, there are indeed distinct duties driven by distinct God-given roles that men and women fill. The man is

---

Covenant God, Focus on the Bible Commentary (Fearn, UK: Christian Focus, 2007), 94.

[40] I am using *fathers* and *mothers* advisedly, as it is preferable to the gender-neutral *parents.* We may at times use the latter term, but the Bible identifies us as fathers and mothers.

not, as we have noted, called to be the homemaker and child raiser of his family. He is called to provide for his family.[41] But before the Lord gives the gift of children (whether natural or adopted), the man and the woman have much freedom of vocation. When children are young and in the home, many Christian couples will decide to prioritize investment in their little ones over investment in financial security, the former outweighing the latter by a great margin in the biblical worldview. But as the children grow, there is some gray area faced by a Christian couple, and a Christian woman has freedom in following her husband's leadership to take on a range of activities and even callings, all while retaining her unique identity as a biblical woman.

A man's leadership of his family is the foundation of his ministry. Not every man becomes an elder, but every man of God is required to lead his family well. As part of his leadership of the home, the man provides for and protects his wife and children

---

[41] Contrast the increasingly popular model of the dadmom, who stays at home to care for the kids while the wife provides for the family. Provision is not a matter of ability and earning-power; provision is part of manly identity and the role given to men by God in the home. This is true of every role given to men and women; filling our place in the cosmos ordered by God is contingent neither on our desires nor our particular talent levels. It is contingent on divine decree, which is reflected in the constitutions of men and women (in general terms). There are exceptions, as when a man cannot provide through disability or loss of job. There is no shame for men in such situations, and the church offers help and support to men who face these straits. But wherever possible, a godly man seeks to provide to the fullness of his ability. This is not only his calling from God; this is part of what God made him to do.

(Eph 5:22; 1 Tim 5:8–14). These are his God-given duties; this is a crucial part of his Christian identity. These duties are burdens, glad burdens, that he takes upon his shoulders to the fullest possible extent.[42] As the Lord forges in him solid character grounded in love for his family, the man will begin to aspire to eldership. This is a "a noble work" (1 Tim 3:1). God calls men, and only men, to the teaching office of the church of the Lord Jesus Christ. Men should not hold back from wanting to shepherd the flock of God; they should desire this. Here we see part of the theme that runs throughout the entire Bible: God wants men to leave boyhood behind. He wants men to hunger for holiness and show eagerness to lead. Manhood in the biblical mind is calibrated for action, for initiative, for responsibility.

The elder must meet a high standard. He must have proven, tested, godly character (1 Tim 3:1–7). He needs to lead his family well; he must interact with others well; he should be producing the fruit of the Spirit in his daily life; above all, he must be a man under control.[43] If the ungodly man has little control

---

[42] "He is still the representative of the family outside the home, insofar as he gives the family his name, his position, his honor, functioning by acting in its name and serving its interests. . . . The husband lives in society, the wife lives in her family . . . Just as the husband is independent in his work and must nevertheless labor with a view to the interests of his family, so too the wife is independent within the family . . ." Bavinck, *The Christian Family*, 95.

[43] "Third, 'self-control' (see 2:9, Excursus) is required of the overseer. One of the cardinal virtues in Greco-Roman ethical thought, it was appropriated by Hellenistic Judaism and supplied with a theological basis in the Torah (see on Titus 1:8). Paul deepened this basis by linking

over his appetites, the elder of Christ's church has a firm grip on them. He is no flawless individual, but God has worked in him such that he lives in thrall to Christ. He images not Adam, but Jesus. In a shifting, dissembling world, he is trustworthy, solid as oak, virtuous, ready to aid the needy, one who teaches the truth and seems a walking demonstration of the truth in all his life.

Men should not try to be superstars. Men should aspire to have the characters of an elder. This is the standard young men need; this is the high call the rising generation should hear. Our culture encourages men to sit down and step back, but that is not the solution to what ails us. The church needs to train men to be men and women to be women. The gospel of grace does not redeem us to live as androgynous beings. The gospel of grace renders us Christ-captivated men and Christ-captivated women. We receive our bodies, our vocations, our identities from God, and we take definition from the Bible, which is a surer word than our emotions, our backgrounds, even our trainings. The gospel forms women who embody femininity, who exude a "gentle and quiet spirit" (1 Pet 3:4), who have markedly distinct priorities from unsaved women. The gospel forms men who embrace manhood, who heed Paul's charge to the Corinthians to "act like

---

it to the Christ-event (Titus 2:12). The term covers a range of meaning (prudence, moderation, sobriety), but gives the general sense of control over one's behavior and the impulses and emotions beneath it. Although it appears here as a requirement for leadership (Titus 1:8), it was expected of all believers (2:9, 15; Titus 2:2, 4, 5, 6)." Philip H. Towner, *The Letters to Timothy and Titus*, The New International Commentary on the New Testament (Grand Rapids: Eerdmans, 2006), 251–52.

men" (1 Cor 16:13 ESV), and who structure their entire existence around scriptural prerogatives.[44]

We pray for our families and our homes and our marriages to brim with vitality. We ask God to help us honor him as husbands and wives. We pray for children and depend on divine grace if this blessing does not come naturally, knowing that God alone gives the gift of life. If blessed with children—whether natural or adopted—we relish the opportunity, hour by sometimes-grueling hour, to raise them for his honor and renown. The world may be telling us that there is no such thing as fixed marriage and a "nuclear" home, but we have received a surer word, and we have a much greater reward than man's applause. We not only obey God by going back to biblical teaching on these matters; we show others an enchanted picture of love, ordered love, that comes by the grace of God and is lived out for the glory of God.

---

[44] This phrase—"act like men"—echoes what we hear in the Old Testament, as when David says to Solomon, "be strong, act like a man" (1 Kgs 2:2 NIV). According to Bill Mounce, the word translated "act like a man"—ἀνδρίζομαι—"occurs in the New Testament only here. Its etymology is clearly from the root ανδρ, from which we get ἀνήρ, 'man,' predominantly (if not exclusively) used of males." Bill Mounce, "'Act Like Men' (1 Cor 16:13)," *Mondays with Mounce* (blog), February 10, 2012, https://www.billmounce.com/monday-with-mounce/"act-men"-1-cor-16-13. The fact that the root of this word is grounded in maleness suggests men are expected to be models of courage in the Christian community. This is no new teaching of Paul. We should be careful to preserve the linguistic connection of manliness to courage found in the Greek text. See also Andrew David Naselli, "1 Corinthians," *Romans–Galatians*, ESV Expository Commentary Series, vol. 10 (Wheaton, IL: Crossway, forthcoming), 191.

This theology was once transformative, changing common first-century Greco-Roman practices by giving women considerable agency and restraining the brutal approach of husbands to their wives.[45] Christian teaching also altered the ways ancient people viewed girls and women, opposing the culture of infanticide that claimed the lives of so many baby girls.[46]

Because it is controversial in the modern West as it was in the ancient Roman Empire, a biblical theology of the sexes will again transform and liberate us. The church's call in the twenty-first century is not to soften our conception of the sexes, but to present biblical teaching with fresh joy and fresh confidence in the power of God to convert and transform those who naturally crave falsehood and oppose truth. The Word of God is true; the Word of God, the whole counsel of the divine, is good.

The Rise of Pagan Sexuality and the Church's Response

It will not surprise many readers to know that the church's doctrine on the aforementioned matters differs from prevailing secular values. If believers have the joyful privilege of actively

[45] If a Roman woman was found guilty of adultery, by Roman law she could be exiled to an island. If a husband caught his wife in the act of adultery, per the teaching of Cato he could kill her. See Bruce Winter, *Roman Wives, Roman Widows: The Appearance of New Women and the Pauline Communities* (Grand Rapids: Eerdmans, 2003), 42.

[46] See Nancy R. Pearcey, *Love Thy Body: Answering Hard Questions About Life and Sexuality* (Grand Rapids: Baker Books, 2018), 69–74.

savoring divine design and intentionally depicting divine order, then we may know that those not found in Christ may well find delight in the opposite. Not every unbeliever, of course, targets marriage; many live according to the natural plan of God, even if they do so without a doxological motive. But the natural man has a wild and disobedient heart. In the twenty-first century, we have witnessed the rise of ideology that seeks to replace divine order with a counterfeit—with what we may call *neopaganism*. This movement spiritualizes sexuality in a design-denying way while rendering sexual practice nothing more than a momentary phenomenon. Sex is both everything and nothing at once.[47]

No idea has swept over recent American cultural life like that of *transgenderism*. It is not that the phenomenon of "gender dysphoria" is new; nor is it new that men and women have sought to cross over the boundaries of their own sex and embrace the identity or appearance of the opposite sex. These instincts are in many societies, though nearly always on the fringe.[48] What is new in our time is the full-fledged push to normalize transgender identity.

---

[47] For an eye-opening survey of secular perspectives on sex, see Pearcey, 130–34. Sex has become a religion for many, Pearcey contends. I think she is right. Yet we cannot fail to see that for many Western people, sex is also seen as nothing more than a biological desire with no greater moral significance. In this sense, sex is both universalized and particularized—sometimes, confusingly, by the same person.

[48] We find examples of such behavior in ancient Greece, Rome, and Egypt, for example. See Harry Benjamin, *The Transsexual Phenomenon* (New York: Julian, 1966).

Transgender represents the rejection of a *gender essentialist* vision of humanity. Gender is not fixed and formed; gender is fluid and formless. This is what we hear; in truth, transgender ideology depends upon a fixed understanding of the sexes. Rather than a reworking of gender, in which gender is truly a construct, transgender ideology introduces a third category to human bodily identity. This third category is the transgender person, who is neither traditionally male nor female. They are people caught between the sexes, questing after their true selves.

This conception of the human person fits fluidly with our disenchanted age. We will save our biblical critique for the pages ahead, but at this point, we note that the human person has no greater design in the eyes of many today. God did not create the human race; the human race evolved from gaseous substances. The blank-slate philosophy commonly traced to the Enlightenment funds our modern conception of the amorphous self.[49] Humanity has no broader obligations to a Creator; there is thus no script to follow that leads to personal wholeness and human flourishing. We must each form our own philosophies,

---

[49] As an example of such thinking, one could look to John Locke, *An Essay Concerning Human Understanding*, ed. Roger Woolhouse (New York: Penguin, 1997), 109: "Let us then suppose the mind to be, as we say, white paper, void of all characters, without any ideas; how comes it to be furnished? Whence comes it by that vast store, which the busy and boundless fancy of man has painted on it, with an almost endless variety? Whence has it all the materials of reason and knowledge? To this I answer, in one word, from *experience*." This is not to intimate that Locke would enfranchise modern gender ideology; rather, we seek to understand the *provenance* of ideas.

finding what clues we can in the known world; so we must each form—or re-form—our own bodies, finding what clues we can in the expressive self.

It is remarkable that transgender identity comes from the same general movement that promoted biologically driven feminism. The sexual revolution of the 1960s made good on the vision of the liberated human person that had long brewed in avant-garde circles in the West, championing in a loose and chaotic way the severing of sex from marriage, the positive virtues of "free love" and unattached romance, the needlessness of marriage itself, the repressive nature of the nuclear family, the right and even goodness of elective abortion, and the need to abandon traditional gender roles. The man should not be the strong leader and head of the home; the woman should not confine herself to the care of her home and her children.

The sexual revolution, in truth, said little in a positive sense about manhood; it mostly encouraged men to step back. But this movement had much to say about women and aimed at their so-called liberation from traditional gender roles and sexuality.[50] Today, the feminist who ardently campaigns for "women's rights" risks sounding like her great-grandmother, bellowing chants from a bullhorn with a stocking cap on her head. Feminism depends upon a hard understanding of womanhood, after all;

---

[50] See the classic text by Betty Friedan, *The Feminine Mystique*, 50th anniv. ed. (New York: W. W. Norton, 2013), 423. Friedan argues that "the women who 'adjust' as housewives, who grow up wanting to be 'just a housewife,' are in as much danger as the millions who walked to their own death in the concentration camps."

modern gender theory, and the pack of thinkers who lead it, have long ago left such constructs behind.[51]

As we watch our culture with a mixture of fascination and sorrow, we find ourselves thinking inescapably theological thoughts about our modern moment. This age is not merely giving us a new way to see the body. It holds out to us a new way to see the human person as post-gender, theorists argue.[52] Like the vision of reality peddled by the serpent to Adam and Eve, our culture can only twist the truth and design of God. Satan cannot actually make a new humanity; this only Jesus, the true image of God, can do. But Satan can tell people that God's design is not best and that there is an alternate vision available. His trickery requires the hearer to overlook the fact that Satan is not an originalist; he is an editor. When we actually dig into the raw theology of transgender identity, we see that it is no new concept at all, rather the blurring of what God himself made.

Transgender ideology is no neutral system. It is, pardon the expression, *transpersonal*. It apprehends and involves the entire human person. A quick recap of its core vocabulary shows that it

---

[51] Not many have pointed out this clash in public, but see Michelle Goldberg, "What Is a Woman? The Dispute Between Radical Feminism and Transgenderism," *New Yorker*, August 4, 2014, https://www.new yorker.com/magazine/2014/08/04/woman-2.

[52] "The end goal of feminist revolution must be, unlike that of the first feminist movement, not just the elimination of male *privilege* but of the sex *distinction* itself: genital differences between human beings would no longer matter culturally." Shulamith Firestone, *The Dialectic of Sex: The Case for Feminist Revolution* (1970; repr., New York: Farrar, Straus and Giroux, 2003), 11.

tweaks common understandings of our instincts, our bodies, and our very identities. According to modern gender dogma, derived from no religious source and handed down by no divine figure, we all possess a *sexual orientation*. This refers to the enduring patterns of attraction we have for others. We also have a *gender identity*, our inmost understanding of ourselves as male, female, a blend of these, neither of these, or something else besides. Gender identity is how we perceive ourselves and what we call ourselves. Our *gender expression* refers to the way we present our gender identity through things such as behavior, clothing, haircut, or voice. Our *anatomies* are merely the genitalia and core physicality we possess per our birth sex. If we are transgender, finally, our gender identities and expressions differ from our birth sex.[53]

The task before us looms large. In light of this modern ideology, what does true wisdom, the very Word of God, teach us about handling gender dysphoria and embracing the body the Lord has given us? In the next section, we attempt a brief survey of biblical teaching relevant to this controverted material. We see that in both the Old and New Testaments, the Word of God clearly addresses bodily presentation and urges the followers of God to take care that they honor God's creative design.[54]

---

[53] American Psychological Association, *Answers to Your Questions: For a Better Understanding of Sexual Orientation and Homosexuality* (Washington, DC: Public and Member Communications, 2008), http://www.apa.org/topics/lgbt/orientation.pdf.

[54] It is no mean thing to cite the Old Testament law today. While we do not abide by the old-covenant law today, we still reverence it. It is the foundation of the New Testament's moral and theological teaching.

The term *transgender* is new, but cross-dressing and cross-gender identity are not. The law given to ancient Israel addresses such behavior directly and unconditionally. In the course of several prohibitions of ungodly behavior, Deuteronomy says this: "A woman shall not wear a man's garment, nor shall a man put on a woman's cloak, for whoever does these things is an abomination to the Lord your God" (Deut 22:5 ESV). We see here that the instinct to wear the clothing of the opposite sex is not new; it is nearly as old as the earth.[55] We feel the strength of this prohibition in the original language.[56] Other nations surely experimented with their sexuality, so to speak, and vented their

If we take it out of consideration—whether for apologetic reasons or for spiritual formation—the New Testament makes little sense because the New fulfills the Old, and the Old points ahead to the New. Even when the old covenant proffers guidance that we no longer obey, for we now obey the law of love in Christ (1 Cor 13:34), we glean understanding of the divine will from the law. It instructs us, enables us to understand God's holy character, and serves as the reference point by which to measure new covenant teaching. The preceding corrects the view that Christians should "unhitch" themselves from the Old Testament and its teaching. See Andy Stanley, *Irresistible: Reclaiming the New that Jesus Unleashed for the World* (Grand Rapids: Zondervan, 2018).

[55] Old Testament scholar Jason DeRouchie calls attention to the fortress-grade strength of this prohibition: "God chose to frame these prohibitions as durative, so that we should read the 'not' as a 'never': 'A woman shall *never* wear a man's garment, nor shall a man *ever* put on a woman's cloak.'" Jason S. DeRouchie, *How to Understand and Apply the Old Testament: Twelve Steps from Exegesis to Theology* (Phillipsburg, NJ: P&R, 2017), 445.

[56] "From God's perspective, there is never a permissible time for the type of cross-dressing that this passage addresses." DeRouchie, 445.

raw desires. They had no clear divine ethic.[57] But the children of God did. The law of God shaped and overcame whatever natural proclivities the fallen man or woman, tempted to cross-dress, might have.

The text speaks strongly to essential identity as a man or woman. The use of *abomination* here only reinforces this principle. Adultery, incest, homosexuality, temple prostitution, and unlawful marriage all occasion the use of this term, revealing the appalling nature of ungodly behavior (Lev 18:22, 27–30; 20:13; Deut 24:2–4; Ezek 16:22, 58; 22:11; 33:26). All sin dishonors the Lord in full, but abominable behavior offends God in a special way. The implication is clear: the man or woman who wears the clothing of the opposite sex makes a conscious decision to contravene the design of God.[58] The circumstances behind this choice do not matter; the lifetime experience affords no

---

[57] "First, transvestism tends to be associated with certain forms of homosexuality; second, in the ancient world, it is probable that transvestite practices were associated with the cults of certain deities. In either or both of these instances, the practice of transvestism would be *an abomination to the Lord your God*. . . . If transvestism was indeed associated with foreign religious practices, it should be noted that things associated with foreign religions are described as an *abomination* in Deuteronomy (see 7:25 and 18:12)." Peter C. Craigie, *The Book of Deuteronomy*, The New International Commentary on the Old Testament (Grand Rapids: Eerdmans, 1976), 288.

[58] There may be a connection between apparel and battle here; in other words, the Lord is prohibiting both the wearing of the opposite sex's clothing and a woman doing so in order to enter into battle. See Jeffrey H. Tigay, *Deuteronomy*, The JPS Torah Commentary (Philadelphia: Jewish Publication Society, 1996), 200.

exception to the command; the person's motives merit no mention. The grouping of cross-dressing with sexual immorality shows us that this practice is part of a complex of behaviors that are wrong through and through, and no explanation can change this truth or erase God's law.[59] Jason DeRouchie summarizes the point powerfully: "In Deuteronomy 22:5, *loving others and God means that people will maintain a gender identity that aligns with their biological sex and will express this gender in a way that never leads to gender confusion in the eyes of others.*"[60] As in ancient times, so today.

Having looked closely at the Old Testament's handling of cross-dressing, we consider similar commentary in the New Testament. In 1 Cor 11:3, 7–15, a passage filled with interpretive opportunities, Paul reinforces and even strengthens the old covenant's teaching.

> But I want you to know that Christ is the head of every man, and the man is the head of the woman, and God is the head of Christ. . . .
> A man should not cover his head, because he is the image and glory of God. So too, woman is the glory of man. For man did not come from woman, but woman came from man. Neither was man created for the sake

---

[59] See Eugene H. Merrill, *Deuteronomy*, The New American Commentary, vol. 4 (Nashville: B&H, 1994), 297–98.

[60] DeRouchie, *How to Understand and Apply the Old Testament*, 448 (italics in the original). Gender identity may seem to differ from biological sex, but the two are one.

of woman, but woman for the sake of man. This is why a woman should have a symbol of authority on her head, because of the angels. In the Lord, however, woman is not independent of man, and man is not independent of woman. For just as woman came from man, so man comes through woman, and all things come from God.

Judge for yourselves: Is it proper for a woman to pray to God with her head uncovered? Does not even nature itself teach you that if a man has long hair it is a disgrace to him, but that if a woman has long hair, it is her glory? For her hair is given to her as a covering. (1 Cor 11:3, 7–15)

This is easily one of the most breathtaking passages in the entire Bible. In an unprecedented and unrepeated way, Paul connects Trinitarian reality to marriage to manly and womanly identities.[61] Paul is not merely teaching that manhood and womanhood have distinctive characters. He teaches that the order of marriage depends upon the very life of the Godhead itself.

This section builds out our biblical understanding of the sexes. To understand the identity and duties of husbands and wives, we not only look at the man and the woman themselves;

---

[61] Paul's concern is with gender distinction, for "11:2–16 is not simply about 'the head covering of women,' but about *men* and women, freedom and *respect for the otherness of the other in public worship.*" Anthony C. Thiselton, *The First Epistle to the Corinthians: A Commentary on the Greek Text*, New International Greek Testament Commentary (Grand Rapids: Eerdmans, 2000), 805.

we lift our gaze higher, impossibly higher, to the heavens where God dwells. The Father who is said to be "head" of the Son has highly exalted the one who submitted to his will (11:3; see also 15:28). Sent by his Father, Jesus obeyed the divine will—truly the one will of the Godhead appropriated by each of the three divine persons—perfectly, giving us a stirring picture in his incarnation of what submission looks like (John 7:18).

We might read this section almost as a stray remark. But in truth, verse 3 frames what follows in 1 Corinthians 11. There is order in the cosmos. The relationship between divine Father and divine Son shapes relationships between covenant partners. The head of the crucified and resurrected Christ is God the Father. Christ is the head of every man. A husband is the head of his wife. In a few deft strokes, the apostle Paul sketches once and for all time the superstructure, the ontological architecture, of reality itself. The Trinity is infinitely above us, but not disconnected from us. Reality is Trinitarian at base. We thus look to the Son's incarnational example in particular to think rightly about our hair, our families, our living worship of God.

Paul gave this burst of revelation, this peek into the working of the Godhead and the fabric of creation, to citizens of a city rife with the denial of biblical order. The temple prostitutes, the worship of Greek gods, and the libertine feel of the city meant that born-again Christians in Corinth needed spiritual guidance to reform their understandings of their bodies and selves.[62]

---

[62] Corinth not only featured sexual libertinism on an epic scale, but "was a major centre of the Dionysian cult, a religion where male

The city famously "Corinthianized" visitors, converting them to a dissolute and debauched existence; the church salvifically Christianized hearers, converting them by the power of the Spirit and remaking them in the image of Christ.[63] When men and women came to faith, however, they needed help. They hailed from a pagan context; now they had to have biblical instruction or else they would not know why God made them or glorify God.

To help a Christian woman understand her identity, the apostle called the woman to differentiate herself from the man by having "long hair" (11:14). This is "her glory," and is "given to her as a covering" (11:15). In the biblical mind, even hair is

---

adherents would don feminine apparel in imitation of the god himself, who was closely associated with feminine clothing—the other name by which he is known, Bacchus, is derived from the word *bassara*, a woman's dress (Farnell 1971:160)." Gillian Townsley, "Gender Trouble in Corinth: Que(e)rying Constructs of Gender in 1 Corinthians 11:2–16," *The Bible and Critical Theory* 2, no. 2 (2006): 17.7; see also Lewis Richard Farnell, *The Cults of the Greek States* (Oxford: Clarenden, 1909), 5:160.

[63] Corinth "had no rivals as a city of vice. 'To live like a Corinthian' meant to live a life of profligacy and debauchery. It was customary in a stage play for a Corinthian to come on the scene drunk." The Corinthians famously worshipped Aphrodite, the goddess of love, and "Her temple on the Acrocorinthus had more than a thousand *hierodou-loi*—priestesses of vice not found in other shrines of Greece, and she attracted worshipers from all over the ancient world." J. D. Douglas and Merrill C. Tenney, *Zondervan Illustrated Bible Dictionary* (1987; repr., Grand Rapids: Zondervan, 2011), s.v. "Corinth."

theological.[64] The woman must not see herself as the same as the man; she came from man, and should thus present herself as a woman under authority. This passage features some complexities, but Paul's point is evident enough: the man and the woman should not look the same.[65] A man growing his hair long functions as a veritable "disgrace" according to the apostle (11:14). He should not look like the woman; the woman and the man should present themselves differently; they are not the same and are not free to blur the boundaries between the sexes.[66]

---

[64] "Whatever is appropriate for the man would be inappropriate for the woman—and vice versa. This strict antithetical relationship seems to suggest that "[c]lear gender boundaries is the point." Roy E. Ciampa and Brian S. Rosner, *The First Letter to the Corinthians*, The Pillar New Testament Commentary (Grand Rapids: Eerdmans, 2010), 513.

[65] Andrew Naselli covers nicely the relationship between nature and personal presentation: "Paul appeals to 'nature' (Gk. *physis*)—that is, 'the regular or established order of things,' hence, the NIV: 'the very nature of things.' Paul bases his appeal to nature on a creation principle and a cultural practice: 1. *Creation Principle.* God created males to look and act like males, and he created females to look and act like females. As a general rule, males (and not females) instinctively feel shame at the idea of embodying feminine characteristics in their culture. Nature teaches men to look and act like men in their culture and teaches women to look and act like women. 2. *Cultural Practice.* Revelation 9:8 describes locusts as having 'hair like women's hair.' That sort of statement is intelligible because cultures express masculinity and femininity through hairstyle (and clothing and cosmetics) in various ways." Naselli, "1 Corinthians," 110.

[66] We distinguish such instincts and behavior from the condition known as *intersex*, which is a genetic condition stemming from a world affected by Adam's sin. A child with an intersex condition possesses genitalia of both sexes from birth. This condition is not a voluntary

This teaching, as we have noted, flies in the face of our androgynous culture, just as we may assume it did in ancient Corinth. When people lose sight of God's handiwork and natural order, when they correspondingly debauch themselves through sexual immorality of various kinds, we may know with certainty that they will not look kindly on the Bible's portrait of an ordered Godhead, an ordered human race, and an ordered home. They will in point of fact find themselves convicted by such living declarations of reality, and this conviction may well occasion serious shame and anger as a result. Faced with the truth of God found in both Scripture and

---

choice, so is experienced involuntarily and from birth. If a Y chromosome is present, the child should be treated as a man. The counsel of Denny Burk is sound on this matter, and worth quoting at some length: "First, parents should be extremely reluctant about—if not altogether against—corrective surgery when the child is an infant. This is especially the case when the surgery would involve the modification of the child's genitals or reproductive organs. . . . Second, try to determine as soon as possible the chromosomal makeup of the child. If there is a Y chromosome present, that would strongly militate against raising the child as a female, regardless of the appearance of the genitals and other secondary sex characteristics. It would also suggest that medical treatments designed to make the child into a female are out of line. Third, understand that not all doctors and medical professionals share your biblical convictions. Worldviews affect the treatment of intersex conditions. Some doctors may view gender as a social construct and therefore would not let biological markers (such as a Y chromosome) determine the child's gender. Fourth, parents need to take an active role in understanding the condition and pursuing treatment options in keeping with their biblical convictions." Denny Burk, *What Is the Meaning of Sex?* (Wheaton, IL: Crossway, 2013), 180–82.

nature, they may well lash out and accuse the church that loves divine design of hating them and wishing for their downfall. They may well take the goodness of God, twist it, and turn the people of God into a movement of hate, all for believing and living according to the reasonable wisdom of the Word of God. They may reeducate their children, raising them to prize androgyny and downplay God-given sex, training them to fiercely oppose Christians (and other religious types who believe relatively similar doctrine) as the very speck in the societal ointment.

But all this is tragically wrong. The church that trusts and obeys the Bible is doing just what it should do.[67] The husbands and wives who live according to the revelation of God, and structure their homes to glorify him, do not hate their unbelieving neighbors by virtue of their actions. The believers who speak up in public to defend what is biologically and scientifically true, and draw tremendous scorn and even persecution for it, have done no wrong. The church of Jesus Christ is not a hateful counterculture. It must repent of sin wherever it finds it, but the church of Jesus Christ is the *true* culture.[68] We minister even to

---

[67] For help in formulating a compassionate pastoral approach to individuals experiencing gender dysphoria, see Andrew T. Walker, *God and the Transgender Debate: What Does the Bible Actually Say About Gender Identity?* (Epsom, England: Good Book, 2017).

[68] See Stanley Hauerwas and William H. Willimon, *Resident Aliens: Life in the Christian Colony* (Nashville: Abingdon, 1989), 17–18. This is a sound perspective on the church's identity vis-à-vis the world.

those who hate us and oppose us, offering them the ministry of truth, which is itself an act of love.[69]

Paul's words to the ancient Corinthians may seem outdated and outmoded. In truth, this section from 1 Corinthians 11 is one of the most needed passages for the modern church in the entire Bible. To a significant and tragic extent, ancient Corinth's ways are our culture's ways. We cannot mute Paul's testimony; we must study it, live it, and praise God by doing so. Jason DeRouchie puts a fine point on the matter, connecting transgenderism to idolatry:

Idolatry gives glory to someone other than YHWH; witchcraft looks to means other than God's word to discern his will or what will happen in the future, and dishonest gain diminishes the value of God's image in others. We must conclude, therefore, that something about transgender expression and gender confusion directly counters the very nature of God.[70]

---

[69] We are, as Richard John Neuhaus and Chuck Colson formulated it, *contra mundum pro mundo*, "against the world for the world." See Owen Strachan, *The Colson Way: Loving Your Neighbor and Living with Faith in a Hostile World* (Nashville: Thomas Nelson, 2015), 178; Richard John Neuhaus and Peter Berger, *Against the World for the World: The Hartford Appeal and the Future of American Religion* (New York: Seabury, 1976).

[70] Jason S. DeRouchie, "Confronting the Transgender Storm: New Covenant Reflections from Deuteronomy 22:5," *Journal for Biblical Manhood and Womanhood* 21, no. 1 (Spring 2016): 65, https://cbmw .org/topics/transgenderism/jbmw-21-1-confronting-the-transgender -storm-new-covenant-reflections-from-deuteronomy-225/.

The Old Testament on Homosexuality

The four major challenges the church faces today in its sexual ethics are feminism, postmarital sexual libertinism, transgenderism, and homosexuality. Each of these four ideologies is the reversal of biblical teaching and divine design. We shall conclude this chapter by making their connections explicit. In what immediately follows, we consider the third of this group in the light of Scripture. Though a secular culture urges the church to embrace homosexuality, the Bible speaks directly against such a move.

The Scripture introduces the matter of homosexuality in a story, a hair-raising one:

> The two angels entered Sodom in the evening as Lot was sitting at Sodom's gate. . . .
>
> Before they went to bed, the men of the city of Sodom, both young and old, the whole population, surrounded the house. They called out to Lot and said, "Where are the men who came to you tonight? Send them out to us so we can have sex with them!"
>
> Lot went out to them at the entrance and shut the door behind him. He said, "Don't do this evil, my brothers. Look, I've got two daughters who haven't had sexual relations with a man. I'll bring them out to you, and you can do whatever you want to them. However, don't do anything to these men, because they have come under the protection of my roof."

"Get out of the way!" they said, adding, "This one
came here as a foreigner, but he's acting like a judge!
Now we'll do more harm to you than to them." (Gen
19:1, 4–9 HCSB)

The scene in Sodom recalls the sinful schematics of Eden. It
begins with God's own messengers, the two angelic visitors left
in Lot's care after the Lord departed in Genesis 18. Heaven has
come to earth, so to speak, but has no happy reception upon
arriving. The men of Sodom, amassed as a whole, circle Lot's
dwelling in sinister fashion. They show no friendliness to Lot
and his guests, nor do they engage in even perfunctory pleasantries. They call out in command form, bidding Lot to send out
the angels as a sexual offering for them.[71]

Lot tries to reason with the crowd, which bristles with awful
intent. He identifies the homosexual desire expressed by the
Sodomites as "evil," but then contributes his own evil suggestion to the scene, urging them to accept the sexual sacrifice of
his daughters. Not only has Lot tried to put his own children in
harm's way, but he has done so with girls who have no familiarity
with sex. These are young women, in other words, and they will

---

[71] According to Gordon Wenham, the sexual nature of this awful
episode is exegetically apparent. "In itself 'knowing' is quite an innocent term, but the context here makes it apparent that sexual intercourse
is meant (19:8; cf. 4:1)." *Eerdmans Commentary on the Bible*, ed. James
D. G. Dunn and John W. Rogerson (Grand Rapids: Eerdmans, 2003),
s.v. "Genesis." Consult also Walton, *Genesis, Exodus, Leviticus, Numbers,
Deuteronomy*, 92–93 (see chap. 1, n. 22).

be powerless before the ferocity of the wicked men of Sodom. The crowd, it is plain, has given itself over to ungodliness, and the call by Lot to reconsider their collective action only angers them more.[72]

The next morning, a rain of fire visits Sodom and Gomorrah. The Lord made these cities a spectacle of destruction. Sodom's burning embers show us how high the stakes are with sin, and they reveal that sexual sin—and specifically the sin of homosexuality—is no isolated problem. Homosexuality involves profound human pride, the rejection of heaven's own counsel, and may well occasion anger—rage, more accurately—in the face of even the weakest of moral confrontations.

What Sodom displayed in a vivid tableau, the levitical law codified. God does not approve of homosexuality. He leaves no place for it in his law and strictly forbids homosexual conduct. Leviticus puts in concrete terms God's prohibition of ungodly sexuality:

> You are not to have sexual intercourse with your neighbor's wife, defiling yourself with her.
> You are not to make any of your children pass through the fire to Molech. Do not profane the name of your

---

[72] Kidner captures the severely negative cast of the text toward the men of Sodom: "At this early point in Scripture the sin of sodomy is branded as particularly heinous. The law was to make it a capital offence, grouped with incest and bestiality (Lev. 18:22; 20:13), and the New Testament is equally appalled at it (Rom. 1:26, 27; 1 Cor. 6:9; 1 Tim. 1:10)." Kidner, *Genesis*, 145 (see chap. 2, n. 24).

God; I am Yahweh. You are not to sleep with a man as with a woman; it is detestable. You are not to have sexual intercourse with any animal, defiling yourself with it; a woman is not to present herself to an animal to mate with it; it is a perversion.

Do not defile yourselves by any of these practices, for the nations I am driving out before you have defiled themselves by all these things. The land has become defiled, so I am punishing it for its sin, and the land will vomit out its inhabitants. (Lev 18:20–25 HCSB)

Homosexuality is not an isolated offense in the mind of God.[73] In Leviticus, it possesses the character endemic to numerous other disgraceful acts of sexuality.[74] But this passage's focus reaches

---

[73] "Homosexuality is condemned throughout Scripture (Gen. 19; Lev. 20:13; Judg. 19:22ff.; Rom. 1:27; 1 Cor. 6:9). *Abomination*, a term of strong disapproval in Hebrew (*tôʿēbāh* [תּוֹעֵבָה]), is used five times in this chapter (vv. 22, 26, 27, 29, 30) and in 20:13. It is more common in Deuteronomy (17 times), in Proverbs (21 times), and in Ezekiel (43 times). Other writers use it less often. It comes from a root meaning 'to hate' or 'abhor.' An abomination is literally something detestable and hated by God (e.g., Prov. 6:16; 11:1)." Gordon J. Wenham, *The Book of Leviticus*, The New International Commentary on the Old Testament (Grand Rapids: Eerdmans, 1979), 259.

[74] "This term is used in Leviticus for sexual practices that defile the people engaging in them, as well as defiling their environment. This eventually leads to God withdrawing his presence from people. As Wold has shown, Boswell's claim that תּוֹעֵבָה is used in Leviticus only to prohibit temple prostitution cannot be sustained because ritual impurity is not just generated by ritual transgressions, but by the effect of

beyond even sex itself. The fact that the killing of children in worship of Molech draws mention here shows us that the Lord is condemning an entire worldview, and not only discrete sins. The passage tells us just this: "the nations" that God wars with have committed all these evils.[75] They do whatever they want, following the lusts of the flesh, whether these lusts lead them to adultery, child sacrifice, bestiality, and more.[76]

The levitical text leaves no room for affirmation of homosexuality in any form: "You are not to sleep with a man as with a woman; it is detestable" (Lev 18:22). The verse that follows strengthens the point: "You are not to have sexual intercourse with any animal, defiling yourself with it; a woman is not to present herself to an animal to mate with it; it is a perversion" (18:23). The man who has sex with another man commits a transgression so defiled it is akin to having sex with an animal. The act, in other words, is wrong because the act is not ordered to God's holy purposes. God has not made sex for the boundless pursuit of pleasure. God made sex for covenantal union and for the population of the earth unto his own doxology.

---

sexual, moral disorder on the sacred domain." John W. Kleinig, *Leviticus*, Concordia Commentary (St. Louis: Concordia, 2003), 379–80.

[75] Vasholz notes the connection between *abomination* language and paganism. Robert I. Vasholz, *Leviticus: A Mentor Commentary*, Mentor Commentaries (Fearn, UK: Mentor, 2007), 216.

[76] Homosexual practice was not uncommon in the ancient Near East. "A Mesopotamian omen (concerned with results rather than morality) prognosticates: 'If a man has anal sex with a man of equal status—that man will be foremost among his brothers and colleagues.'" Walton, *Genesis, Exodus, Leviticus, Numbers, Deuteronomy*, 311.

Homosexual encounter compromises this design and confounds this holy will.[77]

The New Testament on Homosexuality

The book of Romans is known as Paul's theology of the gospel. Before searching out the glories of soteriology, the apostle Paul addresses the depravity of the Gentiles. The Gentiles live out rebellion against God that at its core is bodily, sexual, and pagan:

> For though they knew God, they did not glorify Him as God or show gratitude. Instead, their thinking became nonsense, and their senseless minds were darkened. Claiming to be wise, they became fools and exchanged the glory of the immortal God for images resembling mortal man, birds, four-footed animals, and reptiles.
>
> Therefore God delivered them over in the cravings of their hearts to sexual impurity, so that their bodies were degraded among themselves. They exchanged the truth of God for a lie, and worshiped and served something

---

[77] Israel was to stand out from all the other nations by its sexual righteousness. "Homosexuality, with some restrictions, was accepted in the ancient Near East. By contrast, Moses allows no exceptions, apparently a unique stand against that wider culture. . . . There is no warrant to assert that the dictum against homosexuality applied only to religious practices. The whole passage deals specifically with illicit sexual relationships without that kind of qualification." Vasholz, *Leviticus*, 216.

created instead of the Creator, who is praised forever. Amen. (Rom 1:21–25 HCSB)

When we teach youth the doctrine of sin, we rightly focus on how all people choose to disobey God. This is true. But the apostle's opening disquisition on sin in Romans 1 verges into much more colorful territory than the flannelgraph might go. Paul begins his assessment of Gentilic spirituality and theology by noting that they owe everything to God, and even know of his existence, but have turned from him. Thus we see that paganism—as we have called the leading countertheistic conception of humanity—begins with willful ignorance, but also with ingratitude. As Thomas Schreiner has suggested, "The root sin that dominates human beings and unleashes God's wrath is specified in verses 21–23. These verses describe the same reality in various ways, but the fundamental sin is the failure to glorify God and give him thanks."[78]

The sexual sins we must address to obey Scripture never emerge as isolated iniquities. What may look like raw lust never is. Behind homosexuality, Paul teaches, we find a proud and thankless heart that in truth hates the Lord. Whether we know it or not, this is true of our sinful hearts. In Adam, we both turn from God and hate him. No one is neutral; no one is positively disposed to God before God saves him.[79]

---

[78] Schreiner, *Romans*, 87 (see chap. 1, n. 49).

[79] "The sexual drive itself is wholesome and good. It is God's way of providing both pleasure and progeny. [But w]hen directed toward a

The Gentiles do not embrace the serpent's antivision of
humanity by mistake. They think themselves wise, the perennial
temptation of the Greco-Roman peoples. They fall into the serpent's trap in Eden: they choose against God, who is immortal,
privileging the creature over the Creator. They do so, it appears,
out of a visceral desire to see their object of worship (Rom 1:23).
This is a bad bargain to make, for their resulting lord—their
functional god—ends up being one of several very humble
beasts. The Gentiles did not want God. They wanted the creation rather than the Creator, and they divinized it accordingly
(and still do). "God delivered them over" to sexual sin, enabling
their plunge into the depths of depravity.

There is the truth, and there is "a lie" (1:25). The pagan vision
of humanity is a lie, from the first to the last. Paganism offers
humanity a degodified theology and spirituality enrobed in wonder and happiness. But Scripture tells us what paganism, or for
our modern purposes neopaganism, represents. It is replacement
theology and replacement spirituality. Better said: neopaganism
is *displacement* theology and spirituality. It is idolatry.[80] Following

person of the same sex, it abandons its God-given purpose and becomes
a degrading passion." Robert H. Mounce, *Romans*, The New American
Commentary, vol. 27 (Nashville: B&H, 1995), 83.

[80] Douglas Moo connects this behavior to idolatrous impulses: "In
many Jewish polemical works, the gross sexual immorality that the Jews
found rampant among the Gentiles was traced directly to idolatry. Thus,
to cite Wisdom of Solomon: "the idea of making idols was the beginning of fornication, and the invention of them was the corruption of life"
(14:12)." Moo, *The Epistle to the Romans*, 113 (see chap. 1, n. 50).

Paul's line of thought, creation's God-denying worship of design-less humanity and unbridled sexuality displaces the truth—it attempts displacement, that is. It cannot actually do so, of course; you can no more remove God from the world than you can convince water to stop following gravitational pull. But the Gentiles will not cease to try. They love the lie, they think it serves them, and they will promote it vociferously.

Here we come to the conclusion of this sorry sketch. Homosexual desire and activity does not occur as a discrete act. According to the apostle Paul, homosexuality functions as the logical end of pagan theology. As Douglas Moo suggests, such depravity flows from "the perversion of true knowledge of God," a willful turning away.[81] We cannot understand it merely as the misfiring of sexual interest or as misguided but understandable longing. In the scope of Romans 1, the Bible's most substantial swatch of teaching on ungodly sexuality, Paul sees homosexuality as the outcome of hostile pagan unbelief:

> This is why God delivered them over to degrading passions. For even their females exchanged natural sexual relations for unnatural ones. The males in the same way also left natural relations with females and were inflamed in their lust for one another. Males committed shameless acts with males and received in their own persons the appropriate penalty of their error.

---

[81] Moo, 114–15.

And because they did not think it worthwhile to acknowledge God, God delivered them over to a worthless mind to do what is morally wrong. (Rom 1:26–28 HCSB)

Homosexuality does not count only when expressed in actions. It is "degrading passions" that fire godless sexual practice. Paul makes no mention of monogamy here; the condemnation in question does not reduce to multi-partner homosexual encounters, nor does the apostle make any mention of adult men taking advantage of boys (though this was an immoral feature of the upper-tier Greco-Roman world). The passions in question drive women to have sex with women, and men to have sex with men. The text leaves no room for any redemptive component to these encounters; there is no way in which God receives glory in homosexual activity per Romans 1.[82]

As the poisoned fruit of the pagan growth process—from the seed of ungrateful unbelief to the flowering of wicked desire in physical behavior—homosexuality brings about the awful deliverance of God to "a worthless mind," a mind that has a moral

---

[82] The Christian sexual ethic is distinct from secular society, and it has always been so. In the first century, "Christianity was preaching new and different principles—and one of these principles was its condemnation of homosexuality in itself, considered (in this case following the Jewish tradition) as an abominable and perverse form of sexuality, offensive to the Lord, and one which, whatever its manifestations, could not be tolerated because it was always and everywhere 'against nature.'" Eva Cantarella, *Bisexuality in the Ancient World*, trans. Cormac Ó Cuilleanáin, 2nd ed. (New Haven, CT: Yale Nota Bene: 2002), 208.

sense working in precisely the wrong way. The pagan Gentile thinks that doing wrong is doing right; he cannot see that his personal behavior and advocacy of such behavior heaps up damnation for him.[83] He thinks he will be rewarded, now and later, for his deeds, and so he not only plunges into homosexual sin and myriad other ungodly acts driven by fallen desires, but he "applaud[s] others who practice them" (Rom 1:32). John Murray captures the fearsome consequence of such wickedness: "God's displeasure is expressed in his abandonment of the persons concerned to more intensified and aggravated cultivation of the lusts of their own hearts with the result that they reap for themselves a correspondingly greater toll of retributive vengeance."[84]

How true and terrible these words are. Left without the revelation of God, we will emulate the Gentiles in Scripture (pagans), and naturally follow these instincts all the way down the line, whether to Creator-glorifying living or creation-worshipping

[83] Fitzmyer links this behavior with pagan idolatry: "Pagan idolatry results in human degradation through lust, perversion, and sins against nature. Although God's wrath will manifest itself definitively at the eschatological judgment, it is already revealing itself in human history. God does not allow the impious pagan to prosper; he gives human beings up to their sin, withdrawing his blessing and allowing moral degradation to pursue its course in sin that disgraces humanity and disturbs human society." Joseph A. Fitzmyer, *Romans: A New Translation with Introduction and Commentary*, Anchor Yale Bible, vol. 33 (New York: Doubleday, 1993), 284.

[84] John Murray, *The Epistle to the Romans*, The New International Commentary on the Old and New Testament, vol. 1 (1959; Grand Rapids: Eerdmans, 1997), 44–45.

living. Our sexuality is not a mere matter of which behaviors to act on and which to stifle. Our sexuality syncs with our spirituality and enfleshes it. Every sin separates us from God by an infinite gap; every sin draws the just wrath of God. But we need to see this clearly: committing adultery with a member of the opposite sex is against God's will. But committing a homosexual act is not only against God's will, but against God's design. It is as thorough a repudiation of the goodness of God as humanity can offer.

Understanding the Nature of Desire in the New Testament

The preceding material informs our understanding of homosexuality in a fully sufficient way. Our contention here is not that every sinner possessing same-sex attraction consciously walks through all the steps traced by Paul in his commentary on Gentilic pagan activity. Many sinners, in point of fact, do not think for a moment about the ancient Near East, the garden of Eden, and Greco-Roman temple prostitutes. When sinners sin, they are usually thinking about their lusts. They may not know a single word of Scripture; many people in our twenty-first-century world still have not heard a single verse of the Bible. Further, some sinners come from deeply troubled backgrounds and may have suffered horribly without any initiation on their part.

The Bible does not speak much about the psychosocial backdrop of our immoral behavior. It does not let us off the hook for immorality due to our past experiences. Surely, Jesus Christ offers us invincible and boundless compassion through his gospel message, and he bids every sinner come and be received into the loving family that is his church. But this is not all God's Word teaches us about immorality. The Scripture goes deeper— it digs into not only our behaviors, but also our desires. We see this in Jas 1:13–15, an often-overlooked passage that allows us to glimpse the alchemy of depravity.[85] In this text, we peer into the awful—but arresting—process by which sin forms in the human heart:

> No one undergoing a trial should say, "I am being tempted by God," since God is not tempted by evil, and he himself doesn't tempt anyone. But each person is tempted when he is drawn away and enticed by his own evil desire. Then after desire has conceived, it gives birth to sin, and when sin is fully grown, it gives birth to death. (Jas 1:13–15)

The key phrase for our purposes is that the sinner is *exelkomenos* (ἐξελκόμενος) and *deleazomenos* (δελεαζόμενος)—"lured and

---

[85] The following discussion is adapted from my journal article on this subject. See Owen Strachan, "A Referendum on Depravity: Same-Sex Attraction as Sinful Desire," *Journal for Biblical Manhood and Womanhood* 20, no. 1 (Spring 2015): 24–34, http://cbmw.org/wp-content/uploads/2015/04/4.1_Referendum-Depravity_Owen-Strachan.pdf. See also Denny Burk and Heath Lambert, *Transforming Homosexuality: What the Bible Says about Sexual Orientation and Change* (Phillipsburg, NJ: P&R, 2015).

enticed," respectively—by *tēs idias epithymias* (τῆς ἰδίας ἐπιθυμίας), "his own lusts."[86] This is a dark picture of how desire eventuates in sin, which brings on death.[87] Before the fallen instinct is fully manifested, before it comes to full fruition, a toxic process occurs in the human will. We should take note here: what James describes is not only unfortunate or disordered. It is sinful.[88]

The language James uses to describe the workings of desire leads us to this conclusion. We allowed ourselves to be "lured and enticed" by our own fleshly desire. This is a chilling metaphor. We are not drawn out-of-bounds by someone else when we allow ourselves to be tempted. Instead, we are "dragged away" in a "violent sense," as one commentator puts it.[89] The focus in Jas 1:14 is resolutely, even stubbornly, on our own actions. We are not hauled away by someone else's volition. *We* are the agent here. "We entice ourselves with the object we desire," as we could put it. Whether or not we are fully conscious of this process

---

[86] This word need not signal necessarily evil desire; see, for example, its usage in Luke 22:15, Phil 1:23, and 1 Thess 2:17. It refers either to moral or immoral desires, and the *telos* (τέλος) of the desire is crucial for understanding which form of desire is in view in a given text. The context makes clear that it is used here of immoral desires. See D. Edmond Hiebert, *James* (Chicago: Moody, 1992), 93.

[87] One Catholic scholar notes that this force is nothing other than "evil desire." Patrick J. Hartin, *James*, Sacra Pagina (Collegeville, MN: Liturgical, 2009), 91.

[88] In the broader Greek literature, the Stoic Epictetus uses this imagery to depict the temptations of pleasure. See Ralph P. Martin, *James*, Word Biblical Commentary, vol. 48 (Waco, TX: Word, 1988), 36.

[89] Kurt Richardson, *James*, The New American Commentary, vol. 36 (Nashville: B&H 1997), 81.

(which often occurs very quickly), we act as our own tempters and enticers.

Our sinful wills, fallen because of Adam's unrighteous act, entrap us. Another exegete suggests that the latter term referenced above, *deleazomenos* (δελεαζομενος), harkens to the enticing call of the prostitute, a call presented (and critiqued) in Prov 7:6–23.[90] This makes sense: when we sin, the text suggests, we effectively play the role of the prostitute to ourselves. We fall into unrighteousness not through any external operation, but when our wills have "sanctioned the performance of the sinful act."[91] It is as if our fallen instincts call out to our better natures, our new natures, to abandon our God-given virtue. Yes, we must do battle with evil elements who would undo us, but in James's hamartiology, we ourselves rank as the first problem in committing sin.

With such a vivid textual portrait, the takeaway seems obvious: we regularly act as our own worst enemies. We are the problem, not someone else. We have an inborn hunger for evil.[92] We search for it. Outside of the working of God's grace, we possess a gnawing eagerness to tempt ourselves toward it. So when we sin, it is because we want to do so. What Douglas Moo calls "illicit desire" pushes and goads us into doing what is wrong.[93] These

---

[90] Hiebert, *James*, 93.

[91] Hiebert, 94.

[92] For more on this metaphor, drawn from "the art of fishing." See Simon J. Kistemaker, *James and I–III John*, New Testament Commentary (Grand Rapids: Baker Books, 1986), 49.

[93] Douglas J. Moo, *The Letter of James*, The Pillar New Testament Commentary (Grand Rapids: Eerdmans, 2000), 74.

are not someone else's illicit desires. They are, as we saw above, *tēs idias* (τῆς ἰδίας) —"our own."

Our desires, therefore, are not usually neutral.[94] John Calvin concurs that James "treats here of inward temptations, which are nothing else than the inordinate desires which entice to sin. . . . For this reason James calls us to confess our own guilt, and not to implicate God."[95] In Calvin's handling, we cannot only identify acts and deeds as sinful. We must broaden our categories:

> It seems, however, improper, and not according to the usage of Scripture, to restrict the word *sin* to outward works, as though indeed lust itself were not a sin, and as though corrupt desires, remaining closed up within and suppressed, were not so many sins. But as the use of a word is various, there is nothing unreasonable if it be taken here, as in many other places, for actual sin.[96]

Sin cannot only be the "outward work" for Calvin. Opposing what he called the "Papist view," Calvin argued that "corrupt desires," though "closed up within and suppressed," are nonetheless "actual sin." They call for confession and repentance. That which produces external deeds has internal roots. We are reminded

---

[94] R. V. G. Tasker, *The General Epistle of James*, Tyndale New Testament Commentaries (Grand Rapids: Eerdmans, 1957), 46–47.

[95] John Calvin, *Commentaries on the Catholic Epistles*, trans. and ed. John Owen (Edinburgh: Calvin Translation Society, 1855), 288.

[96] Calvin, 290.

of Luke 6:45 (ESV), where Christ makes this very point: "The good person out of the good treasure of his heart produces good, and the evil person out of his evil treasure produces evil, for out of the abundance of the heart his mouth speaks."[97]

In James's understanding, our lustful desires "conceive"—*syllabousa* (συλλαβοῦσα)—sin and then "bear"—*tiktei* (τίκτει)—it (1:15). This text shows that the metaphorical child to be born is the same in the womb as out of it. Lustful desires conceive sin and then birth it. The process from start to finish is immoral. Lust is not neutral in the womb, so to speak, only to become externally evil once acted upon in concrete form. Sinful instincts pop up in us, we experience desire for an object that is ungodly, and we then produce fully formed sinful actions.

So it is in Matthew's Gospel: "You have heard that it was said, 'You shall not commit adultery,'" Jesus says. "But I say to you that everyone who looks at a woman with lustful intent has already committed adultery with her in his heart" (Matt 5:27–28 ESV).[98] The takeaway here is plain: there is no God-glorifying outlet for a desire that fails to honor God. When we feel homosexual desire, we must confess it to God and immediately repent of it. We cannot class this passion as only "disordered" or "fallen."

---

[97] Thanks to Grant Castleberry for this textual connection.

[98] The lustful desire condemned here is a "deep-seated lust which consumes and devours, which in imagination attacks and rapes, which mentally contemplates and commits adultery." D. A. Carson, *Jesus' Sermon on the Mount and His Confrontation with the World: An Exposition of Matthew 5–10* (Grand Rapids: Baker Books, 1999), 46.

If a desire is oriented to that which is sinful, we must treat the desire itself as sin (see also Mark 7:14–23). It may be that such desires are few and fleeting or that they constitute a pattern. The frequency or the intensity of same-sex desire is not the issue. It is the experience of same-sex desire, just like the experience of heterosexual lust or unrighteous anger in one's heart, that calls for confession and repentance.

In our battle against temptation, we look to Christ. Jesus fought Satanic temptations with the word of God (Matt 4:1–11). We may and must do the same. Yet we must also confess that we struggle in a unique way. Jesus, because he had no sinful nature, did not face what we could call *internal temptation*. Yes, he was tempted "in every way" as we are (Heb 4:15). He was confronted externally by all sorts of prospects and opportunities: the chance to lust, the chance to make himself an impressive king in worldly terms, the possibility of concluding that his cause was hopeless. But Jesus never sinned. He had no internal compulsion to blaspheme God as we do. He was the God-man.

This truth does not—and must not—blunt the beauty of Christ's mastery of temptation. It does not discourage us or put him at an impassable remove from us. To the contrary, it inspires worship and thankfulness in us. Jesus's obedience to his Father (John 15:10) compels us to worship him and to pray to be like him. It shows us that though fallen forces might feel stronger than our new natures, we never need to give into temptation of any kind. Jesus overcame temptation, and so can we.

The Church's Approach to
Transgender and Homosexuality

Almost four decades ago, Francis Schaeffer commented on the church's response to the sexual revolution. He saw it whole, not in pieces:

> They have very gradually become disturbed over permissiveness, pornography, the public schools, the breakdown of the family, and finally abortion. But they have not seen this as a totality—each thing being a part, a symptom, of a much larger problem. They have failed to see that all of this has come about due to a shift in world view—that is, through a fundamental change in the overall way people think and view the world and life as a whole.[99]

Schaeffer was right. The church has rarely put the pieces together in the area of sexual ethics. We know about the sexual revolution, yes, and we speak against given sins. But we still largely fail to see that our major worldview competitor is not an isolated transgression or even a political lobby. Our major worldview competitor is a system. We call this system *neopaganism*.

Paganism is the antiwisdom of the serpent which deconstructs ordered reality—the God-made world—and replaces it

---

[99] Francis A. Schaeffer, *A Christian Manifesto* (Wheaton, IL: Crossway Books, 1982), 17.

with a new order, an antiorder ruled by the devil.[100] In this anti-order, there is no Creator; no divine design; no male or female; no script for sexuality; no God-designed family with a father, mother, and children; no need to protect and care for children at all; no Savior, Lord, or theistic end to the cosmos; and no judge of evil.

The theologian Peter Jones calls this the religion of *one-ism*. This contrasts with what Jones calls *two-ism*, the biblical approach to reality, in which God fundamentally stands above and apart from his creation, grounding all distinctions, judging all the earth, placing his image in the earth under divine authority to live according to divine design. One-ism, by contrast, reduces the world to an ash-gray sameness: "there are real no distinctions, everything is made of the same stuff, matter is eternal, and it has this spark of divinity within it." Accordingly, we worship the creation: one-ism is "the basis of nature worship, there's no category for sin, because think of a circle, everything is within the circle, rocks, trees, good and evil, man and God. Everything is one, and so in that circle, we can do whatever we want to." We must thus "invent gender and marriage," making each whatever we desire them to be, while expressing "tolerance for all religions" and "all lifestyles." A pagan person per Jones's critique distrusts hard-and-fast morality, downplays absolute truth, holds a self-generating view of existence and cosmological origins, vouches

---

[100] For background on modern paganism, see Peter Jones, *Pagans in the Pews: How the New Spirituality Is Invading Your Home, Church and Community* (Ventura, CA: Regal, 2001).

in some form that spirituality is a matter of internal alignment rather than external obeisance, views redemption as a project of self-actualization ("I want to be my best self"), and sees no higher purpose to death and the trajectory of the cosmos.[101]

In this framework, transgenderism makes perfect sense. We understand the cultural push to normalize it as part and parcel of a much bigger worldview. Transgenderism does not emerge in a vacuum; it serves as one part of a system that begins without God but with a hard-to-identify "spark" of divinized force moving through the universe. Sensualism is spiritualism. Transgenderism seems not merely one small part of this new realm; transgenderism, one could argue, is actually the apotheosis of the whole worldview, for what is clearly distinguished in anatomy becomes one.

As we observed earlier, the four major challenges the church faces today in its sexual ethics are feminism, postmarital sexual libertinism, transgenderism, and homosexuality. Each of these is a part of neopaganism. Feminism overturns the biblical ideal of the woman; sexual libertinism severs sex from marriage and encourages men and women to act sexually without respect to morality; transgenderism rebels against the very concept of divine design in terms of identity and appearance; homosexuality revolts against sacred order in terms of sexual identity and practice. These four ideologies represent an antiorder, a worldview

---

[101] Peter Jones, "Paganism in Today's Culture" (lecture, Ligonier Conference, Reformation Bible College, Sanford, FL, February 19, 2015), 38:37, https://www.ligonier.org/learn/conferences/after-darkness -light-2015-national-conference/paganism-in-todays-culture/.

that is in truth no worldview at all. If most modern people do not bow to stone deities, this in no way means that they are not cheerful participants in neopagan worship. They may not be directing their spiritual and bodily rebellion toward a given god, but they are nonetheless following the antiwisdom of the serpent and denying the role of God in the constitution of human identity and the ordering of the human body. Neopaganism is no longer the exception in the West; more and more, it is the norm. But few, to cite Schaeffer, see it in whole. They only see it in pieces, and thus they are ill-equipped to respond.

Neopaganism is the major competitor for the hearts and minds of Western people. The church finds itself in a decadent age. Some years ago, Jacques Barzun noted the decadence of the West, defining it as follows: "When people accept futility and the absurd as normal, the culture is decadent. The term is not a slur; it is a technical label."[102] Decadence and paganism go hand in hand. Today, the absurd grows increasingly normal. Resistance feels futile. Hope for real change seems in short supply. Sinners seem too far gone for the average church to reach.

In times such as these, we need to go back. We need to remember the power of the gospel and the importance of biblical preaching. Our context feels particularly depraved, but if we will open our eyes to biblical experience, we will quickly see that the apostles and the early church faced tremendous fallenness in their time. To the Corinthian Christians, a group living amid

---

[102] Jacques Barzun, *From Dawn to Decadence: 500 Years of Western Cultural Life, 1500 to the Present* (New York: HarperCollins, 2000), 11.

mind bending sinfulness and idolatry, the apostle Paul communicated profoundly needed truth. Writing to a people burned over by the influence of ancient paganism and spiritualized hedonism, and still struggling to detach themselves from their fleshly lives, the apostle Paul wrote:

> Don't you know that the unrighteous will not inherit God's kingdom? Do not be deceived: No sexually immoral people, idolaters, adulterers, or males who have sex with males, no thieves, greedy people, drunkards, verbally abusive people, or swindlers will inherit God's kingdom. And some of you used to be like this. But you were washed, you were sanctified, you were justified in the name of the Lord Jesus Christ and by the Spirit of our God. (1 Cor 6:9–11)

These are preposterously beautiful words. In the Greek, the opening to verse 11 reads simply *kai tauta tines hete* (καὶ ταῦτά τινες ἦτε)—"Such were some of you," as we could translate it, though Thiselton is even closer to the mark when he argues for "This is what you used to be" as the proper translation.[103] The

---

[103] "The most important point about the initial sentence in v. 11 is the continuous imperfect indicative of the form ἦτε. The NRSV, NJB, **this** *is what* **you used to be**, is exactly right, as against REB, AV/KJV, *such were some of you* (NJB changes JB's *were*). While *were* is not strictly incorrect, Paul's reference to *continuous habituation* is implicit in the imperfect (see above on vv. 9–10). The *neuter* plural demonstrative pronoun ταῦτα emphasizes Paul's sense of shock and undermines the

Corinthian church, as we have already shown, faced terrific pres sure in its struggle for spiritual conformity to Christ. A libertine culture filled with people drawn into the dregs of sexual immorality pulled at the fledgling church in Corinth. But the preaching of the gospel had its effect. The very people who lost their souls in pursuit of licentious pleasure were those whom Christ washed, sanctified, and justified through the Spirit's operation.[104]

The apostle Paul gave the Corinthians no better news than this: in their fight for holiness, they did not struggle against sin as those enslaved to it. They had new names, new positions, new status before God, new natures, and they were by divine grace new creations.[105] They had become captives of Christ. The one

---

unnecessary discussion about lists of qualities versus lists of actions. The English **this** *is the kind of thing that you were* brings together the notion of a state of being with the performance of actions which instantiated it." Thiselton, *The First Epistle to the Corinthians*, 453.

[104] The paraphrase by Naselli is helpful here: "In this passage Paul follows the same pattern as 5:7–8 (see comments there): he tells the Corinthians how to behave (vv. 1–10) and then roots that behavior in what is already theologically true of believers (v. 11). Paraphrase (an implied exhortation): "You are washed, sanctified, and justified, so live like it. Become what you are! Be clean, not filthy. Be holy, not profane. Be righteous, not unrighteous." Naselli, "1 Corinthians," 57.

[105] David Garland captures the newness of the believer: "The implication is that Christianity not only offers a completely new sexual ethos and a new ethos regarding material possessions but also brings about a complete transformation of individuals. God's grace does not mean that God benignly accepts humans in all their fallenness, forgives them, and then leaves them in that fallenness. God is in the business not of whitewashing sins but of transforming sinners (Fee 1993: 39)." Garland, *1 Corinthians*, 216–17.

force in the cosmos stronger than the power of sin had rescued and redeemed them. They still felt the pull of the flesh, just as Christians from every sinful past will today, but the Corinthians had left their wicked identities behind. They could not label themselves according to their old proclivities or fuse a fallen self-conception with a regenerate one. There were no "alcoholic Christians" or "male-prostitute Christians" or "gay Christians" or "transgender Christians" or "thieving Christians" in the church at Corinth. Paul taught this body, fighting for godliness as it was, that there was only one name that fit them now: Christian.[106]

So it is today.

---

[106] Roy Ciampa and Brian Rosner spell out the new nature of the believer, one that can have no union with the old self and a sinful identity: "If for Christians the future has invaded the present, a decisive break has also been made with the past; the once/now motif is just as important as the already / not yet." Ciampa and Rosner, *The First Letter to the Corinthians*, 244–45. Evangelicalism needs a recovery of confidence in the newness of the new nature. I write this knowing that God-loving, Bible-following evangelicals will differ in their application of this reality, and that where men and women have turned away from homosexual behavior and relationships, we give thanks to God. Even as we seek to show that the Bible enfranchises neither homosexual activity nor homosexual identity, still we rejoice to know Christians who have left behind the lusts of the flesh.

CHAPTER 5

RACE AND ETHNICITY

It is not light that we need, but fire; it is not the gentle
shower, but thunder. We need the storm, the whirlwind,
and the earthquake.

—Frederick Douglass

The Bible begins with the oneness of humanity. In the Garden
of Eden, there is no enmity and strife in the God-made world.
There is difference, for the man and the woman are not the same
and the creatures bear many distinctions—great and small—
from one another. Oneness is not sameness in Eden. Creation
forms one symphonic sound of praise—the song of life—in its
superabundant diversity.

How beautiful that the Bible ends with one gathered and reconstituted people—and one united song of praise. In the age to come, the four living creatures and the twenty-four elders come before Christ the Lamb. They lift their voices in worship of the crucified, resurrected, and reigning Messiah:

> You are worthy to take the scroll
> and to open its seals,
> because you were slaughtered,
> and you purchased people
> for God by your blood
> from every tribe and language
> and people and nation.
> You made them a kingdom
> and priests to our God,
> and they will reign on the earth. (Rev 5:9–10)

The blood of Christ, this passage makes clear, has definitively "purchased people" from "every tribe and language and people and nation."[1] The blood of Christ covers sinners from all people groups that populate the earth.

---

[1] This is an effectual purchasing: "The object of the Lamb's redeeming activity is described in the concluding line of v 9. This is not a redemption of all peoples without exception but of all without distinction (people *from* all races), as 14:3–4, 6 makes clear. The general consensus is that this phrase is to be traced back to the almost identical expression repeated in Daniel. There the wording refers generally to the inhabitants of the world." G. K. Beale, *The Book of Revelation:*

Though the word *race* is not used here, it is clear that the peoples of the earth have not previously gathered together as they now do to praise Christ. In other words, the text does not explicitly speak of the once-divided, once-scattered nature of these peoples, but it implies their apartness. We do not have a specifically racial reason listed for this apartness, but we do note that the peoples of the earth once divided themselves into manifold groups over all the face of the earth. Now, in Christ, God has made them one family. Those who once built their own fiefdoms and policed them by spoken word and physical weapon, are now a spiritual kingdom. The death of Christ has made the many one, as the rebels have become priests unto God.

Notice where the Bible begins and ends with respect to race and ethnicity. The story between these two poles is a complex one, to say the least. The concept of race is opaque, but we cannot fail to see that millennia of sinful human beings have used their natural uniqueness against one another. In Christ, God is bringing these enemies together in one new man. Robert Mounce observes about Revelation 5 and the language we use to describe our differences,

Those who are purchased are from every tribe, language, people, and nation. It is fruitless to attempt a distinction between these terms as ethnic, linguistic, political, and so on. The Seer is stressing the universal nature of the

A Commentary on the Greek Text, New International Greek Testament Commentary (Grand Rapids: Eerdmans, 1999), 359.

church and for this purpose piles up phrases for their rhetorical impact. In contrast with the exclusivism of Judaism that prided itself on having been chosen out from among the nations, the church was genuinely ecumenical, recognizing no national, political, cultural, or racial boundaries.[2]

Mounce is not dismissing any distinguishing markers between humanity. He is, however, showing that the text points not to our apartness as believers, but to our oneness in Christ.[3] Sinful people have for centuries taken a gift of God—diversity—and used it as either a weapon or litmus test of humanity. This is not right. It is certainly not the will of God, as Revelation 5 discloses and as this chapter will make plain. That which sinful man all too easily turns into a curse, God has intended as a gift. Recovering

---

[2] Robert H. Mounce, *The Book of Revelation*, rev. ed., The New International Commentary on the New Testament (1977; repr., Grand Rapids: Eerdmans, 1998), 136.

[3] "The fact that Christians were drawn from many ethnic groups in the Roman empire but did not (unlike most Hellenistic religions) constitute an ethnic group themselves led early Christian authors to refer to Christianity as a new people or a *tertium genus*, "third race," in contrast to Jews and Greeks (Origen *Contra Cels.* 8.2; Justin *Dial.* 119; *Diogn.* 5–6; Tertullian *Ad nat.* 1.8). Paul referred to "Jews, Greeks, and the Church of God" (1 Cor 10:32), and Christians also regarded themselves as aliens whose true citizenship was in heaven (Phil 3:20; 1 Pet 1:17; 2:11; see Elliott, *I Peter*, 21–58)." David E. Aune, *Revelation 1–5*, Word Biblical Commentary, vol. 52A (Dallas: Word, 1997), 362.

this vision of God-made diversity will take great biblical concentration, great humility, and Spirit-shaped intentionality.

The Origin of Group-Based Separation and the Mission of Israel

If we would accomplish such a lofty end, then we must search out biblical teaching on the matters of race and ethnicity. Our consideration of this subject takes us back to the original design of God. It is important to note that the God of the Bible loves diversity, difference, and the many-splendored beauty of a world that operates in perfect harmony yet contains too many creatures and living beings to count. The God of Genesis 1 and 2 clearly does not wish to populate this realm with a dreary sameness. He is the God who makes one human race but two sexes, birds who pop their feathers in comic displays of courtship, plants seemingly painted with a master colorist's hues, ocean beasts of heart-stopping size and swiftness. In all his creative work, God is telling us and teaching us about his love of this multifaceted cosmos. He loves his handiwork; he derives great glory from it.

The human race falls, however, and things take a terrible turn at that point. The children of Adam take different paths. The line of Seth is faithful, whereas the line of Ham travels a grimmer road. None of Adam's children, however, is untainted by sin. Now, mankind sees his humanness not as a living exercise in doxology but as a vehicle for creaturely pride. The mind God has given the post–Genesis 3 man is used to blaspheme and scheme against God. The heart filled with affections implanted for the thrilling pursuit of God now chases and idolizes lesser things. The soul given for the very experience of the divine, for spiritual communion with God, is employed in the worship of the creation and not the Creator. Nowhere does the exaltation of man through the prideful use of God-given abilities more show itself than at Babel, or Babylon.

> The whole earth had the same language and vocabulary. As people migrated from the east, they found a valley in the land of Shinar and settled there. They said to each other, "Come, . . . let us build ourselves a city and a tower with its top in the sky. Let us make a name for ourselves; otherwise, we will be scattered throughout the earth."
>
> . . . The LORD said, "If they have begun to do this as one people all having the same language, then nothing they plan to do will be impossible for them. Come, let's go down there and confuse their language so that they will not understand one another's speech." So from there the LORD scattered them throughout the earth, and they stopped building the city. Therefore it is called Babylon, for there the LORD confused the language of the whole earth, and from there the LORD scattered them through-out the earth. (Gen 11:1–9)

This is an act of judgment by God. Pride drove the Babylonians to construct their tower and build their city. Self-idolatry occasioned the decisive response of Almighty God as the people's "language" was confused,[4] and the Lord himself "scattered" the peoples across the earth.

The Lord's action was fully just. The people should have used their intellects and technical skills to praise the Lord. They had the opportunity to celebrate him by honoring the dominion mandate through the employment of their talents. Instead, they sought to praise themselves, to stand out. They went so far—literally—as to try and establish their greatness as on par with God's. This is pride in its most noxious, extreme form. The raw materials of the God-made world, given by the Lord for meaningful work in his name, were instead used to dishonor the Creator. Now, speech—which was given for the worship of God and the unity of the race—will separate the peoples. So it was that God sent the peoples out, splitting them in an unalterable way. No human person, however idealistic and well-intentioned, can undo what the necessary work of God's judgment wrought. If the flood meant that the earth essentially shrank to the population

---

[4] Nahum Sarna suggests that the Lord has rendered their work mere foolishness: "The word play *babel-balal*, approximating 'Babel-babble,' in English, hides a subtle satirizing of Mesopotamian notions. Not the 'gate of god' as the inhabitants of Babylon interpreted the name, not the navel of the earth, as they conceived their city to be, but a site of meaningless gibberish, the center from which human divisiveness radiated, and the cause of disastrous alienation from God." Nahum M. Sarna, *Genesis*, The JPS Torah Commentary (Philadelphia: Jewish Publication Society, 1989), 84.

of the ark of Noah, then Babel means that the earth essentially expands to an unprecedented degree. The first act of judgment made the earth small; the second act of judgment made it impossibly big. Unity is no longer possible in natural terms.[5]

Genesis 11 shows the particular shape fallen life takes in a world bearing God's curse. We are not merely sinners in isolated form, staying in our own self-enclosed spaces; we spread across the world—clashing with one another, hostile with one another, misunderstanding one another—and we enter into long and open war with one another. For no greater reason other than our natural communal pride, we hate one another and even try to kill those who are different from us.

This was not God's good intention for humanity.[6] But the Lord fulfills his covenant purpose in the midst of this terrible dissolution. He loves tiny Israel, and he calls this people—founded

---

[5] See Wenham on the resulting confusion and isolation: "To see the cessation of building and the dispersal of the nations as incompatible motifs is to miss the profound grasp of culture that this story exhibits. Without mutual communication through a common language it is impossible for men to cooperate either commercially or socially. Towers cannot be built nor communities live together unless those concerned can understand each other." Wenham, *Genesis 1–15*, 241 (see intro, n. 11).

[6] Kidner looks ahead to Pentecost as when Babel begins to be undone in terms of comprehensibility of speech. "Pentecost opened a new chapter of the story, in the articulating of one gospel in many tongues. The final reversal is promised in Zephaniah 3:9: 'Yea, at that time I will change the speech of the peoples to a pure speech, that all of them may call on the name of the Lord and serve him with one accord' (RSV)." Kidner, *Genesis*, 119 (see chap. 2, n. 24).

in Abraham—to be a light among the nations. For example, his holy law necessitates kindness and hospitality to aliens: "When an alien resides with you in your land, you must not oppress him. You will regard the alien who resides with you as the native-born among you. You are to love him as yourself, for you were aliens in the land of Egypt; I am the LORD your God" (Lev 19:33–34). God nowhere endorses nativism. His people are called to be distinct from the world, but they are never justified in wearing their Israelite status as a badge of pride. They were, in fact, to reach beyond their own kin, their own family, and show mercy to others.[7] If anything, being an Israelite entailed a life of utter humility. Those who were not a people, God made a people. [8] Those who had no inherent greatness, God made great. The nation was to find its identity not in the fact that it merited God's favor—for it assuredly did not—but in the mere and marvelous choice

---

[7] See the teaching of Isa 56:3–7, for example. On this point, Scot McKnight observes that "The 'Gentile mission,' on the other hand, characterized earliest Christianity in that it aggressively sought out converts to Christianity from any people group all over the Roman Empire (*see* Roman Empire) and beyond. . . . The relationship of Jews to Gentiles was diverse, showing signs of both integration and resistance, and this diversity varied considerably with respect to time and place." *Dictionary of the Later New Testament and Its Developments*, ed. Ralph P. Martin and Peter H. Davids (Downers Grove, IL: InterVarsity, 1997), s.v. "Gentiles, Gentile Mission."

[8] DeRouchie calls attention to the identity of Israel as both royal and priestly: "the nation was set apart as God's royal priest-son, called to magnify his majesty in the world." DeRouchie, *How to Understand and Apply the Old Testament*, 372 (see chap. 4, n. 55).

of it by God. The nation, however, would not be confined to one people, but would expand to include all peoples.[9]

It is at this point that we should clarify the terms we use in this chapter. There is considerable discussion over the meanings of *race* and *ethnicity*. In general terms, *race* is seen as a social construct based on skin color, while *ethnicity* refers to one's cultural background. Dalton Conley describes it this way: "First of all, race is primarily unitary. You can only have one race, while you can claim multiple ethnic affiliations. You can identify ethnically as Irish and Polish, but you have to be essentially either black or white."[10] The idea of "multiple ethnic affiliations" seems generally sound, it but leaves us wondering how to integrate race and ethnicity. Is one more important than the other? Are neither important? What is important?

---

[9] One of the clearest indications of this global plan in the Old Testament are the predictions about the temple. Drawing off of Jeremiah 3, G. K. Beale notes, "Israel will finally fulfil [*sic*] the Genesis mandate 'to multiply and increase' at the time of her latter-day restoration (Jer. 3:16). . . . Though this fulfillment is coupled with a promise of a future temple, it is one that will not be like any earlier structures. Not even the centrepiece of the old temple, the ark of the covenant, will exist in the renewed Jerusalem. Only God's presence will exist as the new sanctuary." Beale, *Temple and the Church's Mission*, 112–13 (see chap. 1, n. 34). The trajectory of biblical theology runs one way: toward spiritual fulfillment and, ultimately, physical-spiritual fulfillment in the new heavens and new earth.

[10] Dalton Conley, quoted in "Ask the Experts," online forum for *Race: The Power of an Illusion*, produced by Larry Adelman, aired April 2003, on PBS, https://www.pbs.org/race/000_About/002_04-experts-03-02 .htm.

Many people today are confused and even trepidatious about trying to clarify these complicated matters. This is especially true in a context—I think of America—that has a very difficult past on racial and ethnic matters.[11] The concept of race, it must be said, is relatively recent and has a troubled heritage, as it was used to separate blacks from whites in America and justify slavery.[12] But even as we home in on this past evil, we note the terrible history surrounding the Holocaust as the greatest historical evil perpetrated by one people group over another. In Germany, people who looked remarkably similar nonetheless were separated from one another. Aryans considered Jews inferior and

---

[11] This troubled past is not confined to the experience of one group. Cf. Frank H. Wu, *Yellow: Race in America Beyond Black and White* (New York: Basic Books, 2002); Roxanne Dunbar-Ortiz, *An Indigenous Peoples' History of the United States* (Boston: Beacon, 2014); Esmeralda Santiago, *When I Was Puerto Rican: A Memoir* (New York: Vintage, 1993). In citing these books, as with the nonevangelical texts in this chapter, I do not indicate agreement with every facet of these works. It is, however, valuable to read widely in this and any field, particularly when personal experience is as connected to a theme as in the subject before us.

[12] For more on the history of race in America, see Cornel West, *Race Matters*, 25th anniv. ed. (Boston: Beacon, 2017); Anthony Bradley, *Black and Tired: Essays on Race, Politics, Culture, and International Development* (Eugene, OR: Wipf and Stock, 2011); Thomas Sowell, *Race and Culture: A World View* (New York: Basic Books, 1995); Sowell, *Wealth, Poverty and Politics*, rev. ed. (New York: Hachette, 2016); Shelby Steele, *The Content of Our Character: A New Vision of Race in America* (New York: Harper Perennial, 1990). I encourage readers to read widely in this field and sift various perspectives for wisdom, considering differing viewpoints with empathy and inquisitiveness.

commenced their slaughter, leading to millions upon millions of deaths.

Racial inferiority is a terrible concept; ethnic inferiority is a terrible concept. It is manifestly obvious that both ideas have been used in a sin-infested world to oppress and harm and terrorize image-bearers, sometimes for very long periods of time. Christians, then, do well to go back to basics and recognize that divisions between people groups begin after the fall, as the exiles of Eden scatter and the lines of Adam proliferate. These divisions pick up great force after Babel, when the Lord judges a proud humanity by confusing their tongues, thus leading to greater separation. None of these sad developments represents God's ideal, which would have been realized in a nonlapsarian Eden. The people of earth would not, in other words, have increased in tribe-centric bitterness and enmity. They would have grown more diverse, we may reason, but not more divided.[13]

What, then, are we left with for our vocabulary? How should we speak of racial and ethnic divisions? It seems best to note that whatever approach we take to the diverse peoples

---

[13] One of the predominant terms used in the New Testament to speak to people groups is *ethnos*: "(τὰ) ἔθνη people groups foreign to a specific people group (corresp. to Heb. גּוֹי in LXX; a nationalistic expression." *A Greek-English Lexicon of the New Testament and Other Early Christian Literature*, ed. Frederick W. Danker, 3rd ed. (Chicago: Univ. of Chicago Press, 2000), 276–77. The point is evident: the New Testament documents do not depend upon a concept of race akin to a modern one even as the New Testament (as with the Old Testament) recognizes the presence of diverse people groups on the earth. The primary marker of these groups is their non-Israelite status.

of the earth, the Bible-following church cannot see diversity as a problem but as a sign of God's beautiful creativity. Some may use terms such as *race* and *ethnicity*; whatever our practice, we cannot not use them as weapons against others, as the creators of these categories may have intended. Because of our underlying anthropological unity, many today prefer to speak of ethnicity over race, for while there are different people groups of the earth, with different cultural practices, the human race is unitary. There are not essential biological differences between people of varying skin pigmentation, though some still divide humanity along these lines.

The peoples and ethnic groups of the earth should not and need not strive with one another. Sinners have from the fall of Adam used racial and ethnic diversity to separate, not strengthen, the human race.[14] This will continue until the end of the age. Confessing this does not amount to a dismissal of this broader matter, but rather grounds the problem in the fall of mankind. Until the end of the age, the church references these terms and categories not so that we may divide and conquer, but to marvel and unite those from different backgrounds. In the world, these matters separate and embitter; in the church, however we choose to formulate our terms, these matters seen in proper biblical

---

[14] For more on the history of slavery in America, see Eric Foner, *The Fiery Trial: Abraham Lincoln and American Slavery* (New York: W. W. Norton, 2010). For more on the lived experience of African Americans under Jim Crow laws, see William H. Chafe, Raymond Gavins, and Robert Korstad, eds., *Remembering Jim Crow: African Americans Tell About Life in the Segregated South* (New York: New Press, 2001).

perspective should unite and reconcile.[15] If these are hopeful words bordering on the naïve (considering global history), we take comfort in knowing that hope is the very essence of the Christian life and the kingdom's story.

The People of God Amid the Peoples of the Earth

In attempting to understand race and ethnicity as covered in Scripture, we return to the story of the covenant people of God. There is no sense in which the Jewish people—the Israelites— were allowed by their covenant status to see themselves as ethnically superior to other groups. Yet it is also true that the people of God were favored by the Lord due to his desire to display his mercy and kindness in them. Israel was not loved because it was faithful to Yahweh; Israel was faithful to Yahweh because it was loved. Surely, if any person repented in the old covenant period, God received him regardless of background. In fact, God delights to welcome those outside the nation of Israel as his own people—we think of resourceful Rahab or righteous Ruth.

The other tribes and nations of the ancient Near East did not concur with Yahweh's covenantal interest, however. They

---

[15] Usage of terms vary among godly evangelical theologians and leaders. The major issue before the church today, it seems, is whether we will approach race from a biblical perspective while always thinking contextually. Our challenge is to be distinctly *Christian* in this enterprise, meaning that we do not think about these matters as the unbeliever does, and that we bring to any discussion of these matters the fruits of the Spirit and the hope of Christ.

went to war against the tiny nation. In response, the Lord was not shy to call his people to become a great nation, to oppose evil, and to go to war against wicked rulers and fearsome warriors. Initially, it was the Lord himself who fought for Israel, destroying Pharaoh's forces in the roiling waters of the Red Sea. As the mission advanced, and the covenant mission took shape, the Lord led Israel into battle, calling his people to join him at arms. The book of Joshua charts the progress of the people of God as they take much of the promised land given them by God. This was a martial mission, to be sure:

Then Joshua told the Israelites, "Come closer and listen to the words of the LORD your God." He said: "You will know that the living God is among you and that he will certainly dispossess before you the Canaanites, Hethites, Hivites, Perizzites, Girgashites, Amorites, and Jebusites when the ark of the covenant of the Lord of the whole earth goes ahead of you into the Jordan. (Josh 3:9–11)

We err if we read these words and empathize more with the pagans than with the people of God.[16] The Israelites found themselves in a perilous spot here and throughout the narrative

---

[16] For more on the context of these people groups, see Marten H. Woudstra, *The Book of Joshua*, The New International Commentary on the Old Testament (Grand Rapids: Eerdmans, 1981), 84–85; also Trent C. Butler, *Joshua 1–12*, 2nd ed., Word Biblical Commentary, vol. 7a (Grand Rapids: Zondervan, 2014), 302–3.

of the Old Testament.[17] Pagan warriors summoned by pagan kings sought the undoing of the covenant nation, both spiritually and militarily.[18] Behind the warlike tribes of the ancient Near East was a greater enmity, a more furious force. If God himself fought for Israel, Satan spurred on the pagan peoples of the earth. We remember the prophetic protoevangelium of Gen 3:15 in narratival moments such as this, recalling that the battle between spiritual powers has not evaporated. God and Satan are clashing throughout the Old Testament. Satan, as he always has, hates those who worship the true God, and he agitates to drive lost groups against the people of God.[19] He does not hate them in a passive sense, but in a terribly active way (Job 1; Eph 6:12). Thankfully, God is infinitely stronger than the devil, and his seemingly overmatched people overcome the forces of darkness again and again and again.

---

[17] To understand the odds faced by the nation in this time, see Butler, 301.

[18] "The people of Canaan are involved in repulsively immoral practices that force Yahweh to judge them. What occurs [in Joshua] is not a God-ordained hate mission. Rather it is divine judgment for sin similar to that which God has reluctantly meted out since the Garden of Eden." Paul R. House, *Old Testament Theology* (Downers Grove, IL: InterVarsity, 1998), 200.

[19] "The Israelites could do nothing but resort to coercive force ('the sword') to protect themselves from Amalekite attack (Ex. 17). . . . And despite their peaceable intentions, the Israelites had to fight against Sihon and Og, who nevertheless came against them with force (Num. 21:21–35)." Paul Copan, "Greg Boyd's Misunderstandings of the 'Warrior God,' The Gospel Coalition, January 26, 2018, https://www.thegospelcoalition.org/reviews/crucifixion-warrior-god-greg-boyd.

The conquest of the promised land is righteous and God-ordained. In the Old and New Testaments, the Scripture never encourages or asks us to apologize for the exercise of divine judgment against sin and sinners. The Christian, then, is not on his heels with regard to the Canaanite conquest or other such texts; the Christian, in fact, must never accept the lie that a God who judges evil is a God we cannot worship. The text presents the opposite view: we cannot worship a God who does not oppose and overcome evil. Surely, the matters in question are beyond the facile workings of the creaturely mind, as all the things of God are; we boggle at the reality of divine judgment, and we feel tremendous sorrow when we hear of image-bearers who choose self-destruction—and eternal torment—over the good paths of God's righteousness. We read of the wicked nations and people groups of the Old Testament, and we shake our heads at their choice of antiwisdom over divine truth.[20] As we do so, we confess freely that whatever God does is right. This confession, however, does not scrub away our horror at what sinful humanity perpetually chooses to do instead of obeying God.

The Old Testament is a crimson book, to be sure. Israel must go to war to survive and to honor God. How glorious, then, that the Old Testament itself presents us with a nascent eschatological vision of theocentric oneness. In texts such as Psalm 67, we

---

[20] The Canaanites, for example, practiced the following and sought to entice Israelites to do the same (with some tragic success in the old covenant era): incestuous marriages between brothers and sisters, homosexuality, bestiality (in Egypt women cohabited with goats), and child sacrifice. Wenham, *The Book of Leviticus*, 251–52 (see chap. 4, n. 73).

get a glimpse of a day when the nations do not rage against God
and do not rise against the house of Yahweh, but rather "shout
for joy" in the Lord's presence:

> Let the peoples praise you, God;
> let all the peoples praise you.
> Let the nations rejoice and shout for joy,
> for you judge the peoples with fairness
> and lead the nations on earth. *Selah*
> Let the peoples praise you, God,
> let all the peoples praise you. (Ps 67:3–5)

This is a striking passage given the martial content of much of
the Old Testament. The "peoples" were made for just this vivifying purpose: to praise and worship God. We find ourselves in
a secular age and must debate matters of earthly government
regarding whether a religion-friendly, a secular, or a distinctly
religious nation is best. These are complex questions, to be sure.
In this text the Psalmist extols the direct government of God
over all the peoples as a source of surging joy and praise. God
judges fairly and leads all people well.[21] For this, he deserves an

---

[21] "So the psalm adds that God decides for people with uprightness,
fairness, or equity. God's upright dealings with Israel are a paradigm for
God's dealings with the world, rather than being an activity that ignores
the needs of other peoples. The verb in the second colon puts the point
vividly. 'Leading' (*nāḥâ*) describes the way shepherds care for their flocks,
and it is a natural verb to apply to God's relationship with Israel (e.g.,
77:20 [21]; 78:14, 53, 72). How strikingly, then, that it here applies to

ongoing celebration. The righteous ruler reigns. Every wicked king has fallen away. God is the chief good of his people, but not in an abstract way—in a direct way. The nations, the peoples, all the diverse groupings of humanity were made for this. They were not made to unite against God but to praise him together.[22]

The Old Testament does not terminate on this note—not by a long shot. As it closes, the nation of Israel is subsumed into the Persian kingdom. The peoples of earth continue their ceaseless provocations and hostilities. There is no peace on earth; there is nothing remotely approaching true and lasting unity among mankind. Indeed, the very idea seems hopeless, for not even Israel itself can maintain lasting bonds. Even before Assyria and Babylon attacked and conquered the people of God, the nation of God crumbled from within. Even Israelite identity—grounded in divine calling—could not hold the people together.

But the Suffering Servant was on the way.

---

the nations. They, too, are God's flocks." John Goldingay, *Psalms*, vol. 2 *42–89*, Baker Commentary on the Old Testament: Wisdom and Psalms (Grand Rapids: Baker Academic, 2007), 302.

[22] The language used here in the Hebrew lays bare how miraculous this gathered praise truly is. "The peoples (*'ammîm*, Heb. עַמִּים), who were the nations in v. 2 (*gôyîm*, Heb. גּוֹיִם), are now the "countries" (*lĕ'ummîm*, Heb. לְאָמִּים), a much rarer third word. The meaning of these words is not sharply distinct; the collocation of the different terms rather underlines in a further way how the whole world is involved in the acknowledgment and confession of God. Indeed, they are not merely confessing and realistically acknowledging how things are but rejoicing and resounding: that is, resounding with joy." Goldingay, 302.

The Glory of God as Seen in the Unifying Blood of Christ

The true King of Israel, and the true Son of God, was not born in a palace. He did not come from a "good family" in earthly terms. Jesus Christ hailed from a home ruled by the Roman Empire, which had totally subsumed the remnants of Israel. Christ came into the world at the ebb of the Jewish peoples' history. Raised in the synagogue, he began teaching among his own people in his fourth decade of life, and he brought a word from God that marked him out as a new teacher with authority—the authority of God himself.[23]

Against all expectations, Jesus did not return Israel to exalted national status. He did not claim political leadership of an ethnic group. He did, however, call all around him to repentance in his name. It was not one's background, family, or works that gave entrance to the kingdom of Christ. It was repentance. After Jesus gathered his apostles (and following his crucifixion, resurrection, and ascension), he sent them to Jew and Gentile alike, confounding the expectations of all of his hearers. Jews learned once for all that Jesus had made a new nation from the foundation of the

---

[23] Jesus did not base his teaching on the testimony of rabbinic authorities, but presented his word as itself authoritative: "And when Jesus finished these sayings, the crowds were astonished at his teaching, for he was teaching them as one who had authority, and not as their scribes" (Matt 7:28–29 ESV). The sense of astonishment is presented in a continuous fashion and could read, "they were more and more amazed." Morris, *Matthew*, 184 (see chap. 1, n. 26).

old one by his blood; Gentiles learned that they were responsible for believing in the God-man, and that they could not escape the duty of repentance in his name.

Shockingly, the two groups are united through repentance in Christ. The judgment that falls upon Jesus at the cross yields salvation for the guilty.[24] But those who are saved are not saved to dwell alone as followers of God. The called-out become one family. Those who have so long fought one another now constitute one body:

> For those of you who were baptized into Christ have been clothed with Christ. There is no Jew or Greek, slave or free, male and female; since you are all one in Christ Jesus. And if you belong to Christ, then you are Abraham's seed, heirs according to the promise. (Gal 3:27–29)

The apostle Paul is not teaching that all differences between humans have fallen away in a kind of salvational melting pot.[25]

---

[24] A new community is created by Christ and his gospel. The common experience of this community is the passing from death to life of every member. Salvation comes through judgment, and only through judgment. See James M. Hamilton Jr., *God's Glory in Salvation through Judgment: A Biblical Theology* (Wheaton, IL: Crossway, 2010), 439–40.

[25] "It is easy to quote the saying in this verse as a slogan that proclaims the erasure of any distinctions within the Christian community. But of course Paul recognizes the continuing reality of the male/female distinction among human beings; 'androgyny,' the creation of a new being neither male nor female, is far from Paul's idea." Douglas J.

Instead, Paul makes clear here that the hard-and-fast boundaries endemic to the old man have fallen away. Now, all who come to Christ find their identities first and foremost in Christ.[26] There could be no Jewish church and no Greek church according to the theology of Paul; such a conclusion would violate the fulfillment of the Abrahamic promise by the death and resurrection of Christ. The blood of Christ could not be distributed to separate groups as if God had set up different spiritual blood banks. The righteousness of Christ "clothed" all who confessed their sin to God.[27] Now, there was only one people of God: the church (with a future in-gathering of ethnic Jews yet to come).[28]

The stars Abraham saw in the sky as the image of the gathered covenant people of God no longer stood thousands of miles

---

Moo, *Galatians*, Baker Exegetical Commentary on the New Testament (Grand Rapids: Baker Academic, 2013), 254.

[26] This identity is not grounded in sentiment or statement of personal allegiance—"I am with Jesus." "'Clothed with Christ' makes best sense if explained in terms of the imputation of Christ's righteousness." Graham A. Cole, *God the Peacemaker: How Atonement Brings Shalom*, New Studies in Biblical Theology (Downers Grove, IL: InterVarsity, 2009), 168.

[27] See Ronald Y. K. Fung, *The Epistle to the Galatians*, The New International Commentary on the New Testament (Grand Rapids: Eerdmans, 1988), 175.

[28] The church is purchased by the very blood of Christ, and so it dwells together in iron unity. This unity is a visible display of the kingdom, which even now rules triumphantly over the counter-reign of Satan. For more on the interplay of cross and kingdom, see Jeremy R. Treat, *The Crucified King: Atonement and Kingdom in Biblical and Systematic Theology* (Grand Rapids: Zondervan, 2014), 193–226.

off from one another. All who loved Jesus were one in the Son. As explosive as this teaching is, we cannot miss that the early church struggled to grasp these truths. Filled with repentant sinners, the church in its youth found itself divided along the old lines.

> In those days, as the disciples were increasing in number, there arose a complaint by the Hellenistic Jews against the Hebraic Jews that their widows were being overlooked in the daily distribution. The Twelve summoned the whole company of the disciples and said, "It would not be right for us to give up preaching the word of God to wait on tables. Brothers and sisters, select from among you seven men of good reputation, full of the Spirit and wisdom, whom we can appoint to this duty. But we will devote ourselves to prayer and to the ministry of the word." This proposal pleased the whole company. So they chose Stephen, a man full of faith and the Holy Spirit, and Philip, Prochorus, Nicanor, Timon, Parmenas, and Nicolaus, a convert from Antioch. They had them stand before the apostles, who prayed and laid their hands on them. (Acts 6:1–6)

Ongoing racial or ethnic tension in the evangelical movement is not new. It is ancient. We know the groups in question had numerous differences of culture, background, historical experience, and preference. Individuals in both camps had difficulties with others on the opposite side. The point is plain: there was ample opportunity for the earliest church to begin pulling apart along ethnic lines.[29]

The apostles did not let this happen. In conduct that charts the way for future elders of local churches, they called forth several "deacons" and charged them with meeting the bodily needs of the congregation. The result was a slate of godly men, many of whom had distinctly Hellenistic names, though Nicolaus appears to be Hebraic. The apostles did so because they understood just how propulsive the cross's power to unify was and is. This power does not render culture and ethnicity nothing, because diversity—properly framed—glorifies God.[30] As the New Testament narrative unfolds, it seems proper to conclude that ethnicity is a vehicle by which God communicates in visible form the uniqueness and brilliance of the exclusivistic gospel. His people have unity in diversity. Their Christic unity does not compromise or foreclose diversity; their unity is a unity of many tribes, many peoples, many groups joining together in worship of David's true successor and Abraham's true heir. Rahab and her children have come in

---

[29] Cole describes the hostility in Acts as the "barrier" between different ethnic groups—a barrier which has already fallen in Christ but which the church sometimes tries to reconstruct. See Cole, *God the Peacemaker*, 80.

[30] This is true however one views race and ethnicity. My burden in this chapter is not to defend a concretized vision of either race or ethnicity, but to show that the Scripture pictures atonement-based unity as a crucial part of the glory of the gospel and the uniqueness of the church.

to the family of God, and they will continue to stream in until the end of the age.[31]

The fullest development of these intertwined threads, the very threads of salvation, comes in Paul's letter to the Ephesians. We have already referenced how Paul teaches the Galatians that they are one in Christ. Christ is the identity of all the people of God. In Ephesians Paul spells this out in greater detail, paying attention to the explosively unitive nature of Christ's cross work:

> So then, remember that at one time you were Gentiles in the flesh—called "the uncircumcised" by those called "the circumcised," which is done in the flesh by human hands. At that time you were without Christ, excluded from the citizenship of Israel, and foreigners to the covenants of promise, without hope and without God in the world. But now in Christ Jesus, you who were far away have been brought near by the blood of Christ. For he is our peace, who made both groups one and tore down the dividing wall of hostility. In his flesh, he made of no

[31] John Murray distinguishes between our own feelings toward others and the "objective reconciliation" wrought by the work of Christ. It is not "subjective enmity" that Christ has primarily done away with in his death, but "alienation" from God. John Murray, *Redemption Accomplished and Applied* (1955; Grand Rapids: Eerdmans, 2015), 33–37. We may conclude that divine atonement deals with divine alienation, and that all who are no longer alienated from God are also no longer alienated from one another. Thus our hearts are freed from hatred of the foreigner. There is truly in Christ no ground for enmity with those who are redeemed by God.

effect the law consisting of commands and expressed in regulations, so that he might create in himself one new man from the two, resulting in peace. He did this so that he might reconcile both to God in one body through the cross by which he put the hostility to death. He came and proclaimed the good news of peace to you who were far away and peace to those who were near. (Eph 2:11–17)

In this time, Jew and Gentile alike could point to a catalogue of calamities in relations with the other side. The Gentiles, not insignificantly, were closed off from "the citizenship of Israel." They had no access to the "covenants of promise," which left them both "without hope and without God." The Gentiles knew none of the blessings of covenantal fellowship with the Lord; they lived "far away" from God and his grace. Here is the apostle's textured delineation of the chasm that separated the Jews and Gentiles. To put it in layman's terms, the two groups were as far apart in spiritual terms as they could be. They had no hope of unity. Perhaps they technically shared citizenship within the broader bounds of a given nation, but they had no means of lasting unification. Hostility dominated. Hatred proliferated. Tension boiled as it does among people of varying backgrounds in the modern world.

But Christ made an end of this separation. By "the blood of Christ," Jew and Gentile become one through repentance.[32] Paul pictures the division shared by the two sides in distinctly

---

[32] See Thielman, *Ephesians*, 157–58 (see chap. 4, n. 30).

physical terms. A great immovable "wall of hostility" separated these ethnicities. One could no more overcome the wall than one could move the stone from Christ's tomb. Note how implacable this hatred is to Paul: it is granite, fixed, and constitutive of its environment. To live near a wall, to have one's existence bounded by a wall, is to experience the curious phenomenon of physical strictures shaping one's mentality and spirituality. A prison is nothing more than a set of walls and barriers, yet it takes an uncommon person indeed to wish to live in such a setting. The "wall" of hatred had, in a similar way, affected and even imprisoned the two sides in a condition of implacable bitterness.

There is only one force that may tear down such a wall: the cross of Christ. Jesus, Paul straightforwardly asserts, "is our peace."[33] What a memorable phrase this is. We have no peace in ourselves; we bring only hostility to our interactions. Peace of the lasting, enduring, uniting kind comes from—and truly in—only one person on earth: Jesus Christ.[34] Jesus brings together what Satan has driven apart. Jesus has not only made it possible for

---

[33] This peace "is probably derived from the idea that those who are 'in Christ' (v. 13) assume some of the qualities of Christ himself (cf. 5:2; 1 Cor. 1:30; Col. 3:3–4)." Thielman, 164.

[34] The implication of this truth is that we do not have true peace with those who are outside of Christ. We do have common ground with fellow sinners in terms of the *imago Dei*, but there is real and meaningful unity with unbelievers. Yet when we reckon with the peace that is in Christ and the alienation that is in Adam, we comprehend that we cannot have full unity of any kind with unbelievers. This is not to say that we should not work for the good of the city of man; it is to say that our efforts cannot bring lasting peace, and we can never cancel the alienation

Jew and Gentile and every group to unite—Paul's language is iron-strong in its description of achieved effect—but Jesus "made both groups one" and "tore down" the aforementioned wall.[35] He brought a new law in himself, and so the law no longer informs the covenant community's worship; it is "of no effect." The Jews cannot mark themselves off by it anymore. Christ himself is the ruler of his people; he is identified again as the very "peace" of all who trust in him as Savior. We do not need to find peace within ourselves; we need simply to be who we are in Christ, and the peace that we have through union with him will seep into all our relationships.

Jesus has triumphed. Jesus has reconciled God and man, and man and man.[36] Jesus takes two estranged peoples and creates "one new man" from them. Thus it is not inappropriate to say, as Henri Blocher does, that "Christ died as the Head of the new

---

we have with those outside the church. Unity—true unity—and peace— true peace—are found only in Christ.

[35] F. F. Bruce notes the wall between Jew and Gentile has been "demolished," a potent phrase. Bruce, *The Epistles to the Colossians, to Philemon, and to the Ephesians*, 296 (see chap. 1, n. 44).

[36] According to Jarvis Williams, Paul is not here suggesting "that Gentiles become ethnic Jews and surrender their ethnic identity by being connected to Israel's Jewish Messiah" but rather that God "includes then as Gentiles into his saving promises to Israel through the blood of Israel's Jewish Messiah." Coming to faith in Christ does not cancel our God-given identities, but rather refashions our identities around Christ. He is our center; he is our all. Jarvis Williams, *One New Man: The Cross and Racial Reconciliation in Pauline Theology* (Nashville: B&H Academic, 2010), 117.

humanity," creating an unbreakable "bond of organic unity."[37] Through Jesus, and only through the saving Jesus, true reconciliation comes. It is "peace" for those who are near and "peace" for those who are far off.[38] This does not render the cross of Christ an optional instrument of possible unity; rather, it unveils in high-definition detail the fully effective, once-and-for-all-time accomplishment of the death of the God-man. No other figure can do this. No one else can unify hostile peoples. Jesus is the only true hope of those who desire unity of any kind in the world. This is a good desire, and we can achieve it in a provisional way, but anyone who wants true peace must look to Jesus and Jesus alone.[39] Jesus has drawn the nations to himself and made one new people from them. His finished work shows that he is the fulfillment of Abraham's promises, and it reveals that he is not merely beginning the new creation.[40] He *is* the new creation, and in the age to come, all his people who are spiritually in-gathered

---

[37] Henri Blocher, "Jesus Christ *the* Man: Toward a Systematic Theology of Definite Atonement" in *From Heaven He Came and Sought Her: Definite Atonement in Historical, Biblical, Theological, and Pastoral Perspective*, ed. David Gibson and Jonathan Gibson (Wheaton, IL: Crossway, 2013), 578–79.

[38] By "far off" Paul does not mean those who reject Christ, but those who were formerly alienated from God.

[39] "Jew and Gentile drawn to Christ are drawn to one another." Cole, *God the Peacemaker*, 180.

[40] See Jason S. DeRouchie, "Father of a Multitude of Nations: New Covenant Ecclesiology in OT Perspective" in *Progressive Covenantalism: Charting a Course Between Dispensational and Covenant Theologies*, ed. Stephen J. Wellum and Brent E. Parker (Nashville: B&H Academic, 2016), 31–32.

and indwelt by the Spirit will physically live with him in the remade cosmos.[41] This Ephesians passage thus has soteriological and eschatological implications of the most profound kind.[42]

Paul concludes these comments in verses 18–22:

> For through him we both have access in one Spirit to the Father. So then you are no longer foreigners and strangers, but fellow citizens with the saints, and members of God's household, built on the foundation of the apostles and prophets, with Christ Jesus himself as the cornerstone. In him the whole building, being put together, grows into a holy temple in the Lord. In him you are also being built together for God's dwelling in the Spirit. (Eph 2:18–22)

There are not different ways to God; Jew and Gentile alike "both have access in one spirit to the Father," access granted by the finished work of Christ. This means that diverse peoples are "members of God's household," a single building, a living and holy

---

[41] Oren Martin, *Bound for the Promised Land: The Land Promise in God's Redemptive Plan*, New Studies in Biblical Theology (Downers Grove, IL: InterVarsity, 2015), 134–51.

[42] See also Oren Martin, "The Land Promise Biblically and Theologically Understood," in *Progressive Covenantalism: Charting a Course Between Dispensational and Covenant Theologies,* ed. Stephen J. Wellum and Brent E. Parker (Nashville: B&H Academic, 2016), 272–74; Gentry and Wellum, *Kingdom through Covenant,* 713–16 (see chap. 2, n. 54).

temple in Christ. We do not occupy different edifices; we are all growing up into a "holy temple" through our spiritual connection to Christ.[43] God, Paul told the Ephesians, was in their time building up the structure. He has continued doing so in the two millennia since, though we may struggle to spot this encouraging work in our tumultuous and conflict-ridden world.

In sum, God did the unthinkable in the first century. Through the death of his Son, he cleansed sinners of varying kinds who lived in perpetual hostility toward one another. The Jews and Gentiles in broad terms had not battled for decades or even centuries; the Jews themselves, as we have seen, had a heritage of many centuries of war—often God-directed war—with non-Jewish peoples. Despite this backdrop, the apostle Paul taught the Ephesian Christians that reconciliation was not a possibility with Christians of Jewish background. Reconciliation was an actuality.[44] It had already happened in Christ. With one stroke, one sacrificial offering, Jesus united all believers in all places from all backgrounds for all time. His atoning death first united

---

[43] Paul's use of temple language signifies that Jesus is the fulfillment of old covenant categories—specifically that of the Lord's dwelling place—and shows us that we cannot in any way cut the cord that runs between the old and new covenants. The old no longer binds us, but it surely still instructs us.

[44] The pastoral reflection by John Piper is piercing on this matter: "Vertical and horizontal reconciliation happen together and inseparably through faith in Christ." John Piper, *Bloodlines: Race, Cross, and the Christian* (Wheaton, IL: Crossway, 2011), 125. Throughout his treatment of Ephesians 2, Piper uses definitive language with regard to the work of Christ and the resulting cessation of hostility.

men to God, and from this theistic foundation, it brought unity among all repentant peoples.

If this seems to load a great deal of weight on the cross, it surely does. The cross is so powerful it is effectively a second work of creation by God. There is a new race, a new humanity, a new people of God. Jew and Gentile are one in Jesus. We await the fullest expression of this unity in the new heavens and new earth, but we cannot fail to see that the end-times have broken into our time. We are now, as Benjamin Gladd and Matthew Harmon observe, the "eschatological people of God" and thus "fellow citizens with the saints and members of the household of God."[45] The strongest possible "horizontal" enmity has ceased in the cross of Christ. Division predicated on longstanding grievances has come to a close through faith in the Messiah. The enmity between distinct groups has been defeated in the household of God by the propitiatory work of Christ. The "eschatological people" of God are united now, even as our unity awaits the fullest and most final expression in eternity to come.

Believers from Jewish and Gentilic backgrounds did not always have an easy time mixing in the early church. Tensions sometimes flared. So it has been for many centuries since. The church has struggled throughout its history to obey these few verses of Paul and to comprehend the catalytic effect of this

---

[45] Benjamin L. Gladd and Matthew S. Harmon, *Making All Things New: Inaugurated Eschatology for the Life of the Church* (Grand Rapids: Baker Academic, 2016), 118.

treatment of ethnic hostility. But looking back, we cannot fail to see success, too, in the great global project of the reconciliation afforded by the cross work of Jesus Christ. There is no family like the family of God in human history. There is no movement that crosses boundaries like the Christian mission. Christianity cannot be painted into a corner as the exclusive faith of one ethnicity or region; it is a global faith, a movement united by repentant belief in the atoning death and vicarious resurrection of Christ, yet diverse in terms of its reach, scope, and ultimate ingathering of people from every tribe and tongue.[46]

The Theological Way Forward for the Church in a Hostile World

The preceding New Testament material should give us great God-centered hope for reconciliation and oneness in Christ. If it was possible for two groups with such longstanding enmity to gather as one in the first century, it is possible for diverse peoples to do so today. We cannot assume, however, that such efforts will happen without effort and without distinctly theological thinking. Toward that end, here are three matters for the twenty-first-century church to consider as it seeks to make good on the biblical picture of oneness in Christ.

---

[46] See Brian Stanley, *The Global Diffusion of Evangelicalism: The Age of Billy Graham and John Stott*, History of Evangelicalism, People, Movements and Ideas in the English-Speaking World (Downers Grove, IL: InterVarsity, 2013).

First, the church must be honest about sin, both historic and personal. The American racial heritage is checkered and deeply troubling. The fact that Christians participated enthusiastically in the slave trade and the institution of slavery takes our breath away today. Looking back, we can only conclude that our spiritual forebears too often lost sight of and even muzzled the doctrine of humanity on the matter of racial and ethnic equality. The concept of *chattel* slavery is a low point in the annals of American history. The violent suppression of post–Civil War freedoms on the part of minorities in the American South defies belief, and the Jim Crow laws that persisted in America into the mid-twentieth century show us that our country has much to reckon with in our time. We cannot easily dismiss these sins and evils and wrongs. Our racist past may seem distant, but it is not. The people whose salvation story roots in the Israelites gaining liberation from the Egyptians must know this: our American forebears became the Egyptians to their own brothers and sisters. How terrible this truth is. It demands sobriety, honesty, and humility from us today as we seek to heal wounds that remain open.

Second, the church must model humility in its reconciliatory work. Humility helps us unify divided groups through Christ's cross and resurrection. Whatever our past holds, the biblical way forward is to find oneness in the finished work of Christ. If we cannot find unity in our union with Christ, we simply will not attain unity. We will remain divided. The church will look much like the world in its approach to ethnicity and difference. We will see our past as an impassable wall, when in truth, the wall has fallen already through the powerful work of Christ.

The Lord is powerfully glorified by Christians who have past grievances against other groups who lay those grievances down in the life of the church. Doing so requires that we refuse to embrace the "shame culture" that proliferates in our time and that we, instead of shaming one another, forgive one another. Forgiveness speaks a better word than shame. We think here of the Jews and Gentiles who shared church membership in the first century. No doubt many of them had ample reason to hate their counterparts; they might have had long-standing tensions, terrible family experiences, and deep-seated bitterness along racial and ethnic lines. Church membership did not mean blinking away these experiences. It did, however, mean that the believer clung to hatred of others—even justified hatred in human terms—no longer. So it must be for healing. Christ is our framework. Humility and the fruits of the Spirit are our plan. We are witnesses of the power of the atonement and the resurrection. One of the ways we display that the work of Christ is powerful is through diverse but unified fellowship.[47] The Lord has not only risen from the grave, but he has created a resurrection body by so doing.

Third, the church cannot adopt anything other than a Christocentric approach to unity. In the twenty-first century, we are in a fractured social climate. Christians today cannot solve every societal problem. But the church is called, like the

---

[47] Kevin J. Vanhoozer, *The Drama of Doctrine: A Canonical Linguistic Approach to Christian Theology* (Louisville: Westminster John Knox, 2005), 357.

ethnically divided Jewish and Gentile Christians of the first century, to make good on the unity that Christ has already created by his blood. This is no simple project; we cannot snap our fingers and make the terrible memory of slavery and Jim Crow laws and various racial biases in American culture vanish on the spot. But the church also cannot lose sight of the Scriptural truth that we are all one holy temple built by Christ. In this area, as in so many others, that sound doctrine does not inhibit true ecclesial unity but activates it. Knowing who we are in Christ, and comprehending afresh just how powerful his cross is, provides us with the only lasting hope of oneness on this planet.

This last sentence bears special weight. The church should strive to display gospel-created unity. We want to have an influence, ideally a profound one, in our communities. Further, we want individual Christians to rise up and work as agents of salt and light to advance justice among divided peoples. The church, though, must never forget its distinct mission. We cannot undo every evil in this world. Our local churches should be centers of true hope. Even if they strive for holiness, however, they cannot do what only Jesus can. We cannot end the sins of hatred, ungodly division, and ethnocentrism. We can and should fight these ills, yes, but only Jesus can put an end to sin. Only Jesus will put an end to sin.

Our approach to unity is promising for the world, for we are a force as Christians for good in this place. But our approach to unity is in truth Christocentric. Jesus is our hope. Jesus is the one who takes warring peoples and makes them one in his body. Jesus, further, is sufficient for the task—the serious and weighty task—before us. Racial and ethnic division is not easy to overcome. This is why Paul's words are so important for modern Christians. If only Jesus is qualified and able to split the wall asunder, then only Jesus will suffice in the final analysis for our churches. The task of racial and ethnic reconciliation in the end is not on our shoulders. While we have clear responsibilities before us, responsibilities we must not shirk or ignore, we cannot fail to hold fast to this truth. Reconciliation simply is not something we do. It is something that God has done. He has accomplished the work in Christ. The church is united by faith to Christ and one another.

In conclusion, we return to our starting point. In the age to come, the four living creatures and the twenty-four elders sing the song that we ourselves will rejoice to sound abroad. They praise the one who honored the Father's mission and obeyed the Father's will. Jesus made a people who were no people through his death:

You are worthy to take the scroll
and to open its seals,
because you were slaughtered,
and you purchased people
for God by your blood
from every tribe and language
and people and nation.
You made them a kingdom

and priests to our God,
and they will reign on the earth. (Rev 5:8–10)

In surveying the world and its course, it can look as if hatred is the theme of this place. But if we will lift up our eyes and gaze on what God is doing in his church, we will see that hatred is not the driving force of history. It is love, redeeming love, the love of Christ. The love by which enemies lay down their weapons, embrace one another, and worship God together as friends and more than friends—as family.

CHAPTER 6

TECHNOLOGY

Americans no longer talk to each other, they entertain each other. They do not exchange ideas; they exchange images. They do not argue with propositions; they argue with good looks, celebrities and commercials.

—Neil Postman, *Amusing Ourselves to Death*

We find ourselves, whether we like it or not, in a hyper-technological age. Many of us live in constant contact with our devices, in particular our smartphones. We use our devices to praise technology; we use them to critique technology. Even the Neo-Luddites have email and a preferred hashtag today.

From the beginning, God and man have engaged in complex creation, building complicated realities from created matter. The crude tools of the ancient world may not seem technological, but they surely are and were. Clothes, food, shelter, weapons, implements—these and many more products enhanced the lives of their users, allowing greater efficiency in daily tasks, augmenting the creative capacities of mankind, and enabling humanity to probe the mysteries of existence, transcendence, and greatness. Technology is not the focus of the Bible, but the Bible contains numerous instances of technological achievement and technological idolatry. Technology in both Word and world is used to praise God; technology in both Word and world is used to defame and push away from God.

In this chapter, we consider Scripture's conception of technology. We can't use a Bible's index to look up *technology*, but we can put together several passages from across the biblical canon. In doing so, we find that the Word of God both commends and critiques technology. From this perspective, we transition to consider several matters related to a theology of the body, intertwined as these subjects frequently are in our age. In sum, we see that our hyper-technological age bears both challenge and promise for a vibrant Christian anthropology.

Creation, Pride, and the Holy Meal: Complex Crafting in the Bible

God is the original technologist; he performed the first miracle of the Bible: *creation ex nihilo*. Like a massive gong struck with superlative force, the supernatural theme of miraculous, extra-creational involvement reverberates through the rest of the biblical text. God is not the creation, but neither is he removed from it by a fathomless gap. He is near it, watching over it, reaching into it. In the beginning, he makes something from nothing; in the end, he will make something into nothing, executing judgment in order to prepare the world for his blood-bought people.

In creating, the Lord shows us the essential nature of divine activity: out of the overflow of his righteous character, the Lord builds up, complexifies, and creates beauty. He is not indifferent to matter, to existence, to life; he loves matter, he births existence, he sustains all life (Psalm 135; Col 1:17; 2 Pet 3:7). Further, the Lord's creative work does not render a dull creation, nor his craftsmanship a mute and merely existing humanity. The Lord brings the creation into full flowering. Through his powerful work, the birds figure out their flight patterns, the fish know to swim in schools, rain pours out of the sky and returns to the clouds. The creation is not filled with wonder and beauty by accident; it is filled with wonder and beauty because God made it to function well.

The human body is the original technological wonder. Designed by the Lord himself, the body of mankind represents many supercomputers effectively working together—often seamlessly—for human flourishing. The body, truly, is a marvel of symmetry, synchronicity, and specialization. We think, for example, of what transpires in order for our eyes to comprehend, say, the words you are currently reading. Michael Behe's summary—edited for length—is worth quoting, given our tendency to take bodily workings for granted:

> Here is a brief overview of the biochemistry of vision. When light first strikes the retina, a photon interacts with a molecule called 11-cis-retinal, which rearranges within picoseconds to trans-retinal. The change in the shape of retinal forces a change in the shape of the protein, rhodopsin, to which the retinal is tightly bound. . . . When attached to activated rhodopsin and its entourage, the phosphodiesterase acquires the ability to chemically cut a molecule called cGMP (a chemical relative of both GDP and GTP). . . . Another membrane protein that binds cGMP is called an ion channel. . . . When the amount of cGMP is reduced because of cleavage by the phosphodiesterase, the ion channel closes, causing the cellular concentration of positively charged sodium ions to be reduced. This causes an imbalance of charge across the cell membrane which, finally, causes a current to be transmitted down the optic nerve to the brain. The result, when interpreted by the brain, is vision.[1]

I quote this extensive scientific breakdown of the phenomenon of sight because it reveals how much we take for granted and,

---

[1] Michael Behe, "Evidence for Intelligent Design from Biochemistry," in *Christian Apologetics: An Anthology of Primary Sources*, ed. Khaldoun A. Sweis and Chad V. Meister (Grand Rapids: Zondervan, 2012), 101–2.

more importantly, just how complex the ordinary processes of our bodies are. God designed the eye and gave us sight. Simply to read a line of text requires a flawless fourteen-step process, with none of these steps occurring through conscious choice. God, the original technologist, has opened our eyes to the wonder of activated rhodopsin serving in concert with phosphodiesterase in support of the humble act of reading.

Such complexity makes sense to the Christian. We believe that a God of infinite intelligence and unlimited power formed us by his irresistible will. Beyond the individual person, the Lord fitted the man and woman together; he gave the first couple the ability to perform a natural miracle, the creation of a living being. We would not commonly label the feats of pregnancy and childbearing "technological," but neither can we miss that every child is a little marvel, a sign to humanity that complexity and beauty pervade our lives. A husband and wife may join in one-flesh union, and one flesh may result. Only a divine mind could yield such wondrous outcomes.

The early chapters of the Old Testament show us that the Lord uses technology of a kind. He took animal skins and clothed the sin-stricken man and woman in them, an early sign of God-given imputed righteousness (Gen 3:21).[2] Cain built a city after striking down his brother, showing that the human race is

---

[2] For more on the doctrine of imputation, see John Piper, *Counted Righteous in Christ: Should We Abandon the Imputation of Christ's Righteousness?* (Wheaton, IL: Crossway Books, 2002); Murray, *Redemption Accomplished and Applied*, 117–31 (see chap. 5, n. 31).

spreading and clustering (Gen 4:17). Some time later, we learn of the tower of Babel, perhaps the most striking picture of engineering in the Old Testament. In Genesis 11, the people shared aspirations for feats of greatness and built toward that lofty end:

> The whole earth had the same language and vocabulary. As people migrated from the east, they found a valley in the land of Shinar and settled there. They said to each other, "Come, let us make oven-fired bricks." (They used brick for stone and asphalt for mortar.) And they said, "Come, let us build ourselves a city and a tower with its top in the sky. Let us make a name for ourselves; otherwise, we will be scattered throughout the earth." (Gen 11:1–4)

The construction of the city and tower contained both positive and negative elements. The people employed their powers of creativity to enable complex building. They used an oven, a device that requires careful handling, to produce the building blocks of their structures.[3] They deployed different materials, making both bricks

---

[3] The calculated nature of this proud effort shows through when one considers the technical process necessary to make a structure in southern Mesopotamia: "Mudbrick, however, is not durable, so it was a great technological development to discover that baking the brick made it as durable as stone. This was still an expensive process, since the kilns had to be fueled. As a result, mudbrick was used as much as possible, with baked brick used only for outer shells of important buildings or where waterproofing was desirable." Walton, *Genesis, Exodus, Leviticus, Numbers, Deuteronomy*, 60 (see chap. 1, n. 22).

and asphalt, in order to bind the edifice together. Here is human ingenuity on display. As anyone who has worked a day on construction will know, planning and executing a major building project is anything but unintellectual. It involves considerable skill and planning. These God-given abilities were on full display at Babel.[4]

So too was human pride. The very end of the project in question was the display of human greatness. We hear nothing honoring the Lord in this text; we see no indication that the people understood themselves as little creators due to the kind providence of the greater Creator. The people wished to make themselves impressive.[5] They wanted "a name" that would echo throughout the earth. They did not want to spread over the land in the postdiluvian age, taking dominion of it once more, claiming it for God as in his original instructions to humanity. They had lost the mission, the charge of their Maker, so they gave themselves their own decree. Instead of spreading across the earth, they built what amounted to a secular temple, a landmark to human excellence. Instead of magnifying the greatness of the Lord, they decided to put their own abilities on display, seeking

---

[4] The people of God are emulating the pagan nations in their building project. See E. A. Speiser, *Genesis: A New Translation with Introduction and Commentary*, The Anchor Bible, vol. 1, (New York: Doubleday, 1963), 75–76.

[5] The people are of the earth, but we note that the passage presents God as coming down from the heavens in verses 5 and 7. On this point see Herman Bavinck, *Reformed Dogmatics*, vol. 2, *God and Creation*, ed. John Bolt, trans. John Vriend (Grand Rapids: Baker Academic, 2004), 31.

a reputation among the living. Instead of risking their safety in obedience to the holy mandate of God, they hunkered down in Babel, bringing the expansion of human dominion to a crawl.[6]

Technology does not cause this outbreak of evil. Technology facilitates the instinctual expression of evil. The call to take dominion is a call from God to use every bit of horsepower preloaded into our beings to honor God. The follower of the Lord does not read Gen 1:26–28 and come away thinking he should hold back a portion of his intellect, physical strength, or passion from the mandate of God. We read about God's work as Creator earlier in the chapter and then consider afresh his summons to a dominion-taking existence and recognize we have exhilarating possibilities before us.[7]

But Babel shows us what happens when we humans use our God-endowed capacities for ourselves. The mind, body, and soul are made for holistic, all-consuming worship of the divine. In his Adamic sinfulness, however, mankind employs mind, body,

---

[6] Geerhardus Vos argues that the Babel project is an attempt to find a "centre of unity, such as would keep the human race together." This is certainly part of the problem. Geerhardus Vos, *Biblical Theology: Old and New Testaments* (Grand Rapids: Eerdmans, 1948; Eugene, OR: Wipf and Stock, 2003), 59. Citations refer to the Wipf and Stock edition.

[7] The divine work of creation—as opposed to the bloodless evolutionary process—inspires us to create and to organize. Behind the work of creation is the mind of an artist and a technologist. Kuyper makes this distinction plain: "Thus you recognize that the cosmos, instead of being a heap of stones, loosely thrown together, on the contrary presents to our mind a monumental building erected in a severely consistent style." Kuyper, "Calvinism and Science," lecture, Princeton Univ., October 19, 1898, Princeton, NJ, in *Lectures on Calvinism* (1931; repr., Grand Rapids: Eerdmans, 2000), 106.

and soul for holistic, all-consuming worship of the creation, with particular respect to the self. Man takes the physical material and the critical powers embedded in his intellect, and he fashions the things of the earth—the matter made by God himself—as objects of worship and means of pride. The man-made idol draws the sinful heart's adoration, yes, but also represents the created being's attempt to play God, and thereby register certain worldly things as worthy of fealty and praise. Knowing both of these darkened desires—the hunger to idolize what is not God and to take the authoritative liberty of identifying idolatry-worthy ends—equips us to spot the lie in the technology that still tries to tower over us in a postlapsarian world.

We note as well what the people try to build: a city and a tower. The people wish to unite themselves in even deeper communion with one another, a move made easy by their shared language. They use speech, an ability given to them by the speaking God, to share commonality not in God but in their non-God-focused humanness.[8] Their "community" is not necessarily a positive reality.[9] We observe other problems as well. In the tower, the people create a beacon of transcendence. The sinful human heart, it seems, has not lost interest in the concept of grandeur, but rather finds grandeur in created things. Instead of majestic structures pointing to heaven by intention, such edifices point

---

[8] On the uniqueness of human speech, see Tom Wolfe, *The Kingdom of Speech* (New York: Little, Brown, 2016).

[9] Derek Kidner argues that this text shows "that unity and peace are not ultimate goods: better division than collective apostasy (cf. Luke 12:51)." Kidner, *Genesis*, 119 (see chap. 2, n. 24).

downward to man. Even after Adam's fall, humanity still reaches upward but outside of God; we reach upward to lift ourselves upward. God has set eternity in our hearts, but our sins twist even this spiritual instinct, real as it is (Eccl 3:11).[10]

As happens in numerous places when the pride of man rears itself, the Lord judges Babel. He comes down, confuses their speech, and scatters them across the land (7–8). He does not wipe out the technological proclivities of the people, as we see in the storyline of Scripture.[11] But he does introduce a significant degree of chaos into human interaction, frustrating the connective ability of the race he made. In the starkest of terms, people are divided by words. That which gave life to the earth, which created all things in perfect harmony, now splits the race asunder. We still speak, but we do not all speak the same language, and so we find commonality at even a basic level only with strain. All this owes to the human desire to be great, and the expression of this pride through technological prowess.

---

[10] R. Kent Hughes zeroes in on the narcissism of this effort: "the unadorned belief that man by his superior effort could reach God betrays the fatal delusion of all man-made religion. This delusion is at the heart of every religious enterprise apart from the gospel because the world's religions all teach that works bring spiritual advance—as in an improved karma or works-righteousness. Collective apostasy had engulfed the descendants of Shem, Ham, and Japheth as they stacked their bricks up to heaven." Hughes, *Genesis*, 171 (see chap. 2, n. 7).

[11] Kidner suggests that the Lord is acting graciously here, not as a "rival" to the people. He intervenes in act of common grace to stop the spread of sin. Kidner, *Genesis*, 119 (see chap. 2, n. 24).

Already the relationship between mankind and technology is a fraught one. We gain both helpful and unhelpful examples of technological engagement in successive texts. The book of Exodus sets both kinds in close company. In Exodus 31, the Lord specially indicates his blessing on the craftsman Bezalel. He is filled with "God's Spirit, with wisdom, understanding, and ability in every craft to design artistic works in gold, silver, and bronze, to cut gemstones for mounting, and to carve wood for work in every craft" (Exod 31:3–5). Every facet of Bezalel's artisanship depends on serious creative ability and requires the ability to engage in robust engineering. So too with Oholiab and all the faithful designers who labor on the tabernacle; they must create an ark, a pure gold lampstand, multiple altars, and specially woven garments, among other products (6–11). Clearly the Lord is deeply honored by such skilled labor.[12] The tabernacle, the forerunner to the more resplendent temple, is a kind of counter-Babel, however distantly. It showcases human ingenuity of the vertical kind.[13]

---

[12] "This text is important for understanding the relationship that the Creator seeks with creative and skilled people. The Lord created a beautiful and good world. God called people, gifted them, and filled them with the Spirit to participate in bringing beauty into the world as God continues to do in every generation. **Also I have given skill to all the craftsmen.** They came from every tribe, qualified by their created and developed ability. The construction of the tabernacle required all kinds of skilled people: spinners, weavers, tailors, dyers, metallurgists, silversmiths, woodworkers, lapidaries, perfumers, and tanners." James K. Bruckner, *Exodus*, New International Biblical Commentary (Peabody, MA: Hendrickson, 2008), 255.

[13] John Mackay shows that Bezalel received both a command but also a summons to creativity, which is truly the happy lot of every worker

Just one chapter later, Aaron forms an idol, a golden calf for the people to worship. He does so by using "an engraving tool" (Exod 32:4). At one moment, the biblical text shows us technology gone right; at the next, it shows us technology gone wrong. Complex craftsmanship may create the center of national worship, or it may yield the very incarnation of sin itself. This proves true throughout Israel's history; the kings of the nation undertake projects that glorify the Lord even as they build monuments to their own supposed renown. Through it all, the Bible stands at a distance from such prideful making. "Some take pride in chariots," says the Psalmist of a fearsome innovation in ancient warfare, "and others in horses, but we take pride in the name of the LORD our God" (Ps 20:7).

Technology in the New Testament

The New Testament begins with a marvel of engineering that far outstrips any human endeavor. Through the Holy Spirit, Mary conceives the God-man, Jesus Christ. How striking that the greatest anthropological miracle known to human history is performed not by a scientific genius, but by God. The Lord puts the human race on notice in the incarnation. Humanity

---

in God's kingdom. "For instance, he had been told that there were to be cherubim woven into the draperies, but how exactly they were to be portrayed was a matter for Bezalel's artistry. 'Work in wood' is not just cutting wood into planks. It refers to something closer to the skills of a cabinet maker, carving and ornamenting wood." John L. Mackay, *Exodus*, A Mentor Commentary (Fearn, UK: Mentor, 2001), 514–15.

reaches its heights only through the agency of God, not that of man. Karl Barth says it well: "It means that God Himself—acting directly in His own and not in human fashion—stands at the beginning of this human existence and is its direct author. It is He who gives to man in the person of Mary the capacity which man does not have of himself, which she does not have and which no man could give her."[14] Barth uses the word *miracle* to describe this event, an important word for our considerations. What term, after all, is more an affront to the secular mind than *miracle*?[15]

In definite contrast to even the most skilled fallen entrepreneur, Jesus enjoys total and unquestioned sovereignty over the earth. The thrall in which Christ holds the creation owes not to an unlocked technique—an advantage Jesus gains through some form of ontological upgrade—but to the divinized, Spirit-empowered humanity Christ possesses. What technologist would not wish to exercise perfect control over the weather, rule the sea, heal the sick, and raise the dead? That which sinful humanity strains to do and to be, Jesus effortlessly does and is. The Gospels speak to our hyper-technological age not so much by explicit rebuke as by implicit corollary. Jesus—and no feat

---

[14] Karl Barth, *Church Dogmatics*, vol. 4, *The Doctrine of Reconciliation*, ed. T. F. Torrance and G.W. Bromiley, trans. G. W. Bromiley (London: T&T Clark, 2004), 1: 207.

[15] "This is the miracle of the Virgin Birth as it indicates the mystery of the incarnation, the first attestation of the divine Sonship of the man Jesus of Nazareth, comparable with the miracle of the empty tomb at His exodus from temporal existence." Barth, 207.

of human engineering, no burst of technological insight—is the true marvel.

We shall probe these matters further in our final chapter. For now, it is enough to cast a spotlight on the God-man, the one who reminds us that we are no longer justified in looking for a great king, a great feat, or a transcendent human person. We do not squelch interest in technology and complex creation as the church. We do, however, note that the terminus of human greatness has come. The Son of God cannot be outshone. Knowing this fact of facts influences the way we engage the made world. Coming face to face with the truth in embodied form affects our view of technology. Meeting the Messiah through repentant faith corrects the messianic expectations of the modern world. We cheer on advances in science and medicine, workplace efficiency, and even in-game streaming; but we do so with an asterisk in our minds at all times. No matter what Silicon Valley produces, it will never come within 10,000 miles of the throne room of God, where the crucified and resurrected Son of God sits at the Father's right hand.

Human life span may continue to lengthen; if so, good. But the lengthening of our days will not mean and cannot mean that we may become gods ourselves. We hear such promises today, provided we are paying attention to our surroundings. The believer, however, knows that God has done in Christ what no man can do in himself. The point, the apex, and the end of history have already dawned. There is no room for any other messiah, whether political, technological, ideological, or otherwise.

There is no possibility of a miracle greater than the coming of the second person of the Godhead to earth. Stephen Wellum captures the unique nature of Christ's coming as a "divine intrusion—the last great culminating eruption of the power of God into the plight of humanity."[16] Christ's coming was an intrusion in his day, and it is an intrusion in ours.

Jesus, interestingly, did not lead his followers into a cave. When he came and began his ministry, Jesus took the world as it was. He worked a technological trade, carpentry, and built structures with his hands, using his mind to solve numerous problems unique to such work. When he entered his earthly ministry, Jesus made frequent, even surprising, references to the material world, much of it existing due to human technology. He spoke of cities and lamps (Matt 5:14–16); houses built on different foundations (Matt 7:24–27); city gates (Matt 7:13–14); fishing nets (Matt 13:47–50); oil lamps (Matt 25:1–13); and investing money, activity dependent on market exchange (Matt 25:14–30).[17]

[16] Stephen J. Wellum, *God the Son Incarnate: The Doctrine of Christ*, Foundations of Evangelical Theology (Wheaton, IL: Crossway, 2016), 238.

[17] Jeffrey L. Nyhoff and Steven H. VanderLeest, "What Does God Tell Us about Technology?" Being Fluent and Faithful in a Digital World, Calvin College, 2005, https://www.calvin.edu/academic/rit/web Book/chapter1/lesson2/bible.htm.

Perhaps the most unexpected biblical citation of technological achievement emerges from Christ's teaching on the Lord's Supper. The holy meal itself depends upon human engineering:

> As they were eating, Jesus took bread, blessed and broke it, gave it to the disciples, and said, "Take and eat it; this is my body." Then he took a cup, and after giving thanks, he gave it to them and said, "Drink from it, all of you. For this is my blood of the covenant, which is poured out for many for the forgiveness of sins. But I tell you, I will not drink from this fruit of the vine from now on until that day when I drink it new with you in my Father's kingdom." After singing a hymn, they went out to the Mount of Olives. (Matt 26:26–30)

We would not likely associate the Supper with craftsmanship. Yet the very meal that memorializes a spiritual event—the life-giving, life-sacrificing death of Christ—depends upon a most grainy set of tasks: bread making and grape pressing. In order to celebrate together the atoning work of Jesus, the church needed access to those who could harvest wheat, mill it, create the right dough mixture, and bake it. In addition, someone had to grow grapes, harvest them, crush them, and ferment them. Both the baking and wine-making processes involved substantial labor, specialized utensils, and expert oversight.

We would not confuse the Lord's Supper with a science fair project or a religious invention. We would, however, identify the commendation of technology and craftsmanship inherent in the memorial feast honoring the cornerstone act of Christianity, the atonement.[18] This is how enchanted the Christian worldview is: even bread and wine acquire eternal significance.[19] The holy meal, a feast rooted in Passover rescue and offered in celebration of the king who rules from a cross, does not ontologically become supernatural.[20] The bread and wine do, however, point to supernatural realities, even the salvation of the wicked.[21]

---

[18] Zwingli's "memorial" view, Ware shows convincingly, was not nearly as "mere" or symbolic as is sometimes alleged. Bruce A. Ware, "The Meaning of the Lord's Supper in the Theology of Ulrich Zwingli (1484–1531)," in *The Lord's Supper: Remembering and Proclaiming Christ Until He Comes*, NAC Studies in Bible and Theology (Nashville: B&H Academic, 2011), 229–47.

[19] Blomberg notes that this is a "common loaf." There is nothing special about it in spiritual terms, in other words. Craig Blomberg, *Matthew*, The New American Commentary, vol. 22 (Nashville: B&H, 1992), 390.

[20] Jesus bases the meal in Passover but reworks the ceremony: "By identifying the cup of wine as 'my blood poured out' Jesus adds to the symbolism of the broken bread in v. 26: it is his own imminent death that is the basis of his new interpretation of the Passover. The blood of the Passover lamb featured prominently in the original Passover ritual (Exod 12:7, 13, 22–23), but now it will be Jesus' blood which is his people's salvation. But the lamb's blood was smeared on the doorposts, certainly not drunk; the idea would have been unthinkable to a Jew, for whom the consumption of *any* blood was strictly forbidden. Yet now the disciples, who have just been invited to 'eat Jesus' body,' are invited also to 'drink Jesus' blood.'" R. T. France, *The Gospel of Matthew*, The New International Commentary on the New Testament (Grand Rapids: Eerdmans, 2007), 993.

[21] In contradistinction to the low-key way many evangelicals might approach the Lord's Supper (experientially, that is), the Supper may be

The atonement itself witnessed the Son of God dying on a torture device. Here again the Christian faith bumps into technology in a surprising way. This crude innovation—if it may be called that—allowed the Romans to inflict maximal misery on lawbreakers. Jesus Christ died on this awful implement, and he did so as the Father's satisfactory offering for sin (Isa 53:10). This matters because the Son of God did not assuage the just and perfect wrath of the Father against sinners in the abstract. He did not offer a lecture in the synagogues that shifted the balance; he did not simply announce a new way of life anchored in righteous deeds; he did not buy back the guilty through a monetary transaction. The Son of God died on a tree, albeit one fashioned into a death-weapon. We track with Bavinck on this point:

> By the power of love, he laid down life itself and, fully
> conscious and with a firm will, entered the valley of the

---

seen as a triumphant ceremony, a victory meal as after a great battle. The Supper is also a foretaste of the long-promised feasting in the new heavens and new earth, where delicious food and wine flow (see Isa 25:6; Rev 19:6–9). The Supper, John Mark Hicks argues, comes in "fulfillment in the new covenant meal of the inaugurated kingdom (the church) as well as the eschatological banquet. When the church eats this meal, it eats the new covenant Passover (or thanksgiving meal) and it does so with the expectation of eschatological victory. It eats in the light of the resurrected Lord who has conquered death and will remove the disgrace of his people. The supper is a meal shared with the risen Lord. This eschatological victory is won on the ground of the blood of the new covenant and the sacrificial offering of the body of Christ." John Mark Hicks, "The Lord's Table: A Covenant Meal," *Leaven* 3, no. 3 (December 1995): 6.

shadow of death. There he was, and felt, forsaken by God, so that in precisely that fashion he might be able to taste death for everyone (Heb. 2:9). . . . Christ was made to be a sin and a curse for us, that in him we might become the righteousness of God (2 Cor. 5:21; Gal. 3:13). He is the expiation for our sins; he purchased us for God by his blood and cleansed us from all our sins (1 John 1:7; 2:2; Rev. 5:9; 7:14). He offered himself up once for all for the sins of the people and thereby secured an eternal redemption (Heb. 1:3; 2:17; 7:27; 9:12; 10:12). He bore on sins on the tree and redeemed us by his blood. (1 Pet. 1:18; 2:24)[22]

It was a tree that led the first Adam to leave Eden in disgrace; it was a tree that led to the deliverance of all the children of God from sin. If ever a God-fearing person redeemed technology for divine ends, Jesus did.

All Christian doctrine begins with revelation, without which we would not know God.[23] This was no rote affair; the

---

[22] Herman Bavinck, *Reformed Dogmatics*, vol. 3, *Sin and Salvation in Christ*, ed. John Bolt, trans. John Vriend (Grand Rapids: Baker Academic, 2006), 390.

[23] "God's purpose in revelation is that we may know him personally as he is, may avail ourselves of his gracious forgiveness and offer of new life, may escape catastrophic judgment for our sins, and venture personal fellowship with him." Carl F. H. Henry, *God, Revelation, and Authority*, vol. 2, *God who Speaks and Shows* (Waco, TX: Word, 1976), 31. See the reflection on Henry's method by Paul House, "Hope, Discipline, and the Incarnational Scholar: Carl F. H. Henry's Motives, Methods, and

inscripturation of the Bible transpired through a technical pro-cess.[24] Holy men of God received the oracles of God, using their backgrounds, trainings, and personalities to communicate divine truth. This was both a miraculous and a resolutely practical act, as Benjamin B. Warfield lays out:

It is this final act in the production of Scripture which is technically called "inspiration"; and inspiration is thus brought before us as, in the minds of the writers of the New Testament, that particular operation of God in the production of Scripture which takes effect at the very point of the writing of Scripture—understanding the term "writing" here as inclusive of all the processes of the actual composition of Scripture, the investigation of documents, the collection of facts, the excogitation of conclusions, the adaptation of exhortations as means to ends and the like—with the effect of giving to the resul-tant Scripture a specifically supernatural character, and constituting it a Divine, as well as human, book.[25]

Manners," in *Essential Evangelicalism: The Enduring Influence of Carl F. H. Henry*, ed. Matthew J. Hall and Owen Strachan (Wheaton, IL: Crossway, 2015), 115–33.

[24] See Charles E. Hill, ""The Truth Above All Demonstration": Scripture in the Patristic Period to Augustine," in *The Enduring Authority of the Christian Scriptures*, ed. D. A. Carson (Grand Rapids: Eerdmans, 2016), 85.

[25] *The International Standard Bible Encyclopaedia*, ed. James Orr (Chicago: Howard-Severance, 1915), s.v. "inspiration, 8-18."

To record divine revelation, the biblical author took a stylus, which does not grow on trees, and parchment, which one cannot pluck out of the ground. In the power and influence of the Spirit, he wrote the original manuscripts of the biblical documents and passed them on for copying and transcription. Here as in other facets of Christian theology and practice, we see the people of God using the common grace-filled world of God to maximize the glory of God by transmitting the Word of God. More than we may recognize, our faith depends on the products and expertise of enterprising image-bearers.[26]

Our appreciation and our amazement only grow when we consider the spread of the gospel in church history. Without central planning, while frequently under the boot of Roman authorities, the early church sent the gospel message and the biblical manuscripts all around the ancient world. The church did not sit back on its heels, striving to avoid civilized society like a countess in a weed patch, but rather took full advantage of the highly developed Roman transport system—both land and sea—to disperse witnesses and plant churches.[27] Without Roman roads and Roman ships, the church would not have known such explosive growth.

So too with the printing press in the Reformation age. Though poor Gutenberg went into debt to print the works of Luther and others, he succeeded in launching the print onslaught

---

[26] The divine element, as in the incarnation of the Son of God, is the dominant factor in inspiration. But this affirmation must never allow us to omit or take lightly the human factor, superintended as it was by the Spirit (2 Pet 1:19–21).

[27] See Stark, *The Rise of Christianity* (see chap. 4, no. 32).

of the Reformation, creating the tipping point of this move-ment.[28] George Whitefield, the great evangelist, used the grow-ing medium of newspapers to promote his evangelistic events and drew crowds beyond colonial imagining in the eighteenth century.[29] Billy Graham and his colleagues took to the airwaves, the television, and the constricted space of the mid-twentieth-century airplane to tell the postwar world of Christic hope.[30] In our time, most Christian ministries use the internet and engage social media to find and grow their audience. Technological inno-vations, often pioneered by unbelievers, have led to unthinkable reach over several millennia. Israel was influential in its context; the church has the world for its parish.

But the church also must combat technology and suffer its ill effects. The same Roman roads that sped the gospel on its way to unreached peoples carried Christians to suffering and death. The same printing press that unleashed the Protestant voice also enabled the rise of a concomitant movement, the Enlightenment, with its secular body of thought.[31] Edwards

[28] See Elizabeth L. Eisenstein, *The Printing Revolution in Early Modern Europe* (Cambridge: Cambridge Univ. Press, 1983); Albert Kapr, *Johann Gutenberg: The Man and His Invention*, trans. Douglas Martin (Aldershot, Hants: Scolar, 1996).

[29] See Harry S. Stout, *The Divine Dramatist: George Whitefield and the Rise of Modern Evangelicalism*, Library of Religious Biography (Grand Rapids: Eerdmans, 1991).

[30] See Joel A. Carpenter, *Revive Us Again: The Reawakening of American Fundamentalism* (New York: Oxford Univ. Press, 1997).

[31] See Philipp Blom, *A Wicked Company: The Forgotten Radicalism of the European Enlightenment* (New York: Basic Books, 2010).

and Spurgeon printed millions of words; so too did Voltaire and Darwin. The military technology that defended the innocent was used to savage them as well, leading to more deaths in the twentieth century than in all other centuries combined.[32] The Nazis used experimental science to pioneer one dark art after another culminating in the gas chambers, which exterminated millions of Jews and other Europeans.[33] Enhanced medicine and nutritional knowledge originating in the modern world has shot life expectancy into the sky and brought untold happiness to many; but the bright minds of science have also pioneered new ways to kill unborn children, prematurely dispose of the elderly, and warp the body.[34]

A proper theology of technology neither unreservedly cheers nor unequivocally denounces it. As we have seen, both by explicit teaching and by inference, the Bible urges caution in this realm. More than this, our Christocentric Scripture punctures the fundamental delusion of many modern technologists. We cannot live forever outside of God. Though the New Testament does not offer extensive step-by-step directions on how to handle emerging innovations, we cannot miss that it pops the balloon of any messianic expectation outside of the person of Jesus Christ.

---

[32] See Taylor Downing, *Churchill's War Lab: Codebreakers, Scientists, and the Mavericks Churchill Led to Victory* (New York: Overlook, 2011).

[33] See Mark Walker, *Nazi Science: Myth, Truth, And the German Atomic Bomb* (Cambridge, MA: Perseus, 1995).

[34] For a biased but still informative take on modern developments in global health, see Steven Pinker, *Enlightenment Now: The Case for Reason, Science, Humanism, and Progress* (New York: Viking, 2018).

For the believer, it is not simply that Jesus is the exclusive way to God and the road to Calvary the only road to glory; it is that every other messiah fails, and fails utterly. The ultimate response to any technocratic claim of authority is the lordly kingship of the Son of God. We think of the commentary of Michael Horton on this matter: "To say *Christos kyrios* (Χριστός κύριος) is to witness to the fact that the advent of God's lordship visibly in history has occurred, and it is located in the person of Christ. There are no powers, authorities, thrones, or dominions that can thwart his purposes, although they may present fierce opposition until they are finally destroyed."[35]

The Christian, paying careful attention to the Lordship dimension of Christology in the New Testament, cannot fail to exercise shrewd watchfulness when it comes to branding, advertising, and cultural phenomena.[36] In doing so, we observe that technologists often offer us what amounts to a secular eschaton through the sum total of their costly innovations. We think once more of the language of *Homo deus*, which treats death not in spiritual terms but physical terms. Death, like ill health, is a problem we can solve if we focus on eradicating it. In such renderings, death is not a theological problem caused by sin; death is a physiological problem caused by ignorance. But here Christian theology raises its voice once more and answers all the fevered promises of technocracy with one doctrine: resurrection.

---

[35] Horton, *Lord and Servant*, 262.

[36] On the lordship of Christ, see F. F. Bruce, *Jesus: Lord and Savior* (Downers Grove, IL: InterVarsity, 1986).

That which pride-dominated technology seeks as a witness of its greatness, God has already done. Jesus is raised. In anthropological terms, nothing greater can be imagined or done.[37] No matter how powerful man becomes, though, he can never do the works of God.[38]

We do well to reject such thinking on biblical-theological grounds, but the Christian may be skeptical of technologism on logical grounds alone. We are, after all, the original skeptics and the true skeptics; we know just how flawed the world is, how deceitful the serpent and his antiwisdom is, and what lies in the heart of man. We do not unthinkingly engage the world, nor do we unthinkingly come to faith in Christ. To the contrary—against a common view of biblical Christianity—the believer weighs all things, tests all claims, and ponders all ideas. We test views for coherence, correspondence, and logic.[39] God

---

[37] "Not only has the Lord of the covenant been *made* Lord in his resurrection, but he has been *declared* in this event to be the Lord that he has always been (Rom 1:4)." Horton, *Lord and Servant*, 267. No one else may occupy this role; no one else may claim lordship in the earth. By virtue of his resurrection, only Christ holds this title.

[38] Any conversation about technology is thus in some form a conversation about power.

[39] "The proper task of theology is to exposit and elucidate the content of Scripture in an orderly way." Carl F. H. Henry, *God, Revelation, and Authority*, vol. 1, *God Who Speaks and Shows: Preliminary Consideration* (Wheaton, IL: Crossway Books, 1999), 215. Henry proposes two tests for truth claims, the first of which is consistency, a negative test meaning what is logically contradictory cannot be true, as a denial of the law of contradiction would make truth and error equivalent. The second test is coherence, a positive test, meaning the

has given us a written revelation filled with truth, bursting with propositions, and loaded with spiritual meaning communicated through poems, dreams, visions, apocalyptic prophecies, and more. In coming to faith in Christ, repentant believers do not switch their brains off. They turn their brains on.[40] Gripped by the knowledge of God, the believer turns back to the world, ready to probe it, test it, critique it, and call it to the absolute truth of the Lord.[41]

Christian system of truth can indeed be coherently correlated with all other information, including empirical data involving chronology, geography, history, and psychological experience as well. This is my summation of Henry, *God, Revelation, and Authority*, 1: 237. See also Bavinck on a related point, the *principium cognoscendi internum*, which is "the light of reason, the intellect, which, itself originating in the Logos, discovers and recognizes the Logos in things. It is the internal foundation of knowledge." Herman Bavinck, *Reformed Dogmatics*, vol. 1, *Prolegomena*, ed. John Bolt, trans. John Vriend (Grand Rapids: Baker Academic, 2004), 233.

[40] The believer knows truly but always in a creaturely way. See the distinction between *archetypal* and *ectypal* knowledge made by Cornelius Van Til, *An Introduction to Systematic Theology* (Phillipsburg, NJ: P&R, 1949), 203. See also Cornelius Van Til, *The Defense of the Faith* (Phillipsburg, NJ: P&R, 1967), 64. Van Til writes that God "interprets absolutely" while man is the "re-interpreter of God's interpretation," a statement in line with Bavinck's thought. For reference and helpful interpretation, see John M. Frame, *Van Til the Theologian* (Phillipsburg, NJ: Pilgrim, 1976); John M. Frame, *Cornelius Van Til: An Analysis of His Thought* (Phillipsburg, NJ: P&R, 1995).

[41] See Mark A. Noll, *Jesus Christ and the Life of the Mind* (Grand Rapids: Eerdmans, 2011).

Technology and the Body: Posthumanism and Transhumanism

The believer shows real gratitude for technological progress and scientific breakthroughs. We have no quarrel with science, and we know that many of the greatest scientists in human history were people of faith. We do differ with scientism, the view that science alone—without assistance from other worldviews or definitive texts—furnishes us with the truth we need to make sense of the world. The believer is a God-trusting skeptic—one who is skeptical of the claims, presuppositions, and branding of fallen people and fallen institutions. All truth is God's truth, and so wherever we find truth, we affirm that truth. But we do not affirm that all worldviews are correct or that all ideas are equal. They are not.

We need such a perspective when we consider emerging visions of the human body. The first we shall consider is the *posthumanist* view. Michael Plato summarizes this school of thought:

> At its core, posthumanism is a rejection of the human-ist tradition in the west of human exceptionalism (the notion that humans are unique in the world) and human instrumentalism (that humans have the right to control and dominate the natural world). Much of this has its origins in the academic liberation movements of the 1960s and 1970s, especially feminism, postcolonialism and queer theory which first began to challenge tradi-tional western male understandings of what constitutes

humanity. Posthumanism takes the next step and treats the human as no different from any other life or "non-life" form and calls for a more inclusive definition of "humanity" and even life itself. As such, a central concern of posthumanism is the diffusion of "human" rights to non-human subjects such as animals, ecosystems and even inorganic entities such as machines, computer code and geological formations.[42]

The posthumanists do not view humanity as the special creation of Almighty God. Rather, they identify consciousness or "mind" in all things and thus humanize them. According to mathematician and science-fiction novelist Rudy Rucker, "Stars, hills, chairs, rocks, scraps of paper, flakes of skin, molecules—each of them possess the same inner glow as a human, each of them has singular inner experiences and sensations."[43] There is no distinction in posthumanist between God and the world, mind and matter. All things are "smart matter."[44] The posthumanist views the merging of technology and humanity as a positive outcome

---

[42] Michael Plato, "C. S. Lewis's Nightmare: Christianity after the Abolition of Man (Part 1)," *In All Things*, October 11, 2016, https://inallthings.org/c-s-lewiss-nightmare-christianity-after-the-abolition-of-man-part-1.

[43] Rudy Rucker, "Mind is a Universally Distributed Quality," *Edge*, accessed January 24, 2019, www.edge.org/q2006/q06_3.html#rucker.

[44] Plato grounds this thinking in the philosophy of Baruch Spinoza and references films such as *Alien* and *Avatar* that present this view at the popular level. Plato, "C. S. Lewis's Nightmare."

toward which society is headed. Someday, human people will not be needed. Posthumanism is antihuman and nihilistic at its core.

The second anthropological vision we need to reckon with is the *transhumanist* view. Michael Plato defines *transhumanism* succinctly as an ideology that "promotes striving for immortality through technology" and "seeks to improve human intelligence, physical strength, and the five senses by technological means."[45] Frequently, the call for a transhumanist reimagining of humanity marries with the call to control the world's climate. Humanity is seen not as the steward of the earth but as the scourge of the earth. Despite the fact that human lifespan has shot upward since the Industrial Revolution, global poverty rates are at an all-time low, and the standard of living has never been higher, transhumanists argue that humanity must undergo genetic remaking to save the planet.[46]

These claims deserve closer scrutiny. Consider a journal article by Matthew Liao, Anders Sandberg, and Rebecca Roache for the secular resource *Ethics, Policy and the Environment*. The authors are enthusiastic advocates of transhumanism who approach humanity as a problem to be solved and view Earth as the property to be saved. For this to happen, scientists should

---

[45] Michael Plato, "The Immortality Machine: Transhumanism and the Race to Beat Death," *Plough Quarterly* 15 (Winter 2018): 21, https://www.plough.com/en/topics/life/technology/the-immortality-machine.

[46] Many transhumanists also trumpet the coming of the singularity, when artificial intelligence will effectively become sovereign. This idea is worth pondering in view of the distinctly godlike properties it assigns AI. See Plato, "Immortality Machine."

alter the immune system "to induce mild intolerance (akin, e.g., to milk intolerance)" to meat. The authors argue that since the "human ecological footprints are partly correlated with our size . . . Reducing the average US height by 15 cm would mean a mass reduction of 23% for men and 25% for women, with a corresponding reduction of metabolic rate (15%/18%), since less tissue means lower nutrients and energy needs."[47]

In addition to these major changes in functioning, humans should undergo cognitive enhancement. "There seems to be a link between cognition itself and lower birth-rates," opine Liao, Sandberg, and Roache. The authors argue that population should decline across the earth to safeguard dwindling natural resources, and the human race should embrace "pharmacological enhancements" in pursuit of increased "altruism and empathy."[48] What does this mean, practically? It means targeting testosterone, which "appears to decrease aspects of empathy." Surveying these proposed changes to the human person, ethicist C. Ben Mitchell concludes that "For the transhumanists, human beings are maladaptive and need re-engineering. Instead of seeing human creativity, innovation, and market forces applied in stewardly ways for the sake of the truly human good, the technologist (the human) becomes the technological artifact (the modified post-human)."[49]

[47] S. Matthew Liao, Anders Sandberg, and Rebecca Roache, "Human Engineering and Climate Change," *Ethics, Policy and Environment* 15, no. 2 (July 2012): 206, 208.

[48] Liao, "Human Engineering," 209–10.

[49] C. Ben Mitchell, "Tiny, Happy People," *First Things*, April 10, 2012, https://www.firstthings.com/web-exclusives/2012/04/tiny-happy-people.

Mitchell is right. The kinds of arguments made by Liao, Sandberg, and Roache remind us to spot the presuppositions behind a worldview. Whether such thinkers know it or not, they regard the earth as the point of all things, not humanity. The planet needs saving; humanity needs culling. This is chiliast to the core: every day places planetary sustenance in mortal peril. There is no God at the end of this eschatological rainbow. If we do end up saving the planet through meat aversion, cognitive enhancement, and pharmacological enhancements, then we only preserve it. But for transhumanist environmentalists, preservation of the planet is enough to justify the substantial overhaul of the human person.

Many transhumanists do not merely wish for humans to enjoy a slightly better diet or walk a little bit faster. They hold a secular anthropology, they believe in a secular hamartiology, they quest after a secular soteriology, and they live in thrall to a paranoid and deeply secular eschatology. They believe that man is not made by God but is the latest species to achieve evolutionary dominance (not for long, though).[50] They do not view mankind as the God-ordained ruler of the earth but see mankind as a

---

[50] Both posthumanism and transhumanism are responses to Christian humanism. Each is a fruit of the secular Enlightenment. The two systems affirm the importance of altering humanity by technological means, but they diverge in their teleology. Posthumanism seeks the end of humanity and the ascendance of "living matter"; transhumanism quests after the secular transcendence of humanity with the aid of technology. In the former, technology is master; in the latter, technology is servant.

problem that has dawned in the earth, for the human race inflicts far more punishment to the earth than do most animals.

Let us linger for a moment on the soteriology of the trans-humanist. The transhumanists may not use chapter and verse, but many proffer a distinct doctrine of salvation. Salvation does not come by gracious renewal; salvation comes by genetic reengi-neering. Our problem is not inherently spiritual but physical, so scientists should have a free hand to rewire human instincts, thus shrinking human appetite, forgoing procreation, and reducing testosterone. Each of these ideological commitments flies in the face of biblical teaching. God made the earth as the dwelling-place for humanity. Adam did not live in subservience to the animals; Adam was called to rule the animals, and the earth was created to sustain life. Further, we know that God formed Adam by his own hand, that God thus made manhood, and that God does not call for the church to drain men of testosterone but to reorient manhood to pursue a doxological existence.[51]

Once we start looking for cultural reengineering efforts, our blood chills at all we find. In both quiet and harsh ways, our

---

[51] On the subject of testosterone and men, we do well to reflect on the shocking number of boys in America who live on a steady diet of Ritalin and Adderall. Some boys receive genuine help through such prescriptions, but we should think hard about the rush to medicate boys. As an alternative to medication, we should think collectively about strengthening families, returning fathers to their families, and prioritiz-ing father-son engagement in physically rewarding activities. For cul-tural context, see Christina Hoff Sommers, *The War Against Boys: How Misguided Feminism Is Harming Our Young Men* (New York: Touchstone, 2000). Sommers, it should be noted, identifies as a feminist.

secular culture encourages us to see humanity as a virus, a deadly contagion on the earth. Transhumanism represents one enfleshment of such thinking, but the dark apotheosis of such ideology is abortion. Abortion proceeds from a woman or couple's desire to do away with an unwanted child, yes, but it also fits within a eugenicist (and posthumanist) worldview.[52] In philosophical terms, abortion functions as a major part of the effort to keep the population as small as is possible.

Abortion by means of modern technology causes extreme bodily harm. I do not mean primarily that it kills pregnant women, though it surely does in some instances, but that abortion trains women to fight the natural workings of their God-given bodies. Surely, many modern women realize too late that the promises of the sexual revolution do not measure up to their advance billing. The idea of free-and-open no-strings-attached sex does not hold true in many cases for either men or women, but it is women who bear the greatest responsibility for nonmarital sex resulting in a pregnancy. The woman who discovers a child growing within her body in these circumstances feels justifiable fear. She is in no way excused in her sin, but she does now face a major consequence that a man may more easily avoid (to his shame). Her choices become very stark: she may either embrace what has happened and protect and nurture her unborn child, or she may destroy it. In the latter situation, she

---

[52] Every act of abortion is a successful instantiation of a posthumanist vision which sees humanity as a problem to be overcome and even eradicated.

must act against her body; she must hate her own child. She will bring into her body not medicine to care for life, but surgical or pharmacological means to wipe it out. The abortive worldview, indissolubly linked to a so-called sex-positive ideology, does not encourage a woman to love her body, contrary to its claims. The abortive worldview leads a woman to make war on her own body and on the body of her child.[53]

Beyond abortion, our secular society is very hard on the human body. The body has never been more idealized, more scrutinized, more obsessed-over, than in our age. The female physique in particular seems at once an object of open worship and unrelenting criticism. To survey our culture is to witness insecurity and personal obsession in epidemic form. Much of the pressure on women, as with the solutions offered to women to relieve that pressure, is spiritual in nature and dependent on technology. If we alter the body through surgery and drugs, we hear today, we will find happiness. But as we saw in fallen Eden, physical methods cannot solve spiritual problems.

Technology facilitates this tragic undoing. The internet, alongside wireless technologies, has enabled the commodification of the body to a degree unthinkable in previous human history. Pornography, available in myriad forms in our emergent platforms, trains men to embrace their animal lusts and see

---

[53] Cf. Levering, *Engaging the Doctrine of Creation*, 193–226 (see chap. 1, n. 17). Matthew Levering makes several insightful points in his critique of antinatal culture. One need not agree with every detail to profit from it.

women as objects for their own gratification. It warps men and ruins them; research shows that pornography literally rewires the male brain:

> Viewing pornography is not an emotionally or physiologically neutral experience. It is fundamentally different from looking at black and white photos of the Lincoln Memorial or taking in a color map of the provinces of Canada. Men are reflexively drawn to the content of pornographic material. As such, pornography has wide-reaching effects to energize a man toward intimacy. It is not a neutral stimulus. It draws us in. Porn is vicarious and voyeuristic at its core, but it is also something more. Porn is a whispered promise. It promises more sex, better sex, endless sex, sex on demand, more intense orgasms, experiences of transcendence. [54]

Pornography is essentially Pandora. According to Struthers, it "acts as a polydrug" on the male brain, ramping up the emotions, catalyzing the senses, and energizing the body. God is the one who wired the man to desire the woman, but pornography awakens desire outside the context of marriage and effectively entraps the viewer. Men and women alike who view pornography think they are free, but in truth they are enslaved.

---

[54] William M. Struthers, *Wired for Intimacy: How Pornography Hijacks the Male Brain* (Downers Grove, IL: InterVarsity, 2010), 68–69.

Addiction—even nonsexual—to digital culture has dele-
terious effects. Consider the 2017 report by Jean Twenge, a
researcher and sociologist, on social media addiction and suicide rates:

> Not only did smartphone use and depression increase
> in tandem, but time spent online also was linked to
> mental-health issues across two different data sets. We
> found that teens who spent five or more hours a day
> online were 71 percent more likely than those who
> spent only one hour a day to have at least one suicide
> risk factor (depression, thinking about suicide, making a
> suicide plan or attempting suicide). Overall, suicide risk
> factors rose significantly after two or more hours a day
> of time online.[55]

The rising generation, we hear, is composed of "digital natives"
who essentially live online. This bodes ill for those who do.
Fathers and mothers must think with great care about the

---

[55] Jean Twenge, "Teenage Depression and Suicide Are Way Up—
and So Is Smartphone Use," *Washington Post*, November 19, 2017,
https://www.washingtonpost.com/national/health-science/teenage
-depression-and-suicide-are-way-up—and-so-is-smartphone-use
/2017/11/17/624641ea-ca13-11e7-8321-481fd63f174d_story.html
?utm_term=.4558df703633. This article is based on Jean M. Twenge,
Thomas E. Joiner, Megan L. Rogers, and Gabrielle N. Martin, "Increases
in Depressive Symptoms, Suicide-Related Outcomes, and Suicide Rates
Among U.S. Adolescents After 2010 and Links to Increased New Media
Screen Time," *Clinical Psychological Science* 6, no. 1 (January 2018): 3–17.

health—holistically—of their children. Beyond parental responsibility, individuals must make careful decisions in keeping with godliness and self-control. This does not mean that we cannot use Twitter, Facebook, Instagram, and other outlets as believers. But we should engage the digital world with considerable care, reflection, and thoughtfulness.[56]

The Christian can and should avail himself of technology. We depend on it more than we know, and Scripture gives us many signs that God approves of and even incorporates technology into a properly doxological existence. In addition, we do well to try to use worldly things for heavenly good. We may not be able to redeem them—no one is baptizing smartphones in tiny bathtubs—but we can approach them from a distinctly Christian perspective. This perspective will reduce to neither a jaundiced view of technological products nor an unthinking embrace of the same. We will instead view technology in theological terms, remembering the first principles of our faith and seeking God's glory in all our doings.

Conclusion

The Bible takes subjects that the world has disenchanted and reenchants them. Mankind seeks to make a name for itself and

---

[56] Two texts full of wisdom along these lines are Andy Crouch, *The Tech-Wise Family: Everyday Steps for Putting Technology in Its Proper Place* (Grand Rapids: Baker Books, 2017; Tony Reinke, *12 Ways Your Phone Is Changing You* (Wheaton, IL: Crossway, 2017).

builds cities to find nondivine community, but Christians may enter the earthly city and do so as the Christ-infused city on a hill. We are not mere matter to be reengineered at a philosopher's whim; we are embodied people, and through the gracious work of the Holy Spirit, our bodies are temples of the living God (1 Cor 6:19). A baby growing in the womb is not refuse to be cast off, but a child to be warmly welcomed into life. The world itself is made by God, but it is not the object of our salvation. Beauty is given by the Lord and reflects something of God's own excellence, but it must be stewarded well, accompanied by the grace of modesty, and disconnected from straining after an eternal youth that does not exist. Charm is fleeting; beauty is vain; a crown of gray hair speaks to a life well-lived.

In the midst of confusion and chaos, God is building something. He is gathering a people for himself. He will soon renew and remake the earth, and the biblical story that began in a real garden will end in a real city. The details of the end of this narrative await their unveiling, but we cannot miss just how beautiful, and beautifully crafted, the new Jerusalem is in John's apocalyptic vision:

> The foundations of the city wall were adorned with every kind of precious stone:
>
> the first foundation jasper,
> the second sapphire,
> the third chalcedony,
> the fourth emerald,

the fifth sardonyx,

the sixth carnelian,

the seventh chrysolite,

the eighth beryl,

the ninth topaz,

the tenth chrysoprase,

the eleventh jacinth,

the twelfth amethyst.

The 12 gates are 12 pearls; each individual gate was made of a single pearl. The broad street of the city was pure gold, like transparent glass.

I did not see a sanctuary in it, because the Lord God the Almighty and the Lamb are its sanctuary. The city does not need the sun or the moon to shine on it, because God's glory illuminates it, and its lamp is the Lamb. (Rev 21:19–23 HCSB)

This is not a city for spectators standing miles off and gazing through binoculars. This is a city for the people of God brimming with the creative beauty of God. Here technology, or more accurately, the handiwork of God in the created realm, reaches its celestial peak. There, "The nations will walk in its light, and the kings of the earth will bring their glory into it" (21:24 HCSB).

It will be a visual feast, a time to marvel at the gifting of God in the mind and body of man, and a celebration of the creative and recreative power of the Almighty.

CHAPTER 7

JUSTICE

Mankind has a moral sense, but much of the time its
reach is short and its effect uncertain.

—James Q. Wilson, *The Moral Sense*

We hear a great deal about justice in the twenty-first century. On many university campuses, for example, justice serves as the *raison d'etre* of the curriculum. From a Christian vantage point, this development can be a propitious one. Justice, after all, is a richly biblical theme. From nearly the first page of the Bible to its last, various figures in and authors of the text ask after justice, cry out for justice, and—depending on their character—either deal it out or withhold it. Justice is a crucial part of the biblical mind, and it occupies a key place in the God-fired heart.

Although our secularist age speaks much of justice, it rarely asks bigger questions surrounding it. It is right where people have been wronged to lay hold of justice once more. It is good to redress evils. It is virtuous to seek the good life individually and the good society corporately. We cannot help but point out, however, that the very notion of justice fits far better in a Christian worldview than in a secular one.[1] The believer seeks the balancing of the scales because God is just, and as such God will do what is just. We surely image God when we act, however imperfectly, to advance rightness and true fairness in the world. But we do so because we worship the just God. The just God creates justice-loving people. Thankfully, things are not left to us. History's arc is long, but it bends toward Christic justice.

Here, as elsewhere in our survey of modern anthropology, we see two systems of thought crashing into one another. On one hand, modern man seems gripped by the need to make things right in this world. Channeling Flannery O'Connor, we could say that the human person is "justice-haunted."[2] But on the other hand, modern man sleeps in on Sunday. His spirituality,

---

[1] See his work on *closed systems* in James W. Sire, *The Universe Next Door*, 5th ed., A Basic Worldview Catalog (Downers Grove, IL: InterVarsity, 2009).

[2] O'Connor famously wrote that the American South is "Christ-haunted." Flannery O'Connor, *Mystery and Manners: Occasional Prose* (New York: MacMillan, 1969), 44.

such as it is, is this-worldly and distinctly self-disposed. Yet his interest in rightness persists. How strange that these instincts—the thirst for rightness and practiced indifference to the God of righteousness—coinhere in the modern person.

The preceding raises yet another uncomfortable question: whose justice? In Christian doctrine, justice comes to earth in the form of Christ—the God-man who dies on the cross to satisfy the just wrath of God—and dawns in full bloom when the God-man returns to earth to settle all accounts. But in secular thinking, we find no Christ; we know no crucifixion-powered undoing of evil; we learn that we are the collective savior we have so long awaited. Justice depends on us. This is a major claim and not a heartening one.

The Bible speaks into this confusion. It gives full vent to humanity's interest in rightly balanced scales and rightly ordered actions. Scripture is clear-eyed about human failings, yet optimistic in the extreme about the prospect of ultimate justice. We will examine the biblical testimony, observing how the sacred text develops our conceptions of justice and heightens it in the person and work of Christ.

When Cain Slew Abel

The Scripture deals with the question of justice just a few paragraphs into its narration. In Genesis 4, we learn that original sin is not isolated sin. Righteous Abel, the son of Adam, offers a sacrifice pleasing to the Lord, while his brother Cain does not. Cain cannot handle his failing; though warned by the Lord and told to overcome his temptations, Cain makes no effort to fight his instinctual desires.[3] Instead, he vents them:

> Cain said to his brother Abel, "Let's go out to the field." And while they were in the field, Cain attacked his brother Abel and killed him.
>
> Then the LORD said to Cain, "Where is your brother Abel?"
>
> "I don't know," he replied. "Am I my brother's guardian?"
>
> Then he said, "What have you done? Your brother's blood cries out to me from the ground! So now you are cursed, alienated from the ground that opened its mouth to receive your brother's blood you have shed. If you work the ground, it will never again give you its yield. You will be a restless wanderer on the earth." (Gen 4:8–12)

Here as in Genesis 3, the Lord shows up on the spot. The personal presence of God in the wake of gross disobedience teaches

---

[3] Victor P. Hamilton stresses Cain's agency in this text: "Sin's urge is aimed at Cain. The word for *urge* here, *t^šûqá* (תְּשׁוּקָתוֹ), is the same word used in the previous chapter for Eve's feelings toward Adam (3:16). Similarly, what Cain can do to sin—*you are the one to master* [*mšl*] *it*—is described with the same verb used for Adam's actions with Eve ("he shall be master over you," 3:16) . . . The text makes Cain's personal responsibility even more focused by its use of the initial emphatic pronoun: "*you*, you are to master it." Hamilton, *The Book of Genesis*, 227–28 (see chap. 1, n. 12).

us a powerful set of truths about divine justice. God sees all; God acts as judge; no one may successfully unseat God and have dealings with a different judge; the human wrongdoer must come to account with a holy God in the time of God's choosing.[4] In the moment we may struggle to believe that God sees all and that he will judge rightly. But the tragic case of Cain and Abel shows us otherwise.

Cain has wronged Abel, terribly and tragically. Abel should have known many years of happy fidelity to the Lord, raising up a godly line in the wreckage of Eden. But the opposite comes to pass. Abel, the righteous figure, is the first of the brothers to die, while his evil brother lives. The world seems devoid of justice. Gordon Wenham makes the point powerfully:

> Here Abel's blood is pictured "crying" to God for vengeance; צעק "cry" is the desperate cry of men without food (Gen 41:55), expecting to die (Exod 14:10), or oppressed by their enemies (Judg 4:3). It is the scream for help of a woman being raped (Deut 22:24, 27). It is the plea to God of the victims of injustice (Exod 22:22[23], 26[27]). The law, the prophets (Isa 19:20; cf. 5:7), and the psalms

---

[4] "Yahweh refused to entertain Cain's question, making him confront his responsibility for such an appalling deed by asking, **What have you done?** Yahweh then surprised Cain by telling him that there was a witness to his deed. His **brother's blood** was crying **out to** God **from the ground**. It was believed that uncovered human blood cried out for vengeance against the murderer. If no one heard the cry, God was obligated to redress the wrong." Hartley, *Genesis*, 83 (see chap. 1, n. 21).

(34:18[17]; 107:6, 28) unite with narratives like this (cf. 2 Sam 23; 1 Kgs 21) to assert that God does hear his people's desperate cries for help.[5]

The death of Abel is a scream for justice, as Wenham vividly notes. The cry is heard. As he did after the sin of Adam, the Lord personally visits Cain. He stands as Abel's judicial representative. He judges and curses Cain.[6] He then provides for Cain, a gracious action that Cain's deeds in no way merited. When the Lord does so, Cain displays no thankfulness to God. He pities himself, crying out that his punishment is too great for him (Gen 4:13). We take note: even in the presence of justice, even when faced with the manifest mercy of God, the sinner will not necessarily acknowledge the rightness of God.

The people of God must often suffer in this life. They do so in many cases because of evildoers such as Cain, but not always so consequentially. In the case of heavy-hearted Hannah, we glimpse another miscarriage of justice on the personal level. Hannah's difficulties do not draw a wide audience; she was unknown to many in her day, and like most of us, she suffered her indignities alone. Even her loving husband seemed clueless as to the full measure of her plight. Married to Elkanah,

---

[5] Wenham, *Genesis 1–15*, 107 (see intro, n. 11).

[6] "This is the first occasion in Scripture where a human is cursed. This curse indicates the gravity of his crime against God and creation." Mathews, *Genesis 1–11:26*, 275 (see chap. 1, n. 20).

Hannah must share her husband with Peninnah, the other wife of Elkanah. This made for some difficult circumstances:

> Whenever Elkanah offered a sacrifice, he always gave portions of the meat to his wife Peninnah and to each of her sons and daughters. But he gave a double portion to Hannah, for he loved her even though the LORD had kept her from conceiving. Her rival would taunt her severely just to provoke her, because the LORD had kept Hannah from conceiving. Year after year, when she went up to the LORD's house, her rival taunted her in this way. Hannah would weep and would not eat. "Hannah, why are you crying?" her husband Elkanah would ask. "Why won't you eat? Why are you troubled? Am I not better to you than ten sons?" (1 Sam 1:4–8)

Hannah's child would greatly affect the destiny of Israel. But at this point, Hannah knew nothing of that future. She was a woman suffering in silence. Peninnah, no doubt jealous of Elkanah's favorable treatment of Hannah, relentlessly aggravated her.[7] Behind the scenes, with duplicitousness, she slipped the verbal knife in, wounding Hannah over and over again with

---

[7] Peninnah chooses special occasions to do so, suggesting a truly vicious—if veiled—vengeance toward her rival. See Dale Ralph Davis, *1 Samuel: Looking on the Heart*, Focus on the Bible Commentary (Scotland: Christian Focus, 2000), 16–17.

her words.[8] Unwilling to empathize with Hannah's plight, Peninnah served as a living tormentor of her rival. Peninnah's jealousy—though she knew the blessing of fertility and Hannah did not—created a system of ongoing injustice.[9]

Sadly, Elkanah could not see what was right under his nose. He thought Hannah's tears traced back to dissatisfaction with him. Elkanah failed to protect his wife by spotting the problem in his house,[10] but Hannah did not cry for this. She wept and eventually gave up eating because she felt her lack of agency in the situation in a desperate way. Her infertility grieved her; her rival wounded her. We cannot miss the depth of this wound and how Peninnah loved to reopen it.

The Bible does not only concern itself with the meta-narrative of salvation in the coming covenant king.[11] The Bible

---

[8] The expression of Hannah's distress—her tears—is reminiscent of Abel's uncovered blood. Where injustice occurs, weeping and distress and even torment exist. This is an important biblical-theological theme.

[9] Hannah's trial shows that "the Lord may create social and natural tragedies in order to accomplish his purposes that far outweigh the calamity. The Lord sometimes engineers social tragedies, yet he carries them out 'that the work of God might be displayed' (John 9:3). Accordingly, human tragedy can be properly evaluated and appreciated only when viewed with a consideration of the end results and ultimate purposes brought about by God." Robert D. Bergen, *1, 2 Samuel*, The New American Commentary, vol. 7 (Nashville: B&H, 1996), 62–63.

[10] This is a problem created by an ungodly system of marriage. Though the Bible offers no direct condemnation of polygamy, Elkanah's two wives clearly depart from God's archetypal design in Genesis 2.

[11] For a faithful treatment of this theme, see Thomas R. Schreiner, *The King in His Beauty: A Biblical Theology of the Old and New Testaments*

opens a window into the micronarratives of many seemingly random people whom the Lord employs in the fulfillment of his promises. But God does not only care about the end these men and women serve. He cares about each of these men and women individually. Those forgotten or derided by their peers, those whom the world passes by, God notices and helps. Even if justice waits in the wings for a time for the chosen of God, the Scripture is teaching us that God will indeed enact justice for those he loves. From biblical start to biblical finish, the Lord has an eye for the underdog—for rootless Ruth, little David, a single prostitute in Jericho, the tiny nation of Israel itself, humble Mary, anonymous fishermen-turned-apostles, and on the list goes. Those whom no one cares about, God cares about. Those whom no one nominates for leadership, God thrusts forward. Those wronged over and over again, without recourse and without agency, God sees.[12]

This narratival lesson matters greatly for the formation of a proper theology of divine justice. The stories of God-ordained men and women gaining great and greatly unexpected blessings from God do not satisfy every philosophical challenger pondering the problem of evil and the horror of human suffering, but they do show us a God who gets his hands dirty, who hears the

---

(Grand Rapids: Baker Academic, 2013).

[12] One key recurring theme of 1 Samuel is "reversal of fortune." Hannah is the forerunner in many ways of David, and her song of joy in 1 Samuel 2 parallels David's in chap. 22. Tremper Longman III and Raymond B. Dillard, *An Introduction to the Old Testament* 2nd ed. (Grand Rapids: Zondervan, 2006), 158–59.

cry of the afflicted, and who takes an undeniably special interest in the humble. In the kingdom of God, the barren widow may become a mother in Christ's regal bloodline; the low-born may become a king; the persecuted wife, enclosed in a psychological chamber of abuse and wretchedness, may give birth to one of the Bible's greatest leaders.

All this comes to pass because Hannah stumbles to the temple of God and prays a single heartfelt prayer. Continuing the theme of checked-out men, Eli the priest initially takes no notice of Hannah, and then he accuses her of drunkenness in the Lord's house (1 Sam 1:9, 14). But Hannah is not drunk. She has prayed to the Lord out of her agony. Her prayer comes from the depths of her sorrow: "LORD of Armies, if you will take notice of your servant's affliction, remember and not forget me, and give your servant a son, I will give him to the LORD all the days of his life, and his hair will never be cut" (1:11). To compress the story from this point, the Lord hears Hannah. Previously, the text identified him as having closed Hannah's womb; now, the Lord gives Hannah the gift of a son. The Lord has seen Hannah's plight, has acted in response to her desperate but trusting prayer, and has brought incredible good from a trying situation.[13]

---

[13] "When his people are without strength, without resources, without hope, without human gimmicks—then he loves to stretch forth his hand from heaven. Once we see where God often begins we will understand how we may be encouraged. Yahweh's work, however, began not only in barrenness but also in distress (esp. vv. 6–7)." Davis, *1 Samuel*, 16–17. The trial is not accidental; the trial is given to Hannah by God to magnify the kindness of Yahweh.

This story teaches that the Lord is a gracious God. He hears
the prayers of the weak who know him. He takes notice of the
forgotten, those trodden down by others. He is a majestic God,
impossible to capture and tame, high and lifted up; yet he sees the
plight of the lowly and moves with breathtaking speed to answer
the simple prayer of the godly. The Bible shows us here and elsewhere that justice is not abstract. Justice flows from the character
of God. Justice is personal, for it is the Lord himself—a personal
being—who metes it out, and justice redresses wrongs done to an
individual. The God of justice, we learn, is also the God of grace. He
not only ends Hannah's suffering at the hands of a cunning rival,
but he blesses her beyond belief. He raises her son up to be a priest
of priests, a leader of Israel who strengthens the nation by his ministry. The one anointed by Yahweh eventually anoints David, the king
who establishes the throne taken by Christ at his coming (Isa 9:7).

Pain in the Lowest Place: The Imprecatory Psalms

Hannah's story, like Ruth's and Esther's, has a heartening and
historical outcome. But Scripture does not only share stories
with happy conclusions. Perhaps the most puzzled-over portion of the Bible, aside from certain eschatological texts, are the
imprecatory Psalms. Psalm 58, for example, tackles the issue of
justice in the first two verses of its searing lament:

Do you really speak righteously, you mighty ones?
Do you judge people fairly?

No, you practice injustice in your hearts;
with your hands you weigh out violence in the land.

The psalm addresses powerful figures who "practice injustice" with impunity (58:2).[14] They show no instincts for kindness; they do not use their agency or physical strength to lift others up. They use their positions to trample the weak to the ground. Derek Kidner sums up their approach: "Here is a calculated ruthlessness, thought out and meted out . . . with businesslike efficiency."[15] The Psalmist sees evildoers who "go astray from the womb," who have within them "venom like the venom of a snake" (58:3, 4). Injustice, like divine justice, is not abstract. It may take on a bureaucratic form, but injustice derives from personal iniquity. These wicked leaders use great cunning to deal out maximum suffering to the downtrodden.

The Psalmist mourns this awful predicament, and he lifts up his voice to the heavens and calls upon the Lord to judge these wicked figures in colorful, brutal language:

God, knock the teeth out of their mouths;

---

[14] "The opening verses lament that the judging of these rulers is characterized by injustice. It is not done uprightly (lit. 'with equity'), a quality that characterizes Yahweh's judging in the psalms of Yahweh's kingship (96:10; 98:9; 99:4). And not only that, they promote violence. They are described as 'venomous' and out of control." Broyles, *Psalms*, 247 (see chap. 3, n. 45).

[15] Derek Kidner, *Psalms 1–72*, Kidner Classic Commentaries (1973; repr., Downers Grove, IL: InterVarsity, 2008), 226.

Lord, tear out the young lions' fangs.
May they vanish like water that flows by;
may they aim their blunted arrows.
Like a slug that moves along in slime,
like a woman's miscarried child,
may they not see the sun. (Ps 58:6–8)

The violence of the imprecatory Psalms takes us aback. But the Psalmist's visceral request comes from a place every person can understand: injustice. Weakness. The Psalmist has no earthly deliverer. He has no help in human terms.[16] He and his loved ones are prey to the "fangs" of evil men who tear into the needy as lions on the plain. Imprecatory Psalms such as this one show us just how far depravity travels from Eden. Injustice is not a small part of the cosmos; for many people, now and in past days, it is an ever-present darkness.

The Christian faith reckons fully with injustice. In close conjunction with its condemnation of violent oppressors, the Scripture sternly addresses economic injustice. Often these two evils are mixed—physical oppression works hand in glove with economic oppression. Micah 2 gives us an example of such wickedness. In this text, the indictment of God falls not on a pagan nation, but the tribe of Judah:

---

[16] Grogan argues that God hovers in the background of this lament. "[T]hrough God's action, these savage predators can become as harmless as disappearing water." Indeed they will. Geoffrey W. Grogan, *Psalms*, The Two Horizons Old Testament Commentary (Grand Rapids: Eerdmans, 2008), 114.

Woe to those who dream up wickedness
and prepare evil plans on their beds!
At morning light they accomplish it
because the power is in their hands.
They covet fields and seize them;
they also take houses.
They deprive a man of his home,
a person of his inheritance. (Mic 2:1–2)

As in Psalm 58, we find in Micah 2 a discomfiting picture of the wicked. They go to sleep dreaming of evil, making plans for ill-gotten gains. They do not approach their neighbors to transact a fair deal; they do not wish to "deal" at all. They want only to take, to trample, and to get rich. They scheme to land an "inheritance" that is not theirs.[17] They have "power," Micah says, and they use it. This problem recurs throughout the Bible (James 2). In one form or another, sinners always try to take advantage of other sinners—they do so physically, simply because they can,

---

[17] "Sin begins in the heart (Matt 15:19). The following verbs are intended to cast the schemers' actions in a negative light: 'seize . . . take . . . defraud.' Perhaps because of indebtedness they foreclose on fields and houses of other human beings—probably with help from crooked courts (cf. Amos 5:12)." Kenneth L. Barker, *Micah, Nahum, Habakkuk, Zephaniah*, The New American Commentary, vol. 20 (Nashville: B&H, 1999), 63–64.

and they do so economically, simply because their unrighteous hearts thirst for more and find satisfaction in robbing others.[18]

The solution to these woes is not the socialistic relinquishing of personal property or the urging of simplistic niceness.[19] God does not call his followers to stop engaging the market, nor does he unfold a biblical vision of humanity trafficking only in pleasantries. The follower of God must take the world as it comes. He must know that sin has ruined this place but that we should not crumple in despair due to this reality. We should, on the contrary, seize what agency we have. Micah says this explicitly:

Mankind, he has told each of you what is good
and what it is the LORD requires of you:
to act justly,
to love faithfulness,
and to walk humbly with your God. (Mic 6:8)

By the power of divine grace, which is a stronger power than mankind's sinful hunger for personal exaltation, the Christian

---

[18] "The intensity of the Hebrew parallelism suggests that not only do the wicked thoughts take place at night, the intentions and the planning to execute those do also. . . . what gets these people up in the morning is their desire to gain and grab." Stephen G. Dempster, *Micah*, The Two Horizons Old Testament Commentary (Grand Rapids: Eerdmans, 2017), 85.

[19] A good resource here is Jay W. Richards, *Money, Greed, and God: Why Capitalism is the Solution and Not the Problem* (San Francisco: HarperCollins, 2009); see also Grudem and Asmus, *The Poverty of Nations* (see chap. 3, n. 26).

walks in humility, faithfulness, and justice.[20] Surely, these virtues have vertical meaning first, but what begins as worship of the divine flows into works of the day. Shaped by the character of God, we embody this character in life and calling.

The second solution to injustice owes only to God. The imprecatory Psalmist, like Micah, knows this well. The follower of God should live as righteously as possible. But the Christian doctrine of justice extends far, far beyond the individual believer. Most Christians, frankly, have little access to the levers of power. We cannot at a stroke make society just. We cannot with one email reorder a troubled workplace. We cannot with one conversation reconcile one fractured relationship. Indeed, we often find that justice is delayed, arrives in only partial form, or evades us altogether. This is true of our own decisions and those of others. We ourselves fail to deliver justice. Contrary to a self-justifying worldview, we not only play the role of the wronged, but we commit wrongs against others.

On this point we return to the imprecatory Psalm examined above. Psalm 58 does not create in us the expectation that

---

[20] "How can a man approach God? One answer is: with sacrifice, things, good works. The other answer is reflected in v 8. God requires not some external gifts from his worshiper, but a humble communicant who loves to serve God and practice justice toward his fellow-man." Ralph L. Smith, *Micah–Malachi*, Word Biblical Commentary, vol. 32 (Nashville: Thomas Nelson, 1984), 51. See also David W. Baker, T. Desmond Alexander, and Bruce K. Waltke, *Obadiah, Jonah and Micah: An Introduction and Commentary*, Tyndale Old Testament Commentaries, vol. 26 (Downers Grove, IL: InterVarsity, 1988), 213–14.

injustice can escape God. To the contrary, Psalm 58 tells us to expect "retribution" in personal form from a figure who washes "his feet in the blood of the wicked" (Ps 58:10). The same Psalm that debuts in extreme bleakness closes in rapturous expectation. The righteous will have their "reward" (58:11). The wicked will not escape the righteous God. He "judges on earth" (58:11).[21] He brings injustice to an absolute halt. He does so by exerting his divine strength in all the earth, bringing evildoers to their knees, and calling every sinner to account. No one escapes his searching eye or slips out of his mighty right arm. The dealing of justice happens personally, as the divine God himself rights every single wrong that has ever happened on earth's blemished face.[22]

The first major sign that the Lord will accomplish this apocalyptic work comes during the nadir of the covenant people. Mighty Pharaoh holds Moses and the followers of God in his thrall, forcing them to perform back-breaking tasks as slaves in his kingdom. The picture is a poignant one: a pagan ruler has overtaken the people of God. The covenant seems lost, submerged in sorrow, and the people have no immediate hope. They collectively bear a terrific injustice, but God acts through Moses to deliver his people. His deliverance is not simply from a

---

[21] Kidner rightly notes that this "vengeance" is from God. Kidner, *Psalms 1–72*, 228.

[22] It is entirely true, as Kidner point out, that the New Testament in no way moves away from the doctrine of divine retribution. Instead the New Testament "will, if anything, outdo this language in speaking of the day of reckoning (*e.g.* Rev. 14:19f.; 19:11ff)." Kidner, *Psalms 1–72*, 228.

country in geographic terms; it is more than this. As Geerhardus Vos notes, "redemption is portrayed as, before everything else, a deliverance from an objective realm of sin and evil."[23] This is important to the developing metanarrative of the Scripture.

Deliverance comes when Moses holds back the waters of judgment, allowing the people of God to pass through safely. The act of salvation for the Israelites is the very act of judgment for the Egyptians, as they are buried in the deepest parts of the sea (Exod 14:21–31).[24] Divine justice thus sets right what man has made wrong. Divine justice releases the people of God from captivity and closes the reign of terror under which they lived. It also springs the people of God out of a context in which their spirituality is compromised. The Lord did not merely desire to take Israel out of Egypt, but to take Egypt out of Israel.[25] The people were called to be thankful for the Lord's act of judgment, counterintuitive as that may sound to the natural man.

Divine justice redresses imbalanced scales, restoring rightness in a desperate place, but it is not only abstract. It is true that justice must follow from the violation of the right by the wrong. In confessing this, however, we must take care never to sever the abstract from the divinely personal. The crimes of the

---

[23] Geerhardus Vos, *Biblical Theology*, 110.

[24] Hamilton draws a parallel here to the salvation-and-judgment event of Noah in Genesis 7. Hamilton, *God's Glory in Salvation through Judgment*, 95–96 (see chap. 5, n. 24).

[25] It also delivers the people from the pagan nation that enticed them into disobedience against the Lord. See Vos, *Biblical Theology*, 112.

Egyptians caused the people of God to cry out, and God sent a deliverer. Divine justice accomplishes what no human effort, however well-intentioned, can. We learn much about the Lord here. God judges men—a fearsome thing to confess and a truth only a child of God can receive as good news.

The Cross and the Church

The Exodus teaches the people of God that their Lord will fight for them. He is not far off, though he may seem to be during exilic times. Exodus is the momentous forerunner to the Bible's narratival climax: the atoning death of the Son of God.

The death of the Son of God is the Bible's greatest word on divine justice. Sin offends God personally and occasions the exercise of his just wrath. Though humanity deserves nothing less than instantaneous evisceration for its wickedness, the Lord does not destroy mankind following the fall. He sets up a covenantal system whereby a guilty people may confess their sins, repent of them, and know the Lord's forgiving grace. Like Abraham, all who believe in God as their Savior are counted righteous in God's sight (Gen 15:6).[26] The Day of Atonement celebrated the Lord's mercy and grace; though Israel deserved to experience divine judgment, the Lord ordained the death of

---

[26] Abraham, as was every born-again believer, was "justified *by* faith, or *through* faith, or *upon* faith, but never speaks of our being justified *on account of* faith or *because* of faith." Murray, *Redemption Accomplished and Applied*, 132 (see chap. 5, n. 31).

two goats. The first goat was sacrificed as a purification offering for the people, while the second—the scapegoat—took the covenant community's sin into the wilderness (Lev 16:15–22). Sin is judged through death, the death of these goats, thus assuaging the just anger of God on behalf of the covenant people.[27] Sin is dealt with and dispensed with, taken to a place far from the holy nation where "the animal had no chance of returning to Israel and bringing back the guilt of their sins."[28]

The cross of Jesus Christ fulfilled the Day of Atonement specifically and the sacrificial system generally. In his substitutionary death, Jesus met all the terms of divine justice. Sin offended God infinitely, and Christ made infinite and perfect atonement for sin, as only God could do (Heb 1:3). Man's sin drew the righteous curse of God, and so Christ died as a man, representing Adam's helpless race.[29] God did not hold back his burning hatred of sin at Calvary; it was not that he looked down at his bleeding Son, and decided to stay his hand, and love all who sought to emulate Jesus' way. The Son effectively took the wrath of God, poured it into a cup, and drained it to the last

---

[27] Although this sacrifice was acceptable and honorable to God, it did not actually cleanse the guilty objectively before the Lord. This only the cross of Christ could do.

[28] Wenham, *Leviticus*, 233 (see chap. 4, n. 73).

[29] "Only Jesus can satisfy *God's* own righteous requirements, because he is one with the Lord as God the Son; only Jesus can do this *for us* because he is truly a man and can represent us." Stephen Wellum, *Christ Alone: The Uniqueness of Jesus as Savior*, The Five Solas Series (Grand Rapids: Zondervan, 2017), 89.

drop.[30] Put differently, but no less pointedly, God caused Christ "to be sin for our sake" (2 Cor 5:21). He shed his blood, for sin required death of a spotless lamb, and met the perfect terms of holy retribution.[31] In the cross, the mercy of God satisfied the justice of God. Now the grace of God rushes forth like a flood of love and blessing and joy that overcomes evil and overwhelms the repentant sinner.

We look at the cross and say, "There is justice." We look at the cross and say, "There is mercy." God in no way relaxes his holiness at Calvary; his loving gift of his very own Son satisfies in full the holy demands of his nature. God has moved toward man, having long ago predestined all his chosen; so his chosen step forward when the Spirit moves and reckon with the infinite and personal character of their sins against God. By the Spirit's power, mankind bows before God, embracing the terms of divine justice. Man sees that the sentence of eternal death for sin is just;

---

[30] It is essential to confess that this act was directly substitutionary in penalty of the law. Christ did not with us; he died *for* us, in our very place. Consult Steve Jeffrey, Michael Ovey, and Andrew Sach, *Pierced for Our Transgressions: Rediscovering the Glory of Penal Substitution* (Wheaton, IL: Crossway Books, 2007), 244–45.

[31] This is a personal punishment. See Schreiner on Paul's theology of wrath: "Paul was nurtured in the OT, where it is clear that God's wrath is personal. Detaching God's wrath from his character reflects a deism that comports with modern sensibilities but deviates from a proper understanding of Paul." Schreiner, *New Testament Theology*, 836. Beyond Schreiner's immediate discussion, this is true not only of Paul's writings but of the biblical corpus more broadly.

man sees that the cross of Christ satisfies God's sentence, and thereby breaks with all his sin in the name of the Savior.[32]

In so doing, the repentant sinner gains a new verdict: innocent. Once guilty, the sinner could not know the Lord. Now declared righteous, the sinner was a new status through God-granted faith: justified.[33] God has naught against the Christian; there is no judicial sentence that divides the Lord from the believer. And upon regeneration, the converted Christian is united with Christ, found in Him, and possesses all his righteousness.[34] The one who became sinful now becomes, as the text says in language nearly too wonderful to believe, "the righteousness of God" (2 Cor 5:21). When God sees his new covenant people, the tribe washed in the blood of the Lion of Judah, he sees a people who are not only innocent but righteous, holy, and spotless. It is the miracle of miracles; it is the giving of a new nature, the making

---

[32] "If we love people, we will be concerned to secure their basic rights as human beings, which is also the concern of justice. The community of the cross, which has truly absorbed the message of the cross, will always be motivated to action by the demands of justice and love." John R. W. Stott, *The Cross of Christ*, 20th anniv. ed. (Downers Grove, IL: InterVarsity, 2006), 285.

[33] This justification is by faith alone, and not on the basis of any human-generated work. See Guy Prentiss Waters, *Justification and the New Perspectives on Paul: A Review and Response* (Phillipsburg, NJ: P&R, 2004).

[34] See Murray, *Redemption Accomplished and Applied*, 169–70 (see chap. 5, n. 31); also, Constantine Campbell, *Paul and Union with Christ: An Exegetical and Theological Study* (Grand Rapids: Zondervan, 2012).

of a new creation from the old, the bestowal of a new name no one can take away.

The primary justice problem in the cosmos is mankind's sin. The divine solution to the injustice of our wickedness against God is Christ. To see what God will do to evil, we look to the cross, out of which a new, truer, and greater Exodus emerges. The cross is the down payment on the long-promised just response of God to the fall. The cross shows us how God saves, yes, but it also shows us what the Exodus previewed: God does not sleep regarding depravity. He has not lost his righteous identity; he does not fail to see the jagged swath that sin cuts through the earth. He sees it all. He must execute justice, as Calvin makes plain: "For how could he who is the Judge of the earth allow any iniquity [cf. Gen. 18:25]? If the execution of judgment properly belongs to God's nature, then by nature he loves righteousness and abhors unrighteousness."[35] Justice flows from the character of God. In earthly terms, it always has and always will, even if it seems delayed for a time.

The cross signals to us and to all humanity that justice has happened and that justice is coming. In the cry of Christ on the cross, we hear "trumpet blasts of the Apocalypse."[36] We see a demonstration of what God will do to the ungodly whose sins

---

[35] John Calvin, *Institutes of the Christian Religion*, vol. 2, trans. Ford Lewis Battles, The Library of Christian Classics (1960; repr., Louisville: Westminster John Knox, 2006), 951.

[36] I have borrowed this poetic phrase from Phillip Jensen, "On the Death of a Grandson," accessed January 24, 2019, https://phillipjensen .com/upon-the-death-of-a-grandson.

were not covered by the blood of the Son of God. Christ has not made atonement for the vessels of wrath (Rom 9:22); this is why, like fire from the sky, destruction will rain down upon them. They are not forgiven; they have no propitiatory sacrifice; they are without God and without hope.

The fate of the wicked takes our breath away. If we are not careful, the reality of this terrible end may wrongly color our understandings of divine justice. We might forget that eschatological justice means every evil scheme will be undone. All the sad stories will come untrue. Every wicked plot will come unraveled. The justice of God has visited earth, and God has formed a new people through his Son's death. The Son of God died, rose from the dead, and returned to the Father's right hand. He will not stay there forever but will return to the earth. In his second coming, he will not visit this place to save it but to judge it. No one will stop his work on that day. No one will impede it. No one will triumph over the triumphant king. His justice will prove unstoppable, and his hand will prove unstayable.

All this shapes the Christian's understanding of justice in this world. We work for the spread of virtue and righteousness and equity every chance we obtain. We enter the public square as salt and light, seeking to express our love of neighbor in tangible form.[37] We oppose evil and promote good wherever we can. We

---

[37] For framing work on these matters, see D. A. Carson, *Christ and Culture Revisited* (Grand Rapids: Eerdmans, 2008); Owen Strachan, *The Colson Way: Loving Your Neighbor and Living with Faith in a Hostile World* (Nashville: Thomas Nelson, 2015).

take truth wherever we find it, for all truth is God's truth. If we can participate in a movement of justice, even one that includes unbelievers, we do; but we remember our fundamental call as the church is to advance the gospel of God so sinners may escape the wrath of God. There is no justice movement like this one, for it unites God to man and the sinner to the Savior. This is the mission of Christ's church. Individual Christians have manifold opportunities to help their fellow man, to reach out in love as a witness to the struggling and the needy, the broken and the lost; and they act with alacrity to do so. But they do so because of what God has done through Christ on the cross, and they do so knowing their efforts foreshadow the final stroke of divine justice to come.

Through the work of Christ, the New Testament envisages the children of God as "a city on top of a hill," brightly beaming amidst a decaying public order (Matt 5:14). Followers of God should "do good to everyone" with special reference to fellow believers (Gal 6:10 ESV). The church has a unique perspective on kings and crowns, on governments and nations. On one hand, we seek to live peaceably and submit ourselves to those who reign, knowing that authority—even earthly authority—comes from God himself. The ruler "does not bear the sword in vain," and the Christian does not agitate for him to swing it (Rom 13:4 ESV). On the other hand, Christianity cannot help but be a deeply subversive faith, for it places us under allegiance to a dominion so much greater than the earth that it is truly a heavenly dominion.

We are citizens of the city of God, and thus we live as "strangers and exiles" on the earth, no matter what country we hail from (1 Pet 2:11). This does not mean that we conduct ourselves like an anarchist group with a theological identity; it does mean that we can never fall prey to the delusion that the state is god, a temptation once prominent in ancient Rome but alive today. Many today place their hope and trust in governmental uplift, not knowing how theological this view is, or how misguided. The Scripture nowhere encourages us to believe that a man-driven cause will arise, preceding the return of Christ, that will crush human injustice and end public evil. Jesus himself, brought before Caesar's own governing officials, does not make a plea for the fortunes of his followers. Unexpectedly, Jesus offers himself up as a lamb upon the Roman altar. The sacrifice comes, but not in the Jewish system; Jesus dies as a public spectacle upon a Roman cross, slain without any deeper consideration on the part of the offending officials.

The death of Christ surely speaks to kingship, government, and political involvement. The church, saved by this cleansing death, engages its world in two major dimensions, both of which involve the quest for justice and the promotion of divine grace. First, the church gathers weekly to worship the Lord. The church is the body of Christ and thus a living display of justice and grace. In one sense, the church is not political at all; we don't gather together to celebrate the risen Christ each week out of any this-worldly agenda. Parties rise, parties fall; governments come, governments go. The church of the Lord Jesus Christ was not founded for any contemporaneous political cause, however valuable, however worthy. The church engages in something far more important: obedient, doxological worship of the living God, whether it does so in a prison camp, a big air-conditioned building, a tent on the plain, or an apartment in a forty-story residence towering over a megacity.

But in another sense, the church's worship is directly political. The Christian will not bow to Caesar or worship any political figure. We thus rebuke every human society and every major leader. We will submit to governing authorities, but never under any pretense of ultimate submission. This in no way closes the church off to any form of political involvement; it does, though, shape our political involvement, relieving us of the eschatological expectations held by citizens on all sides of the political spectrum. We offer this testimony by existing and by gathering before a higher king, a greater throne, and a soon-dawning order that will stretch over every inch of the remade earth in a reign unseen in all the annals of human history.

The church communicates all this simply by its weekly worship. But the people of God also scatter each week and bring the salt and light to their corrupt and darkened communities and nations. The church is the worshipping church and the witnessing church. Everywhere the believer goes, he or she seeks the spread of truth, beauty, goodness, and justice. We do so from the biblical and theological framework sketched to this point; we do so with the goal of pointing to Christ.

Conclusion

The church's vision of justice and flourishing differs sharply from culture's. Of course, this assumes that our culture has a vision of justice. We do well to query whether a secularist outlook logically yields such an interest; if there is no Creator, and there is no teleology behind human existence, then we may fairly conclude that justice is an apparition and selfishness beckons us as a way of life.

Many do not live this way. Many unbelievers do express interest in making the world right and advancing fairness where they can. We affirm the human instinct for these lofty ends, but we also know that outside of Christ, these passions easily miscarry. Unlike the world, Christianity preaches and promotes true justice, true equity, and true unity. The remarkable aspect of our doctrine of justice is this: it depends on a divine person. Even while we work to spread goodness wherever we are, we remember that the enactment of lasting justice does not finally depend on us. Justice depends on Christ.

We hate injustice, and we oppose it everywhere we find it. We remember when we uncover it that we need Christ. He sets the human heart free; he will soon set the cosmos free from its bondage to evil. We need help; we cannot accomplish what we strenuously desire; our prayer is ever, "Come, Lord Jesus and make every sad thing untrue."

CHAPTER 8

CONTINGENCY

Today, the road all runners come,
Shoulder-high we bring you home,
And set you at your threshold down,
Townsman of a stiller town.
      —A. E. Housman, "To an Athlete Dying Young"

We hear today that we are only limited by our imaginations. We may become whatever we like; we should never stop dreaming; we have no meaningful constraints on our potential greatness; we must power ahead to our goals. While we commend a human spirit bent on savoring life rather than nihilistically extinguishing it, we cannot help but note that such thinking is problematic. In biblical-theological terms, the human person is by definition and design a limited being. From the beginning, even before the fall, humanity knew boundaries. The Lord made Adam, spoke reality to him, called him to obedience, and gave him certain tasks. From his inception, Adam learned his meta-physical dependence on God. He existed only because the Lord desired him to exist. He enjoyed exhilarating freedom and had the run of Eden, but he could not transcend his creatureliness. God was made by no one; Adam was made from dust.

Today, a secularist neopagan culture challenges human frailty. We do not want to exist as creatures; we do not wish to recognize limits on our anthropology. We do not need God, we hear; we should dispense of God in our beliefs, our ethics, our public-square involvement, our parenting, and our quest for pleasure. We will hear no word from heaven about our bodies; we will accept no blueprint when it comes to our identities; we will question everything (except perhaps those teachers who urge us to question traditional thought). We will attempt the age-old project of making ourselves like God, believing we are independent rather than dependent beings.

In this chapter, we will consider three areas that Scripture searches out: contingency, time, and death. By examining these three aspects of our existence, we will understand what God desires us to do and to be. Our study takes us back to the foundations and restores in unapologetic terms our humanness. We were not made to be gods; we are creatures made by God and for God. When we see our limits and come to terms with them, we prepare ourselves for a great discovery: the excellency of God and his Son, Jesus Christ.

Just a Creature: Contingency in Biblical Perspective

In our discussion of mankind as the image of God, we have covered the creatureliness of mankind. We shall not retread that ground but will build off our study of Genesis to fill our conception of contingency—man's dependent nature. Scripture treats this subject not only by explicit declaration, but through historical object lessons. Few receive a more direct lesson in human weakness than the Babylonian king, Nebuchadnezzar:

At the end of twelve months, as he was walking on the roof of the royal palace in Babylon, the king exclaimed, "Is this not Babylon the Great that I have built to be a royal residence by my vast power and for my majestic glory?"

While the words were still in the king's mouth, a voice came from heaven: "King Nebuchadnezzar, to you it is declared that the kingdom has departed from you. You will be driven away from people to live with the wild animals, and you will feed on grass like cattle for seven periods of time, until you acknowledge that the Most High is ruler over human kingdoms, and he gives them to anyone he wants." (Dan 4:29–32)

We might first read this as a divine denunciation of human pride. Surely, the arrogance of Nebuchadnezzar rises like a stench in the Lord's nostrils.[1] But it is not only pride that God hates. It is the very idea that the Babylonian king rules over all and can do as he likes. Pride and the denial of human contingency work in tandem, of course, but the Lord deals Nebuchadnezzar a stunner of a lesson in embracing his limits. The human king has none of the "vast power" that he imagines. He may sit on a throne, but he deserves no "majestic glory." He believes that he is self-sustaining, has no limits, and may do anything he wishes; but in an instant, the Lord's decree removes everything Nebuchadnezzar has. There is only one true ruler. He gives kingdoms, and he takes them away.

Without further ado, the Babylonian became a kind of animal. He lost everything he had. Thinking himself a god, he morphed into a beast. Failing to see his human creatureliness, he dipped even lower, eating grass, having no shelter, growing nails as long as claws (Dan 4:33). He did gain understanding, though; when God brought his field study to a close, Nebuchadnezzar clung to no delusions of his greatness. Only God is great, he avowed: "For his dominion is an everlasting dominion, and his

---

[1] The text makes clear the king's narcissism: "The first person pronouns are conspicuous in v. 30. 'I [emphatic in Aram., 'I, myself'] have built as the royal residence, by *my* mighty power and for the glory of *my* majesty' (italics added). In his pride the king took for himself the glory that rightly belonged to God and invited divine judgment." Stephen R. Miller, *Daniel*, The New American Commentary (Nashville: B&H, 1994), 18:141.

kingdom is from generation to generation" (4:34). In God's great kindness, this rediscovery of human finitude leads to great monarchical blessing. The king not only regains his regal spot, but he watches as "even more greatness came" (4:36).[2]

This thread runs throughout Scripture: God exalts the humble and abases the proud. It is not often that a person experiences both sides of this truth so viscerally, but Nebuchadnezzar does. He goes lower than many people would in a nightmare, yet he knows greater power in his second reign than even the mega-ambitious could imagine. All this comes from God. Following self and selfish ambition is the path to obliteration and ultimate loss. Following God and dying to self opens the gateway to glory, the way Christ himself traveled in obedience to his Father.[3]

---

[2] "It is worth noticing where Nebuchadnezzar's eyes are directed at the beginning and end of his time of judgment. At the beginning of the episode he is on a lofty perch, the rooftop of his house, from where his eyes roam sideways and downwards, comparing his glory to that of other men and glorifying himself. He thought of himself as the center of the universe, the tree from which everything else receives its sustenance. This is exactly what pride does: it locates the self at the center of the universe, glorying in its own achievements, and putting everyone else in second place." Iain M. Duguid, *Daniel*, Reformed Expository Commentary (Phillipsburg, NJ: P&R, 2008), 69–70.

[3] We think here of the "theology of the cross" championed by Martin Luther which opposes the "theology of glory." In the former, we follow Christ and lay down our lives; in the latter, we seek to be great like God. See Martin Luther, "Heidelberg Theses," in *Luther's Works*, ed. Helmut T. Lehmann, vol. 31, *Career of the Reformer I*, ed. Harold J. Grimm (Minneapolis: Fortress, 1957), 40.

The Bible teaches us the same ideas from a different slant in the book of Ecclesiastes. In the closing scene of this mournful but instructive book, the author pictures for us the ebbing of creation and the vicissitudes of old age. In the days when "the sun and the light are darkened," when "the guardians of the house tremble, / and the strong men stoop, / the women who grind grain cease because they are few" (Eccl 12:2–3), the narrator witnesses the seeping away of the earth's strength. Tremper Longman notes that we witness here "the deterioration of old age. Everything falls apart."[4] In these elegiac days, "the dust returns to the earth as it once was, / and the spirit returns to God who gave it" (12:7). At this time, the Teacher takes the measure of this place, and concludes, "Absolute futility . . . Everything is futile" (12:8).

We find much to ponder here, but what stands out for our purposes is this: human strength will fail. The vigor of this sphere will dim. Seen from natural eyes, this world will not make good on our once-lofty expectations. The writer accomplishes several purposes in his meditation on finitude; among them, he punctures the man-centered confidence of the human heart. Considered apart from God, this world will not improve. A golden dawn of vigor and happiness will not break out in coming days. Things fall apart; things break down. The strong become the weak, the weak go to their grave, and no one remembers them.[5]

---

[4] Tremper Longman, *The Book of Ecclesiastes*, The New International Commentary on the Old Testament (Grand Rapids: Eerdmans, 1998), 270.

[5] Duane Garrett suggests that this passage is charting the breakdown of the human body: "The 'keepers of the house' are the hands,

Here is human contingency in existential expression. It is not merely that we are dependent on the divine; it is that without the divine nothing works, nothing makes sense, and nothing good will come to fruition.[6] We need God. We depend on him for existence, but just as significantly, we depend on him for purpose, meaning, and the discovery of hope. Take away the Lord, and all is futile. Ecclesiastes 12 offers us the philosophical counterpart to the spiritual and theological presentation of human depravity; it portrays what happens when man gets what he wants and God seemingly disappears from the frame.[7] If God

---

which tremble in old age; and the 'strong men' are the major muscle groups of the legs and back. Beyond that, it is impossible to be specific in anatomical details. The 'grinders' are teeth, which have ceased to chew food because they are few. Those who look out of windows are again the eyes, although growing 'dim' may refer to a lack of sparkle in the eye rather than inability to see well." Duane A. Garrett, *Proverbs, Ecclesiastes, Song of Songs*, The New American Commentary, vol. 14 (Nashville: B&H, 1993), 341–42.

[6] "The coming of the clouds is also an eschatological motif; in Ezek. 32:7, for example, the sun is covered with a cloud. That the 'light' and the 'sun' grow dark hints at the undoing of creation itself, bearing in mind the allusion here to Gen. 1. In Eccles. 1:5 part of the endless cycle of nature is that the sun sets, only to rise again. Here, however, it is darkened. Thus, Qohelet clearly has something much larger in mind than old age or death." Craig G. Bartholomew, *Ecclesiastes*, Baker Commentary on the Old Testament: Wisdom and Psalms, (Grand Rapids: Baker Academic, 2009), 348. It seems likely that this is a layered text, with physical breakdown paralleling cosmic breakdown. Without God, everything truly does fall apart.

[7] "In this book God reveals to us exactly what life is when God does not reveal to us what life is." This is very nearly paradoxical, but

is not true, then the prophets of despair have the best theology going. But God *is* true, and we exist by his mere pleasure, and so hope triumphs over despair.[8]

In reckoning with hard truths, acknowledging our contingency ranks as a close second to affirming our depravity. Even after coming to genuine faith in Christ, we may struggle to cede God his sovereignty. It is not that we deny him his attributes for his own personal exercise; it is that we may still wrestle mightily with our total dependence on his will when it comes to our fate. Texts such as Romans 9 confront us with a stark portrayal of human destiny:

> You will say to me, therefore, "Why then does he still find fault? For who can resist his will?" But who are you, a mere man, to talk back to God? Will what is formed say to the one who formed it, "Why did you make me like this?" Or has the potter no right over the clay, to make from the same lump one piece of pottery for honor and another for dishonor? And what if God, wanting to display his wrath and to make his power known, endured with much patience objects of wrath prepared for destruction? And what if he did this to make known the

---

quite right. Peter Kreeft, *Three Philosophies of Life: Ecclesiastes—Life as Vanity, Job—Life as Suffering, Song of Songs—Life as Love* (San Francisco: Ignatius, 1989), 23.

[8] "To forget the Creator of youth is to invite bitter regrets and an empty existence in old age. To remember the Creator is to follow the path of wisdom and extend the joy of life." Garrett, *Proverbs*, 340–41.

riches of his glory on objects of mercy that he prepared beforehand for glory—on us, the ones he also called, not only from the Jews but also from the Gentiles? (Rom 9:19–24)

This more than any other Scripture challenges the human heart. When we come to faith in Christ, we accept that God rules all things. He is in control. He is God, and we are not. But Scripture goes further than blandly asserting that the Lord possesses general oversight of the cosmos. The apostle Paul teaches that there are only two kinds of human people: those formed "for honor," and those "formed for dishonor." Some God has prepared for everlasting life; others God has readied for everlasting destruction.[9]

The text thus flies in the face of twenty-first-century self-directed, choose-your-own-destiny thinking that teaches contingency is a fairy tale. The biblical view of humanity teaches contingency is a fact. We are not God, but more than this, God has laid out the eternal course every human soul will travel. He

---

[9] According to Douglas Moo, there is no "reference to human works or human faith (whether foreseen or not) as the basis for God's act of hardening (as so many of Paul's 'defenders' have done)." To the contrary, "Paul never offers—here or anywhere else—a 'logical' solution to the tension between divine sovereignty and human responsibility that he creates. . . . Paul is content to hold the truths of God's absolute sovereignty—in both election and in hardening—and of full human responsibility without reconciling them. We would do well to emulate his approach." Moo, *The Epistle to the Romans*, 601 (see chap. 1, n. 50).

is fully sovereign. He has not saved those whom he foresaw will choose him; he has not fitted for wrath those he foresaw would reject him.[10] Our predestining, all-powerful God does what he pleases and is maximally glorified by the exercise of his infinite wisdom. There is no injustice in God's choice; as Berkhof argues,

> If God owed the forgiveness of sin and eternal life to all men, it would be an injustice if He saved only a limited number of them. But the sinner has absolutely no right or claim on the blessings which flow from divine election. . . . Not only have we no right to call God to account for electing some and passing others by, but we must admit that He would have been perfectly just, if He had not saved any.[11]

Salvation depends on him and him alone.

Romans 9 is the Bible's master class on divine providence and divine power. We read in this chapter the clearest possible

---

[10] Against the view that argues that God simply foresees who will choose him, Schreiner responds that "He is the potter who exercises complete authority over the clay. Any attempt to carve out ultimate human self-determination in these verses is eisegesis." Schreiner, *Romans*, 514–15 (see chap. 1, n. 51). The opposite view is found in David L. Allen and Steve Lemke, *Whosoever Will: A Biblical-Theological Critique of Five-Point Calvinism* (Nashville: B&H Academic, 2010). The former view must reconcile the goodness of God with the damnation of the reprobate; the latter view must show how the sovereignty of God allows for the "free will" of the human person.

[11] Berkhof, *Systematic Theology*, 115 (see chap. 2, n. 46).

declaration of the all-wise lordship of God. We may have come to the text expecting to find some limitation on God's agency, but instead we learn the limitations of humanity. Our flesh may thrash against these truths; we may find it bitterly hard to countenance at first. The world has trained us to see ourselves as sovereign and God as the one who counters our moves.[12] But the Bible reveals a God who is sovereign and a human race made for purposes greater than we may presently comprehend.[13]

Wherever we land on the spectrum of views regarding sovereignty and man's will, we should never conclude that man is an automaton. Instead, believers of every perspective can agree that secondary causation matters, that God has given us a will and liberty and the daily experience of human freedom. The Lord does not rule the creation as a cruel taskmaster; our days are filled with possibilities, and the capacity for human invention

---

[12] The "middle knowledge" position attempts to do justice to both divine agency and human agency. See Kenneth Keathley, "The Work of God: Salvation," in *A Theology for the Church*, ed. Daniel L. Akin (Nashville: B&H Academic, 2007), 720–23. This view, along with "conditional election," deserves careful consideration. Faithful Christian scholars and pastors disagree over these difficult issues.

[13] "He has not merely the power; he has the *authority*. There is no warrant for the interpretation or objection that Paul represents God as esteeming mankind as clay and dealing with men accordingly. He is using an analogy and the meaning is simply that, in the realm of his government, God has the intrinsic right to deal with men as the potter, in the sphere of his occupation, deals with clay. But the kind of differentiation is as great as is the difference between God and the potter, on the one hand, and between men and clay, on the other." Murray, *The Epistle to the Romans*, 32–33 (see chap. 4, n. 84).

and activity does not cease to surprise us. We humans are responsible beings.[14] We have all received many gifts, and God's common grace ensures that even those who turn their backs on him partake of many good and joyful pleasures. Biblical faith does not mean we human creatures have no agency; it simply means we understand our considerable agency as defined and delimited by God.[15]

---

[14] "It puts man in his place, not by contrasting creaturely weakness with arbitrary almightiness, but by reminding him of what 'man' is according to Holy Scripture—the creature created in the image of God, the sinner for whose sin Christ died and for whose justification He has been raised from the dead. It is because, whether one is Moses or Pharaoh, member of the believing Church or member of still unbelieving Israel, one is this man, the object of God's mercy, that one has no right to answer God back." C. E. B. Cranfield, *Romans: A Shorter Commentary* (1985; repr., Edinburgh: T&T Clark, 2001), 237.

[15] On this point, all perspectives concur. It is not a matter of whether our creatureliness entails some form of limitation before a holy God; we all must determine where that limitation begins with respect to the agency of God. All traditionally Christian views limit the power of the human will at some point. The Baptist Faith and Message 2000 offers an elegant statement on election and sovereignty in salvation: "Election is the gracious purpose of God, according to which He regenerates, justifies, sanctifies, and glorifies sinners. It is consistent with the free agency of man, and comprehends all the means in connection with the end. It is the glorious display of God's sovereign goodness, and is infinitely wise, holy, and unchangeable. It excludes boasting and promotes humility." The accent here is rightly on the power of God to elect and save. "The Baptist Faith and Message" (summary of faith), Southern Baptist Convention, Atlanta, GA, June 14, 2000, http://www.sbc.net/bfm2000/bfm2000.asp.

Our bodies teach us in natural form what the Scripture teaches principially; we are frail creatures. We all must face this fact in practical ways whether we accept it intellectually or not. The human being is a creature. We are finite. We will not evolve to some higher lifeform. We cannot freeze our brains and return to existence. Even if human lifespan continues to lengthen, we will never transcend our finitude. Even if Adam had not fallen, he would never have shed his human skin and become a god. He could have lived forever—from the point God made him, that is—but he could not have become infinite, become God. Humanity was, is, and will be contingent. We are wholly dependent on God, wholly under divine control, and wholly and unalterably beings made by God.[16]

The Days Pass Like Shadow on the Mountain: Time and Humanity

Part of what it means to be a contingent, dependent being is living in time. Left to ourselves, we cannot be free of the twenty-four-hour clock. We can dislike the rampant march of the hours; we can refuse to submit ourselves to the strictures of a schedule; we may practice habitual tardiness (which takes as much

---

[16] "Death is not the natural end to a merely biological life. Death is an intrusion into the perfect world of the Creator designed by that same Creator to make a point. Death is a punishment for human pride. It exposes our foolish confidence in our freedom to be whoever we want to be." Matthew McCullough, *Remember Death: The Surprising Path to Living Hope* (Wheaton, IL: Crossway, 2018), 68.

forethought as being on time). We can shake our fists at the great clock that counts down our days, but we cannot unmake the time-limited nature of the world.

What may come as a surprise is just how late in time we are. I am reminded of the scene from the Peter Jackson–directed *The Lord of the Rings: The Two Towers* in which the king of Rohan, Théoden, prepares for battle with the mystic wickedness of Saruman's forces. As his armor settles into place, Théoden says, "The days have gone down in the West, behind the hills into shadow. How did it come to this?"[17] The evil army that would undo this mythical kingdom is nearly at the gate. Théoden's own men are ill-prepared for what awaits them. He lost much time during his captivity to Saruman's influence, and now, after waking from a long and terrible slumber, he finds death just beyond the castle walls.

Like an army of Orcs, we experience time as an enemy in our natural condition. Our contingency, in contrast to God's aseity, means we have only so much time before us.[18] At some points in our existence, we may feel as if our lives will go on forever, but they will not. This truth closes in on us as we age and as mortality becomes a preoccupying concern. We think of testimony from the book of Job on this count. After the death of Job's family and the loss of his holdings, Bildad said this:

---

[17] Bernard Hill as King Théoden, in *Lord of the Rings: The Two Towers*, directed by Peter Jackson, New Line Cinema, 2002, film.

[18] See Frame, *Doctrine of God*, 603–8 (see chap. 2, n. 76).

For ask the previous generation,
and pay attention to what their fathers discovered,
since we were born only yesterday and know nothing.
Our days on earth are but a shadow. (Job 8:8–9)

Our youth-culture-oriented society tries to convince us other-wise.[19] It does not receive Bildad's wisdom.[20] It tells us that life stretches endlessly before us, and lack of imagination is the only thing keeping us from realizing our fullest potential. But in poetic, mournful form, Job speaks a wiser word. In our natural states, we are born, we know so little, and our hours disappear as a shadow passes over the ground.

---

[19] On this matter, consider Thomas E. Bergler, *From Here to Maturity: Overcoming the Juvenilization of American Christianity* (Grand Rapids: Eerdmans, 2014).

[20] We do not automatically assume that the elderly are wise, but neither should we make the now-common mistake of assuming they are not and the young have cornered the market on wisdom. "Bildad now draws on the ancient traditions of **former generations** and **their fathers** to support his arguments. Such attention to the results of the investigations (Heb. *kheqer*) of one's predecessors is the foundation of the wisdom enterprise. The experiences and observations of generations of sages, gathered over the ages, were thought to provide ever greater understanding of the divine ordering of the world and the appropriate way to relate to it. Bildad calls Job to *affirm* the traditional teaching of wisdom (which, in Bildad's view, affirms retribution). The Hebrew verb *konen* means 'to establish firmly,' as in the foundation of a building. Bildad is encouraging Job not simply to **find out** about the teachings of past sages, but also to 'buy into' the prevailing ideology instead of picking away at its flaws." Gerald H. Wilson, *Job*, Understanding the Bible Commentary Series (Grand Rapids: Baker Books, 2007), 76.

Scripture exhorts us to wrap our arms around our finitude. We should gain from the days, the months, and the years whatever we can. So the psalmist urges us: "Our lives last seventy years / or, if we are strong, eighty years. . . ./ Teach us to number our days carefully / so that we may develop wisdom in our hearts" (Ps 90:10, 12). The God-fearer does not treat time as if it is owed him. He relishes it as a gift from God. With a thankful heart, he measures out his days. We have no clue how long we will live, but in his day the Psalmist knew that many would make it to seventy or eighty years before dying. Little has changed in the roughly three millennia since the Spirit inspired these reflections. Our quest is the same: how can we number the days? How can we use them to "develop wisdom" and learn the fear of the Lord?

A scriptural theology of time precludes arrogance. Though our flesh might hate to admit it, the very fact that our days are numbered means we are not God. God is infinite; He existed before the earth, before the sun and moon, before morning and evening. The Lord feels no constraints regarding time; he never grows anxious due to the clock; he is in no hurry, and he is never late. What we may scarcely understand—the passage of a thousand years—is a mere turning of the head to the Lord, just a single day in a reign that never ends and never had a temporal beginning (2 Pet 3:3–9). There is no hindrance, no qualification, to the godness of God. He is fully, thoroughly, unstoppably God. He has no limitations to his power or presence. He does not work within constraints; he cannot be boxed in. In contrast to the God we worship, we are mere creatures, and indeed, the clock even now ticks.

The natural man, however, defies this truth even as he lives according to it. In Adam, we make plans for the future and brag about what we will bring to pass. But the Scriptures speak a better word. "Don't boast about tomorrow," we read in Proverbs, "for you don't know what a day might bring" (Prov 27:1). Once more we observe the gap between us and God. God knows everything that will come to pass tomorrow in every part of the world through the actions and thoughts of every living being. He not only knows all that will transpire, but he is bringing all things to their rightful conclusion through his victorious Son (Eph 1:10). The Lord has perfect knowledge of the future, and he communicates his will for the times to come in various biblical books. Revelation does not represent God's hopes for the end of all things. Revelation, in language that is often symbolic and literal, tells us how the end goes.[21] God knows what tomorrow and every day after that until the close of time will bring. We do not.

The biblical portrait of man's temporality drives us not to despair but to worship God. Once reconciled to the reality of our finitude on the earth, we may reverse our natural instincts and adopt a mind-set of savoring all the wonder, mystery, beauty, pain,

---

[21] For helpful theological commentary on the nature of language in Revelation, see Sam Storms, *Kingdom Come: the Amillennial Alternative* (Fearn, UK: Mentor, 2013); Kim Riddlebarger, *A Case for Amillennialism: Understanding the End Times* (Grand Rapids: Baker Books, 2003). For the premillennial perspective, see Russell D. Moore, "Personal and Cosmic Eschatology" in *A Theology for the Church*, ed. Daniel L. Akin (Nashville: B&H Academic, 2007), 858–926.

promise, challenge, and purposefulness of our God-given days. The book of Ecclesiastes commends just this kind of outlook and categorizes all significant human experience into "times":

> There is an occasion for everything,
> and a time for every activity under heaven:
> a time to give birth and a time to die;
> a time to plant and a time to uproot;
> a time to kill and a time to heal;
> a time to tear down and a time to build;
> a time to weep and a time to laugh;
> a time to mourn and a time to dance;
> a time to throw stones and a time to gather stones;
> a time to embrace and a time to avoid embracing;
> a time to search and a time to count as lost;
> a time to keep and a time to throw away;
> a time to tear and a time to sew;
> a time to be silent and a time to speak;
> a time to love and a time to hate;
> a time for war and a time for peace.

Humanity's instinct is to thrash against time. All too often, our minutes do not contain what we wish them to contain. Sometimes we wish only to work; other times, our bursts of creativity, of serendipity, of familial togetherness pass far more quickly than we would like. But redeemed humanity knows that, while fallenness pervades and invades our days in every dimension, we have the opportunity to view time differently than the unbeliever.

It takes wisdom to work out such a perspective, but the follower of God affirms with a glad heart the reality that "there is
an occasion for everything." The miracle that God intends to
give most of us for most of our days is the miracle of the ordinary.[22] Everyday life is God's gift to us. The ordinary existence
is the one suffused with holy dynamism, for it welcomes and
involves birth and death, planting and uprooting, war and peace,
mourning and dancing. The enchanted life that God would give
us in Christ is not what we might have been trained to expect or
desired in our hearts. The enchanted life is the life given to God,
a life that embraces the full range of human experience, including the ordinary and even mundane.[23]

This last claim bears pondering for a moment. Many of us
pull against it, wishing to fashion a more exciting existence. We
do not want to be anonymous and ordinary; we hunger to be in

---

[22] "Verse 1 states the general principle, which is then fleshed out in
the rest of the poem: there is an appropriate season and time for every
activity in the creation. This principle rests, as OT wisdom does, on the
belief in creation and its orderliness." Bartholomew, *Ecclesiastes*, 162.

[23] The entrance to such an existence is the knowledge that God
holds everything in his hand. "The pairing of the varying aspects of
human life indicates the universality of God's control. For the expression of totality in pairs is a common Old Testament idiom. Thus 'man
and woman' (Exod. 36:6) or 'great and small' (Jer. 6:13) is used to say
emphatically 'everybody'; 'sea and land' (Jon. 1:9) is an emphatic way of
saying 'everywhere.'" Michael A. Eaton, *Ecclesiastes: An Introduction and
Commentary*, vol. 18, Tyndale Old Testament Commentaries (Downers
Grove, IL: InterVarsity, 1983), 92.

what C. S. Lewis called the Inner Ring.[24] We want to count, to matter, to make the decisions that move the needle. It may be that God grants us some measure of influence and even fame. If this happens, we should seek to steward whatever leadership we gain for his glory, knowing the dangers inherent to our flesh and our age, the temptations that our hearts all too easily covet. This life, this enchanted life, is not fundamentally about us. It is about the increase of Christ, not the increase of celebrity.

With the increase of Christ's glory as our chief end, we are freed to savor the times appointed for us by the Lord.[25] God is the chief end of our days; if we are obeying the Lord and giving energy and attention to doxological pursuits, we are living the good life.[26] We open our hearts to beauty, and they feel—truly

---

[24] C. S. Lewis, *The Weight of Glory and Other Addresses* (1949; New York: HarperOne, 2001), 141–57.

[25] Here we are reminded of John the Baptist's confession that Christ must increase, and he (John) decrease (John 3:30). Ridderbos captures the spirit of this confession: it is "with a sense of full and unmixed joy that fills him when he sees that his work of preparation has reached its intended goal." Ridderbos, *John*, 147. We do not have the redemptive-historical role of John the Baptist, but we do well to emulate his example.

[26] "That God in seeking his glory, therein seeks the good of his creatures: because the emanation of his glory (which he seeks and delights in, as he delights in himself and his own eternal glory) implies the communicated excellency and happiness of his creature. And that in communicating his fullness for them, he does it for himself: because their good, which he seeks, is so much in union and communion with himself. God is their good. Their excellency and happiness is nothing but the emanation and expression of God's glory: God in seeking their glory and happiness, seeks himself: and in seeking himself, i.e. himself diffused

and deeply—for the first time. This does not only mean feeling glad, contrary to how weekly church services can condition us to think. There are things to hate in this world, as Ecclesiastes says. We hate evil, Satan, and the effects of the fall. We grieve and weep intensely, perhaps even uncontrollably, when a child or a friend dies. This world cuts into us and leaves wounds that become scars that stay with us. God does not dull the deepest passions and emotions of our persons; God awakens our affections when we trust savingly in Christ. The Spirit brings us out of our numbness, out of our emotional comas, out of our unstable patterns, and orients us to the world as it actually is, not as we would pretend it to be. The ministry of grace is also the ministry of reality, so that we see God's grace in the world as it is.

We may do so because when God redeems us, God redeems time.[27] Scripture introduces us to this truth in the Old Testament, as God communicates to his people a promise that—then and now—sounds too good to be true. But the redemption of our sinful past is gloriously real: "I will repay you for the years / that the swarming locust ate, / the young locust, the destroying locust, / and the devouring locust— / my great army that I sent against you" (Joel 2:25). The people wandered from God, yet the Lord assured them that he would "repay" them. He would not only bless them from the time of their repentance, but he

---

and expressed (which he delights in, as he delights in his own beauty and fullness), he seeks their glory and happiness." Edwards, "The End for, Which God Created the World," 459 (see chap. 1, n. 57).

[27] See Stanley Hauerwas, *The Work of Theology* (Grand Rapids: Eerdmans, 2015), 90–102.

would redouble his grace, restore them, and lift them higher than before.

Christian doctrine offers the sinner a truth so good it defies belief. To Judah, the Lord made a similar promise of forgiveness:

"Come, let us settle this,"
says the LORD.
"Though your sins are scarlet,
they will be as white as snow;
though they are crimson red,
they will be like wool." (Isa 1:18)

As in days of old, so in the new covenant era. "The promise, therefore, is of a new, holy nature, not just the cleansing away of the past."[28] The Christian, given the grace of ruin and the grace of repentance, may wash his uncleanness in the blood of the lamb.

In Christ, we gain a new past, a new present, and a new future. Our past is comprehensively washed in the crimson blood of Jesus. This does not erase the wrong things we have done. It does not absolve us of any responsibilities incurred by evil acts we committed or terrible words we said. The cross does not cancel out the consequences of our lived depravity, but it does allow us to see our past lives in a new light of Christ. Our preconversion lives have culminated in the miracle of conversion. We can look back and see how our sins positioned us to receive the grace

---

[28] Motyer, *Isaiah*, 54 (see chap. 3, n. 53).

of God. This truth in no way leaves us viewing sin in a positive light. It does place the glad confession of Joseph to his brothers in our mouth: "You planned evil against me; God planned it for good" (Gen 50:20).

We gain a new present in Christ, to be sure. Whatever has transpired to this point is not of first importance. It is not unimportant, but the moment before us is a moment of fresh possibility. We who have been washed and resurrected by the resurrected Christ now live in resurrection time. The greatest possible work has happened; we are part of a new humanity in Christ, who is not dead but raised. Every moment we live as believers is lived in the fullness of this truth, and thus our moments and our hours are infused with present meaningfulness grounded in the resurrection of Christ and the coming return of Christ. Our days are not grim; we do not simply await our translation to glory. We await it as those who are already resurrected and filled with hope and purpose for the time immediately before us.[29]

Our future, thirdly, is a Christic future. That future is ours already, but we must patiently watch for the final return of the Son of God.[30] We have inherited an eternal inheritance, and through faith in Jesus, we made an infinite down payment on

---

[29] In this paragraph my thoughts are fueled by (though not dependent upon) the concept of "Easter time" in Karl Barth, *Doctrine of Creation*, 2:488–89 (see chap. 1, n. 31).

[30] See George Eldon Ladd, *The Gospel of the Kingdom: Scriptural Studies in the Kingdom of God* (1959; repr., Grand Rapids: Eerdmans, 2000). This work on already/not yet eschatology is of great value in understanding the Christian future regardless of eschatological position.

the new heavens and new earth. Our future is secure, so time has a new significance for us. Our days are a continual offering to God, and in all we do, we live *coram deo*, "unto God." We need not fear the advance of time. Strange as it sounds, we eagerly await going to glory.

In the final analysis, Christians experience and view time differently than unbelievers. Christ makes all the difference. Conversion in his name redeems our future; conversion redeems our present; conversion redeems our past.

The Last Enemy Overcome: A Theology of Death

Death comes to all the children of Adam, and we have no power to stop it in ourselves. The natural human response to death is fear. Death is not tame, after all. No one can master it. No one can peer into it. No one has any idea when it will come. Death is a mystery, a veiled figure just out of sight, and the natural man feels terror—rightly—in its presence. The Scripture shows us that death is indeed the gateway to terrible things, for when we die outside of God's grace, we go to hell, where we experience divine justice for eternity. Little wonder that the natural man busies himself with amusements, tasks, and leisure. We are contingent beings; we live under the metronomic control of time; we will surely die.

The Christian approach to death differs markedly from a secular, unbelieving one. We have seen already that Adam's sin brings a harvest of death, pain, and suffering to his fellow sinners. Created for immortality, mankind now may live only a short span on the earth. The Christian response to death thus begins with meeting our fate head-on. Christianity does not dodge the truth or slip away from reality's clutches. It affirms the truth and embraces reality. We are of all people most fitted for realism about the workings of this world, for we follow the God who speaks what is real and whose creation reinforces his teaching.[31]

In Ecclesiastes, there is "a time to give birth and a time to die; / a time to plant and a time to uproot" (3:2). In one sentence fragment, this wise book telescopes our days. One moment, we celebrate the joy of a child entering the home; in another, we draw our last breaths. We are planted in the earth by God; we will be uprooted from the earth by God. The Christian mourns death; we do not celebrate its presence in this world. We hate death, oppose it, and try to stave it off. But we also know that the path we travel as human beings leads to one destination for us all. We will all die. Sooner than we know, it will be our time.

But this is just the first part of a properly biblical doctrine of death. The second part necessitates that we lift up our eyes to the hills and ponder afresh the truth that Jesus roared back to life three days after his crucifixion. Jesus triumphed over the grave. In 1 Corinthians 15, the apostle Paul expounds on the resurrection of Jesus, identifying it as the key to hope and security for believers. For unbelievers, the resurrection means nothing. But for believers, Christ's resurrection represents God's answer

---

[31] See "A Ministry of Reality: Theology in the Indicative Mood" in Kevin J. Vanhoozer and Owen Strachan, *The Pastor as Public Theologian: Reclaiming a Lost Vision* (Grand Rapids: Baker Academic, 2015), 108–12.

to Adam's peril.[32] Though death has not yet died, Christ was raised to life by God (15). This makes all the difference for us. If Christ laid in the grave still, then we would have no hope, and "we should be pitied more than anyone" (1 Cor 15:19).

But Jesus was raised. Death is overcome.[33] This was necessary.[34] The last enemy will not endure past the end of the age. Jesus' resurrection does not signify that we will necessarily escape death, even as he did not. Until Christ returns, we must all suffer the great consequence of the fall. But we know that

---

[32] Thiselton handles both the corporate and individual dimensions of this broader passage nicely: "[T]he argument that humanity is, simply as a brute fact, bound up in the solidarities, vulnerabilities, and consequences of the life and destiny of **Adam** finds its saving parallel in the gospel assurance that the new humanity is bound up in the solidarities, atoning work, and resurrection victory and promise of **Christ** as the 'last' (i.e., eschatological) **Adam** (see 15:45)." Thiselton, *The First Epistle to the Corinthians*, 1225 (see chap. 4, n. 61).

[33] "In Isa. xxv. 8 it is said that God will swallow up death—the death which came by the hand of the Assyrian. In the Prophet's vision the deliverance from death is limited by the necessities of his own age. The Apostle's view is much wider. He knows that all death will be swallowed up now that Christ has conquered death by rising again. The doom pronounced upon Adam (Gen. iii. 19) is removed; and the result (εἰς) is victory, absolute and everlasting triumph. Death is annihilated, and God is all in all. This thought makes the Apostle burst out into a song of triumph of death which is a free adaptation of another prophetic utterance." Archibald Robertson and Alfred Plummer, *A Critical and Exegetical Commentary on the First Epistle of St. Paul to the Corinthians*, 2nd ed., The International Critical Commentary (New York: Charles Scribner's Sons, 1911), 378.

[34] "Death for Paul is a power that casts its ominous shadow over us all and must be not just removed but defeated." Ciampa and Rosner, *The First Letter to the Corinthians*, 833 (see chap. 4, no. 64).

the resurrection of Christ is not only a story about Jesus, but the trajectory of our destinies as Christians. What happened to Jesus will happen to us. We will go to God immediately upon our deaths, just as the thief on the cross appeared that day with Christ in glory (Luke 23:43). On the last day, the day that comes in "a moment," in the blink of an eye, Jesus will return to earth. Then, "we will be changed," Paul tells us. "For this corruptible body must be clothed with incorruptibility, and this mortal body must be clothed with immortality" (1 Cor 15:52–53). On that day, the people of God will thunder as one voice together:

Death has been swallowed up in victory.
Where, death, is your victory?
Where, death, is your sting? (15:54–55)

The reality of the resurrection means that we need not fear death. The believer has seen how the Father raised Christ. We who have union with Christ, indissoluble identification achieved through the power of the cross and the sealing of the Spirit, will rise as well. We died with Christ; we live with Christ; we will be raised with Christ; we will reign with Christ forever.[35] This is the power of God in us. We Christians freely confess that we do not find ourselves strong enough, fit enough, gifted enough to overcome daily challenges on our own, let alone face down the

---

[35] As P. S. Johnston notes, since death is swallowed up, "Christ's resurrection is thus the prototype of Christian experience." *New Dictionary of Biblical Theology* (see intro. n. 2), s.v. "death and resurrection."

last enemy. We are truly those who know our weaknesses, and who gladly cry out to God for help. In his infinite grace, God grants us all we need. His gift to us is his Son, Jesus Christ. Our life is in Christ. Our death is in Christ. Our hope is in Christ. Our victory is in Christ.

Jesus has broken the back of the foe who held us captive all these years. Jesus is the hero, the head-crusher who has triumphed in the cosmic conflict between Eve's offspring and the serpent's offspring (Gen 3:15; Rom 16:20). Jesus went outside the city gates. He did so with one purpose: to conquer Satan and end his deathful reign. So says the author of Hebrews: "Now since the children have flesh and blood in common, Jesus also shared in these, so that through his death he might destroy the one holding the power of death—that is, the devil—and free those who were held in slavery all their lives by the fear of death" (Heb 2:14–15). Here is the hero the Bible has long awaited. Here is the heir to David's throne, the warrior-king who needs no "mighty men" to guard him (2 Sam 23:8–39 ESV). Here is the good shepherd who keeps the night watch and will allow no wolf to sink fangs into his blood-bought sheep (John 10:11). Jesus of Nazareth has come to deal out death to Satan and death to death.[36]

Satan, Hebrews shows us, does indeed hold sway over the children of men. He has the power of death over the unrepentant, and thus they do not know freedom during their earthly days but "slavery," bondage to unbroken and uncontrollable fear

---

[36] The classic work that articulates this truth is John Owen, *The Death of Death in the Death of Christ* (1648; Carlisle, PA: Banner of Truth, 1999).

(Heb 2:15). For everyone outside of Christ, slavery takes hold of the human person from the start of one's days, and it never releases its throttling grip. But Christ has broken the power of sin, which funds the power of death.[37] When we turn away from our ungodliness and taste the grace of God, we instantly gain eternal life. We still will die, but the devil has no power over us. We still face temptation, but Satan's power is broken for the believer. The Christian is free from Satan's tyranny. We are free from hell, from enslavement to sin, from a tormented conscience.

All this is because of Christ. All the work of salvation is Christ's own work. Jesus is the warrior-savior we have so long sought.[38] He, the greater David, has faced down the devil, the greater Goliath. He, the greater Moses, has triumphed over Satan, the crueler Pharaoh. He has led his people through the waters of judgment, but not by holding them back. He let them crash in on him, and he buried our sin in the depths of that sea. Jesus is the warrior-king who reigned from a cross, who went outside the camp and battled his enemy, and who has rescued and ransomed and redeemed all who trust in him.[39]

---

[37] On the connection between humiliation and freedom from slavery, see Paul Ellingworth, *The Epistle to the Hebrews,* The New International Greek Testament Commentary (Grand Rapids: Eerdmans, 1993), 174.

[38] See Phillip Bethancourt, Christ the Warrior King: A Biblical, Historical, and Theological Analysis of the Divine Warrior Theme in Christology (PhD diss., Southern Baptist Theological Seminary, 2011), https://digital.library.sbts.edu/handle/10392/3732.

[39] The pairing of penal substitutionary atonement with *Christus Victor* is biblically justified, even as we posit that the former is the central accomplishment of the work of Christ, and makes victory over the

This reign has begun. Christ did all the Father called him to do in his incarnation. But the reign of God, realized in all the world, has not yet reached total fulfillment. So it is that the author of Hebrews can say that Christ came that he might "destroy" Satan's work (Heb 2:14), but the apostle Paul can look ahead to the final completion of God's head-crushing plan. At the end of his letter to the Romans, the point when Paul customarily sends greetings and shares niceties, he slips this in: "The God of peace will soon crush Satan under your feet" (Rom 16:20).[40] We may say, reading the Bible as a unified book, that Satan both is crushed already—for the cross has overcome his power—and will be crushed finally in days to come (Revelation 19). God did not forget his promise to the serpent. The Lord has a long memory. He sent his Son to destroy the works of the devil, and he will send his Son once more to terminate Satan.

Conclusion

The creatureliness and fallenness of humanity pose insuperable obstacles to every person. We begin life with three major problems: we are dependent and helpless; we are time-limited and under the gun; we will die and suffer for eternity. Every system of theology, every spirituality, every worldview must engage these

---

forces of darkness possible. On this point see Treat, *The Crucified King*, 247–51 (see chap. 5, n. 28).

[40] Paul has in view both victory over Satan in an eschatological sense and the defeat of the false teachers faced by the Roman Christians. See Schreiner, *Romans*, 820 (see chap. 1, n. 49).

truths. We cannot pretend they do not exist. Though we like to think of ourselves as gods, we must quickly lose this delusion.

Many around us try to deal with mortality by hurdling it on a daily basis. But even if this effort pays off in the short term, it can only fail in the long term. How heartening, then, is the biblical truth that God wishes to do something greater than improve our daily performance. Our health matters, and our bodies are temples of the Holy Spirit. But the greatest victories do not come in this life. They come through the enchantment of our humanity, the very remaking of our person by the grace of God that is in Christ. Christ's cross refigures our contingency, enabling us to not only acknowledge our dependence on God, but savor it. The miracles of the cross and the empty tomb renew our sense of time, catapulting us into each and every moment God has given us, and allowing us to enjoy and experience the full range of multidimensional humanity. The cross and empty tomb steal away our fears of death, teaching us that while death is terrible, it is overcome by Christ. In every facet of our being, God enchants our existences by reorienting them around the events accomplished in Christ.[41]

---

[41] "For Paul, resurrection is the necessary outcome of what God has done in Christ and what he intends to do for his people. Paul's personification of death, following the lead of both Isaiah 25:8 and Hosea 13:14, depicts it not as the inevitable and benign fate of all humans but as 'an alien, inimical power,' nothing less than a tragedy. In the words of Isaiah 25:7, death is 'the shroud that is cast over all peoples, the sheet that is spread over all nations.' Death for Paul is a power that casts its ominous shadow over us all and must be not just removed but defeated.

There is such a thing as a "good death" for the believer. But the "good death" is not that which our secular culture champions. A cultural *euthanatos* (ευθάνατος), propelled by a thoroughly disenchanted worldview, serves the strong. A biblical "good death" serves the weak. The Bible opposes the fundamental principle of the evolutionary mind-set, *survival of the fittest.* In secular thought, the weak must sacrifice themselves for the good of the strong. The Bible teaches the very opposite. The Word of God offers an alternate principle: *sacrifice of the fittest.*[42] In Christian theology, the strong must sacrifice themselves for the good of the weak. Those given many abilities, many talents, do not have the option of withdrawing, holding back, and opting out. "To whom much has been given, much may be gained for oneself," says the culture. "To whom much has been given, much will be required," says the Scriptures (Luke 12:48 NRSV). We see this principle throughout the canon. Abraham called to sacrifice Isaac; Moses charged to lead God's people; the spotless lamb slain on the Day of Atonement; the Suffering Servant crushed for our iniquities; the Son of God satisfying the wrath of God in the stead of sinners.

A key emphasis of this whole chapter has been that what is required for complete victory over God's enemies includes the total defeat of death, 'not a compromise in which death is allowed to have the body while some other aspect of the human being (the soul? the spirit?) goes marching on.'" Ciampa and Rosner, *The First Letter to the Corinthians,* 833 (see chap. 4, n. 64).

[42] Andrew Lisi, "Toward an Understanding of the Atonement as Sacrifice of the Fittest" (master's thesis, Trinity International University, December 2010), https://tiu.academia.edu/AndrewLisi.

The Lord of heaven and earth does not reenchant his people for their own ends. He saves us to speed his kingdom forward, to be strong for the weak, and to give him glory in a world that denies it to him. He saves us above all to rejoice in his Son, the man Christ Jesus, truly human and truly God, a figure so great that we might think him a figment of our imaginations. But as we shall see in our final chapter, he is no imagined figure. He is real; he is risen; he is reigning.

CHAPTER 9

| CHRIST |

Do little things as though they were great, because of the majesty of Jesus Christ who does them in us.

—Blaise Pascal, *Thoughts*

Winston Churchill stood in his study, dictating to secretaries while his close friends sat nearby taking in the daily performance. For Churchill, every evening was another opportunity to play his magisterial role; he loved nothing more than creating phrases that would echo throughout the world, making international headlines, and setting policy across the globe. On this particular night, he found himself interrupted midsentence, one of his least favorite events. His six-year-old grandson, Jack Soames, had somehow slipped past the gatekeepers who ensured Churchill's solitude, and he had a burning question on his mind. Bursting through the door, Little Jack ran up to his grandfather and asked him, "Grandpa, is it true you are the greatest man in the world?" Without missing a beat, his grandfather answered him, "Yes! Now scamper off!"

Many today would laugh at this anecdote from the epic life of one of the twentieth century's greatest heroes for a different reason. They would scoff at the very idea of the Great Man theory of history, viewing it as a hoary concoction of a bygone past. Once, humanity believed in courageous leaders who inspired whole civilizations; now, our cynicism has freed us from such delusions. There are no great men. We no longer laud such figures; we dismiss and disdain them. There is no hero on the horizon.

As we twenty-first-century creatures downplay such virtue, we still look for it. We want society to improve. We still seek the good, or at least a version of it. We still want to follow leaders who are true, though we have been burned many times. We quest after a vision of our lives and our society that is beautiful, frustrated though our hopes have been. We seem confused about where this deliverance will come from; on the one hand, we don't believe in heroes anymore, but on the other, we crave justice just as much as ever. We do not wish to live in a world that is always winter; we want spring to break out and the earth to be enchanted once more.

The human instinct for enchantment need not end in disillusionment and despair. The Word of God tells us our hope comes from the Lord. The biblical metanarrative unfolds with speed and momentum, building the reader's expectation for the Messiah who will rescue God's people, wash them clean of their sins, return them to doxological covenant-keeping, and set up a greater kingdom than any can imagine. This promise comes early in the story, as just after the fall of Adam, the Lord promises a deliverer (Gen 3:15). It takes a long time for this deliverer to visit the earth, but we see the wait was worth it. The Messiah has come.

The Miraculous Conception and Holy Life of the Messiah

Throughout the Old Testament, the Lord trains his people to keep looking to the hills, giving them a range of types, persons, events, and institutions that point them to something greater on the horizon.[1] Noah survives the judgment flood of God; Abraham readies Isaac as a God-honoring sacrifice; Moses leads the nation in a righteous course, executing the Exodus; Joshua strikes down the enemies of God's people and leads them into the promised land; the Day of Atonement displays what sin requires and God provides, namely, the blood of an honorable

---

[1] For a careful handling of discontinuity and continuity regarding typological interpretation, see D. A. Carson, "Mystery and Fulfillment: Toward a More Comprehensive Paradigm of Paul's Understanding of the Old and New," in *Justification and Variegated Nomism*, vol. 2, *The Paradoxes of Paul*, eds. D. A. Carson, Peter T. O'Brien, and Mark A. Seifrid, (Grand Rapids: Baker Books, 2004), 393–436.

and innocent sacrifice; David and Solomon exhibit courage, wisdom, and strength in leading Israel; Esther, Ruth, Deborah, and Rahab play vital roles in the messianic bloodline and political survival of the nation; the major and minor prophets speak the living word of God, declaring reality in a world that denies it; Isaiah sees the Suffering Servant laying down his life for his beloved, washing them clean. The typological list could go on much longer, but this shows us that the biblical narrative builds toward the realization of the people's messianic hopes in the New Testament.[2]

Everything about the coming of Christ is supernatural. The prophecy that enshrouds his incarnation, the timing of his arrival, and especially the nature of his conception mark out Jesus as the God-man. Some today dismiss the importance of the virgin conception and birth, but this New Testament event signifies the thoroughly miraculous cast of the coming of Christ. The Holy Spirit gave conception to Mary; the baby who grew within her womb did so because "the Most High . . . overshadow[ed]" this humble young woman (Luke 1:35). Jesus is a fully human man who is conceived by wholly supernatural means.[3] He is not

---

[2] To gain a framework for typological interpretation, see Aubrey Sequeira and Samuel C Emadi, "Biblical-Theological Exegesis and the Nature of Typology," *Southern Baptist Journal of Theology* 21, no. 1 (2017): 11–34.

[3] Karl Barth suggests that the virgin conception "consists in a creative act of divine omnipotence, in which the will and work of man in the form of a human father is completely excluded from the basis and beginning of the human existence of the Son of God, being replaced by

born as a *tertium quid*, a different species of being, but is truly human and yet truly divine.[4] From the start of his human life, the Scripture drives us to these overlapping conclusions. There is nothing unusual at all about the birth of Christ; Mary delivers him in a stable, yes, but her delivery of her son takes place in normal human fashion. "He was a normal human being" with a human body "identical with our own."[5] Jesus was born as all babies are (Luke 2:7).[6] Though his conception came through supernatural means, the Gospels show that the circumstances of Christ's birth could not have been homelier. He was born in a dusty, dirty stable surrounded by animals. The scene reminds us of Adam's origin; he came into being not in a sealed-off space but in the real world populated by animals and other living things. There is a refreshing authenticity to this birth that we must not miss or underplay.

---

a divine act which is supremely unlike a human action which might arise in that connexion, and in that way characterised as an inconceivable act of grace." Barth, *Doctrine of Reconciliation*, 207 (see chap. 6, n. 14).

[4] Con. Apollinarius, who wrote that Jesus is "a mean between God and man, neither wholly man nor wholly God, but a combination of God and man." Cited in Charles E. Raven, *Apollinarianism* (New York: Macmillan, 1923), 204.

[5] Donald Macleod, *The Person of Christ*, Contours of Christian Theology (Downers Grove, IL: InterVarsity, 1998), 162.

[6] "Luke describes Jesus' birth in very simple, unadorned terms. Many issues are raised by the verse, mainly because of traditional associations tied to the birth event. But the setting presents a very humble beginning for the future messianic king." Bock, *Luke 1:1–9:50*, Baker Exegetical Commentary on the New Testament (Grand Rapids: Baker Academic, 1994), 206.

The biblical text goes out of its way to show us that Jesus did not hover over the ground. He came into the world as we do, though he came as the second Adam who would not send humanity back to the dust, but would lift it out of the ground. From the start, the man Christ Jesus is a singularly divine individual. The Holy Spirit works in a gloriously unique way to give Mary conception of the Christ-child. This holy event marks out Jesus as the God-man. We cannot therefore adopt a wait-and-see approach to the deity of Jesus Christ. The New Testament communicates a wonder-and-see perspective. The magi map a proper approach to Jesus: they behold the child and worship him (Matt 2:1–12). This is a human child, real flesh and blood in a feeding trough, but this child is the long-expected Messiah of God's people. Jesus is not a member of a different race and an alien people. He is not superhuman. We see in the magis' response the recognition that he is the true human. This is the archetype. Reading Scripture theologically, this is the perfect image of God.

Jesus, truly human, lived a normal yet perfect life.[7] Though the Gospels do not give us a long philosophical disquisition on the interplay of his divine and human natures, once the birth of Christ happens, we gain snatches of his day-to-day existence. Jesus "grew up and became strong, filled with wisdom, and

---

[7] This word, *perfect*, may sound controversial today, but if we balk at affirming that Jesus' life was perfect, then the problem is not with the description but with a Christology that may have gone far more "below" than we have noticed. See Carl F. H. Henry, *The Identity of Jesus of Nazareth* (Nashville: Broadman Press, 1992), 20, 94, 102.

God's grace was on him" (Luke 2:40).[8] The normal course of human growth and physical maturation worked in him. Jesus did not live in a kind of superhuman physical frame; in terms of his constitution and his daily life, he was an ordinary man. When twelve, Christ went to Jerusalem with Joseph and Mary but stayed behind in the temple. When his parents found him, Jesus was "sitting among the teachers, listening to them and asking them questions" (Luke 2:46). Here Jesus foreshadowed much of his later engagement with Jewish leaders; he went to them, listened to them, and asked them questions. But he not only posed queries; he gave his own answers, which "astounded" those who heard them (2:47). His own parents, upon finding him, felt similarly. They were "astonished" to find him among the religious leaders (2:48). This seems to indicate that Jesus had not acted in this manner before, and that his father and mother did not expect such behavior from him.

A little bit of Jesus' uniqueness seeped out in this instance, but God yet veiled the glory of his Son. For some time, Jesus stayed out of sight. He grew up, learning wisdom and "in favor with God and with people" (2:52).[9] The fact that Christ learned

---

[8] "V. 40 summarizes twelve years of Jesus' life. Luke refers to the growth and maturity of Jesus in v. 40 in virtually the same words that he used to describe the growth and maturity of John in 1:80, thus implying a normal childhood of Jesus." James R. Edwards, *The Gospel according to Luke*, Pillar New Testament Commentary (Grand Rapids: Eerdmans, 2015), 89.

[9] It is not only God's love that is in view here, but his unique plan for his incarnate Son. "The words 'and the favor of God was upon him' (cf.

wisdom shows us that Jesus did not live as a glowing holo-
graph, spiritually detached from his loved ones. He learned basic
principles of life and intellection.[10] He soaked up the rabbinic
teaching of his Jewish tutors. He took the law to heart and medi-
tated on it. He knew the ordinary challenges of human existence; in his ministerial days, he got tired (John 4:6), "thirsty"
(John 19:28), and "hungry" (Matt 4:2). Jesus had a full-fledged
emotional life. In his ministry, he grew "troubled" (John 12:27),
"sorrowful" (Matt 26:38 ESV), "amazed" (Matt 8:10), and was
overcome with sadness (John 11:35). To the fullest extent, Jesus
was a human being who faced what we face.

Jesus was tempted, tried, and tested just as we are. But Jesus
was different, for he never sinned against the Lord. When his
ministry began, Jesus went into the wilderness through the

2:25) underscore this divine aid. God concerns himself with the child
not only because he loves him, but because he has a plan for him. Thus
supported, Jesus grows and becomes strong. More than this we (unfor-
tunately?) do not know; nor probably did Luke." François Bovon, *Luke
1: A Commentary on the Gospel of Luke 1:1–9:50*, ed. Helmut Koester,
Hermeneia (Minneapolis: Fortress, 2002), 106–7.

[10] "The σοφία is to be regarded as wisdom in the highest and
fullest sense. The intellectual, moral, and spiritual growth of the
Child, like the physical, was *real*. His was a perfect humanity developing perfectly, unimpeded by hereditary or acquired defects. It was
the first instance of such a growth in history. For the first time a
human infant was realizing the ideal of humanity." Alfred Plummer,
*A Critical and Exegetical Commentary on the Gospel according to St.
Luke*, 5th ed., International Critical Commentary (Edinburgh: T&T
Clark, 1896), 74.

Spirit's leading (Matt 4:1). He had a test to pass.[11] Three times Satan tried to induce Jesus to obey him. The second Adam, weak with hunger, did not follow the will of the devil, however. Three times he responded to Satan's temptations by quoting Scripture. Even when the devil himself quoted the biblical text, Jesus saw through the ruse and overcame it with the rightly understood word of God (4:5–7). Offered physical relief, spiritual influence, and earthly splendor, Jesus rejected each in turn. Here we see that Satan offered the Son of God gifts that God alone gives in full; the devil's offerings were a secularized, de-Godified version of what the obedient savior would gain. Through his obedience unto death itself, Jesus won for himself and all his followers ultimate rest, the very power of God in spiritual form, and a remade heavens and earth.[12] Satan tried to give Jesus a shortcut to this threefold inheritance, but Jesus refused his offers, banishing him with a final word: "Go away, Satan!" (Matt 4:10)

In every moment of his life, Jesus exerted power over sin. He never succumbed to temptation. He kept covenant with his God. Jesus shows us what true humanity was intended to be. True

---

[11] "The whole experience takes place under the guidance of the Spirit and therefore according to the purpose of God." Satan himself only carried out what God ordained. R. T. France, *The Gospel of Matthew*, 128 (see chap. 6, n. 20).

[12] "Jesus triumphs and shows himself to be 'the true Israel, the "Son of God" through whom God's redemptive purpose for his people is now at last to reach its fulfillment' (France, *The Gospel of Matthew*, 128)." Grant R. Osborne, *Matthew*, vol. 1, Zondervan Exegetical Commentary on the New Testament (Grand Rapids: Zondervan, 2010), 128.

humanity does not mean sinning. It means acting as a holy child of God. Humanity does not inherently have sin or a sin nature. [13] The true human knew no sin and felt no internal compulsion to sin. There was nothing in Jesus that bent him toward evil. [14] Jesus shows us we will have no pull of the flesh in eternity. We will not curve toward iniquity. We will have perfected holy natures, and sin will have neither power over us nor the opportunity to tempt us.

The biblical text presents us with a sinless, spotless Christ. The Son of God knew no sin and never desired it. Jesus, we conclude, did not have a fallen nature. Some have argued that it was necessary that the Son experience temptation in order to fulfill Heb 4:15, but I believe the opposite. In order for Jesus to be the true human, it was necessary that he not experience attraction in his own person toward ungodly ends. He was "tempted in all things" but without sin.

The term for temptation (πειράζω) in this text is likely a specific reference to the redemptive sufferings of Christ. In general, the verb πειράζω means *to put someone to the test*. But the only other time Hebrews uses the term of Jesus is in 2:18, which is a specific reference to his sufferings: "For since He Himself was tempted [πειρασθείς] in that which He has suffered, He is able to come to the aid

---

[13] Cf. Cortez, *ReSourcing Theological Anthropology*, 145–66 (see chap. 1, n. 40).

[14] Con. Cortez, who argues "it would seem necessary to affirm that Jesus also experienced both external and internal temptation." Cortez, 162.

of those who are tempted [πειραζομένοις]." Many com-
mentators, therefore, interpret the use of the term in 4:15
in light of its use in 2:18 and conclude that both are a
reference to his suffering up to and including the cross.[15]

It is reasonable to conclude that Heb 4:15 speaks specifically
to the cross work of Christ.[16] In addition, Jesus—while fully
human—did not engage sin as we do. He was the Son of God in
human form; he was indwelt by the Spirit (more on this below).
He was "without sin." Even as the text affirms that Christ is
like us, it simultaneously reminds us that he is unlike us. This
two-sided portrait of Christ is not unintelligible or illogical; to
the contrary, it reminds us of the uniqueness of the man Christ
Jesus. Again, we mean here not that Jesus is superhuman (a
third thing), but that he is the true human. He is the antitype,
the ideal, the perfect one.[17] He approaches sin in a holistically
holy way without a hint of impurity, without any sampling of
unrighteousness. He feels the full force of temptation but resists
it entirely. If we struggle to comprehend how this can be true, it
is because we cannot imagine a being so holy as Christ.[18]

---

[15] Denny Burk, "Is Homosexual Orientation Sinful?" *Journal of the Evangelical Theological Society* 58, no. 1 (March 2015): 103.

[16] See Ellingworth, *Hebrews*, 268–69 (see chap. 8, n. 37).

[17] See Wellum, *God the Son Incarnate*, 321–23 (see chap. 6, n. 16). The logic of the incarnation itself matters greatly on this point. The divine Son of God assumes a human nature, not the other way around.

[18] "The man who yields to a particular temptation has not yet felt its full power. He has given in while the temptation has yet something

Here we must connect the ontology and function of Christ.[19] Because Christ is spotless, he can accomplish a spotless atonement—a full atonement for sin, in other words—and he can render his people spotless.[20] The accent in the Scripture is not on the ethical murkiness of the life or character of the Son of God; the accent in the Scripture is on his purity, holiness, and heavenliness. It is true that Christ "became sin" for us in his substitutionary death on the cross, but we note with care Berkhof's analysis of the identity of Christ: "While Christ was made to be sin judicially, yet ethically He was free from both hereditary depravity and actual sin."[21] Christ never transgressed against God. If he had, he could not have cleansed guilty sinners. Clearly, if we do not put Christological ontology and function together with

---

in reserve. Only the man who does not yield to a temptation, who, as regards that particular temptation, is sinless, knows the full extent of that temptation." Leon Morris, *The Lord from Heaven: A Study of the New Testament Teaching on the Deity and Humanity of Jesus Christ* (Grand Rapids: Eerdmans, 1958), 51–52, quoted in Erickson, *Christian Theology*, 737 (see chap. 1, n. 28). My thanks to Burk for this citation.

[19] I am thankful to Midwestern Seminary PhD student Ronni Kurtz for suggesting this terminology. See Ronni Kurtz, "The Soteriological Significance of B. B. Warfield's Doctrine of Hypostatic Union: An Exploration in His Redemptive Polemics," PhD paper, Midwestern Baptist Theological Seminary, accessible at http://www.academia.edu/37243000/The_Soteriological_Significance_of_B.B._Warfields_Doctrine_of_Hypostatic_Union_An_Exploration_in_His_Redemptive_Polemics.

[20] To connect these threads, consult Num 19:2; Heb 9:14; 1 Pet 1:19; Rev 19:8.

[21] Berkhof, *Systematic Theology*, 318 (see chap. 2, n. 46).

great precision, we will construct our conceptions of Christ on faulty grounds, and tweak the work of Christ as well.

The entailment of the above claim is the impeccability of Christ.[22] Wayne Grudem rightly stresses the unique ontology of Christ in arguing for impeccability: "The union of his human and divine natures in one person prevented it," that is, foreclosed the possibility of sin in the person of Christ.[23] This is right, for Jesus was and is the true human.[24] This is the emphasis of the New Testament in its portrayal of Christ, and in the Old Testament in its expectation of the Messiah. Jesus was not merely like Adam in his pre-fall state. Jesus is the greater Adam, the one Adam foreshadowed but could not be. It was impossible for Adam to meet the standard of Jesus. Adam was able to sin, though in no way forced to do so. Even if Adam had not sinned against the Lord, the Father would still have sent the Son as the perfect image of humanity. This does not mean that Adam had to sin; Adam was appointed the first son of God, and Christ was appointed the second and greater son of God.

[22] See Augustine on impeccability: "God forbid that we should ever say that He is able to sin!" "A Treatise on Nature and Grace," in *Nicene and Post-Nicene Fathers*, ed. Philip Schaff, vol. 5, *St. Augustine: Anti-Pelagian Writings*, (Cosimo, 2007), 147. See Burk, "Is Homosexual Orientation Sinful?" 104–5.

[23] Wayne Grudem, *Systematic Theology: An Introduction to Biblical Doctrine* (Grand Rapids: Zondervan, 1994), 539.

[24] For sound reflections on the supposed fallenness of Christ, see Wellum, *God the Son Incarnate*, 232–34 (see chap. 6, n. 16).

The Spirit's Ministry in the Ministry of Christ

Our understanding of Christ as the true man, the one who reenchants our humanity, has yet another dimension. Jesus was not self-sufficiently holy. He had all the theistic resources necessary for total obedience in his person, but if we are to do justice to the Old and New Testaments we cannot miss the Spirit's presence in numerous aspects of Christ's life and mission.[25] So far from a disconnected, lone-ranger Christology, the Bible portrays Christ as the Spirit-empowered Messiah.[26]

Before the incarnation of the Son of God, the prophecy of Isaiah told of the Messiah who would live out his days under the unique power and influence of the Holy Spirit. One day, a shoot would arise from Jesse's stump. The line that slumbered and even seemed to have ended altogether would suddenly awaken. This righteous branch would "bear fruit" that honored the Lord (Isa 11:1). God would uniquely favor this figure: "The Spirit of the Lord will rest on him— / a Spirit of wisdom and understanding, / a Spirit of counsel and strength, / a Spirit of knowledge and of

[25] For a rich and persuasive accounting of this undersourced aspect of Christ's life, see Bruce Ware, *The Man Christ Jesus: Theological Reflections on the Humanity of Christ* (Wheaton, IL: Crossway, 2013), 34.

[26] This view, I believe, does justice to the Trinitarian concept of *inseparable operations*. The three persons work together—inseparably—to carry out the work of God. See Stephen R. Holmes, "Trinitarian Action and Inseparable Operations: Some Historical and Dogmatic Reflections" in *Advancing Trinitarian Theology: Explorations in Constructive Dogmatics*, Los Angeles Theology Conference Series (Grand Rapids: Zondervan, 2014), 60–74.

the fear of the LORD" (2). So too would the Lord empower this figure: "This is my servant; I strengthen him, / this is my chosen one; I delight in him. I have put my Spirit on him; / he will bring justice to the nations" (Isa 42:1).

We have two major options with such testimony. We may view the Spirit's unique blessing on this divine deliverer as symbolic, or we may see it as speaking to the actual dynamic assistance provided by the Spirit to Christ. Isaiah's testimony, taken literally, funds most fully the second of these options. The Spirit, Isaiah prophesied, would play a unique role in this unique servant's ministry. The Spirit would "rest on" the Messiah and give untold blessings to him, just as the Spirit did for the first David. The greater David would gain from the Spirit special strength, wisdom, and obedience.[27] This figure would make good on the gifts of the Spirit and not lose his Davidic kingship. He would bring the line of David to unseen heights.

The Spirit certainly made good on these promises. In Matthew's account, Jesus directly fulfilled Isaiah's words when he warned the people not to publicize his miraculous healings (Matt 12:15–21). Matthew thus identified Jesus as the one who enfleshed the Isaianic promise that the Father would put the Spirit upon his holy servant. He healed and delivered and taught because he was the one highly favored by the Lord. The Spirit worked through him. He did not come to make himself great, but to give hope to hopeless people. He did so as the Spirit-indwelt

---

[27] For the connection between the first and the second David, see Motyer, *The Prophecy of Isaiah*, 122–23 (see chap. 3, n. 53).

one. Leon Morris says it well: "The Spirit is given in some measure to all who serve God, but clearly here it is envisaged that the servant will have a special endowment."[28]

Indeed, the Son intimated that it was the Spirit of God who enabled him to "cast out demons" (Matt 12:28 ESV). So, the disciples saw and knew that the kingdom of God had landed in the world of men. The Son accomplished the will of the Father by the power of the Spirit. In this power, Christ bound the strong man, plundering Satan's household through his work that climaxes in his death on the cross (Matt 12:29; Mark 3:27). Christ so honored the Spirit and so ascribed force and agency to him that he cited blasphemy against the Spirit as the one unforgivable sin (Matt 12:31). The one who dishonored the Spirit dishonored the very power of God in the life and deeds of Christ. To deny that Christ ruled the spiritual realm was to deny that the Spirit lives and moves and exerts power over the devil and his demons. This Jesus could not tolerate or forgive.

The same Spirit moves through the diverse accounts of Christ's life and ministry. In Luke's Gospel, the Spirit gave conception to Mary, overshadowing her (Luke 1:35). The Spirit thus made possible the unique conception of the God-man, signaling that God's favor was upon this child. The Spirit led the Son into the wilderness, where Satan tempted him (Matt 4:1). In John's Gospel, the Spirit descended upon the Son according to the testimony of John the Baptist. The Spirit did not only visit the Son, but "remained on him" (John 1:32 ESV). So it was the

---

[28] Morris, *Matthew*, 310 (see chap. 1, n. 26).

Spirit-empowered Messiah would baptize Spirit-borne disciples (1:33). We should mark this carefully: the Spirit did not come and go according to the Fourth Gospel. The Spirit came and remained on Christ. The actions of the Son of God in obedience to the Father transpired by the empowerment of the Spirit.[29]

Luke makes further connection between the Spirit and Christ. In Luke 4:16–21, Jesus went to his hometown synagogue on the Sabbath, where he applied Isa 61:1 to himself:

The Spirit of the Lord is on me,
because he has anointed me
to preach good news to the poor.
He has sent me
to proclaim release to the captives
and recovery of sight to the blind,
to set free the oppressed,
to proclaim the year of the Lord's favor. (Luke 4:18–19)

---

[29] This statement does not indicate that Christ divested himself of his deity during his incarnation. He surely did not. Christ ruled the cosmos even as a baby (so we affirm the *extracalvinisticum*, as one example.) It is true, however, that the incarnation of the Son of God entailed the assumption of human limitation and mortality. Jesus became tired; his body felt pain; he needed food. We thus do well to affirm that the Son of God exercised the prerogatives of his deity during his incarnation while living fully as a man, a limited being, during his earthly sojourn. For a profitable discussion of different views on Christ's exercise of divine attributes (and the strength of krypsis Christology), see Oliver Crisp, *Divinity and Humanity*, Current Issues in Theology (New York: Cambridge Univ. Press, 2007), 149–53.

After this audacious choice of text, Jesus sat back down, all eyes on him. He then explained why he read this portion of Isaiah's scroll: "Today as you listen, this Scripture has been fulfilled" (4:20–21). This was the public debut of Jesus as the Messiah. He identified himself as the one Isaiah foresaw preaching "good news." He portrayed himself as the one who would release the captives, give sight to the blind, and free the oppressed. The year of the Lord's favor has come because Jesus, the boy from Nazareth, enjoyed the Spirit's anointing. The Anointed One had been sent with the Spirit "on" him so that he might do the works of God.[30]

Other voices beyond the Gospel authors teach us this same wondrous truth. The apostle Peter preaches that the Spirit blessed Christ in unpredented fashion: "You know the events that took place throughout all Judea, beginning from Galilee after the baptism that John preached: how God anointed Jesus of Nazareth with the Holy Spirit and with power, and how he went about doing good and healing all who were under the tyranny of the devil, because God was with him" (Acts 10:37–38). The Father anointed the Son with the Spirit in Peter's telling.

---

[30] "This anointing refers to Luke 3:22 (cf. Acts 10:38) and the divine commissioning for Jesus' ministry. This anointing was not just a prophetic anointing (Luke 4:24) but a messianic one as well (3:22; Acts 4:26–27; 10:38), for Jesus is the bringer, not just the herald, of salvation. Although only Jesus was said by Luke to have been anointed by the Spirit (cf. Acts 4:26; 10:38), he serves here as a model for Spirit-filled teachers and healers in Acts." Robert H. Stein, *Luke*, The New American Commentary, vol. 24 (Nashville: B&H, 1992), 156.

As a result, the Son overcame the evil rule of the devil. God the Holy Spirit was with Jesus. The picture Peter creates of Christ was of a powerful, effectual, able savior. The true king triumphed over the false one, enacting his powerful will wherever he chose. There never was a time in his ministry when Jesus did not have divine power; there never in his ministry was a time when Jesus did not have the Spirit's anointing.

The Spirit empowered Christ not only to do marvelous deeds, but to die. Hebrews reveals that Christ "offered himself" as a holy sacrifice to God on behalf of sinners, and did so "through the eternal Spirit" (Heb 9:14). The Son did not go to Calvary without the Spirit; he gave himself as a ransom for the wicked in the Spirit's power. In the same way, the Spirit raised Jesus to life after his crucifixion, showing us once more just how intertwined the work of the Son and the Spirit are. The Spirit who "raised Jesus from the dead," Paul noted, will also bring our "mortal bodies to life" through the third person of the Trinity (Rom 8:11). Indeed, the Spirit of God "lives in" us as the people saved by Christ (1 Cor 3:16). Our bodies "are God's temple," just as Christ himself was filled with the Spirit.

The Spirit-empowered Messiah overcame every temptation.[31] He fulfilled, in totality and entirety, the will of God in his

---

[31] We should not understand Christ's victory over evil as a privation in his existence but should see it as a signal glory of the Son of Christ. It is in the simplest but most profound terms the implication of his holy identity. Along these lines, Bavinck argues that Christ's "inability to sin (*non posse peccare*) was not a matter of coercion but ethical in nature and therefore had to be manifested in an ethical manner." Bavinck, *Sin and*

life, death, resurrection, and ascension. He never sinned; he only pleased his Father; he resisted the temptations of the devil. Jesus thus shows us what we may be by divine grace. Yet Jesus was not a lonesome dove; the dove descended on him and remained. He did not come to earth to deal death to darkness as a lone ranger. He came to earth and ministered and lived all his days as the One uniquely blessed by the Spirit. He shows us how we may live, obey God, and make it all the way to glory despite many trials and conflicts in our pilgrimages. The fact that the Spirit blessed Jesus and now dwells with us maximizes our hope, confidence, and delight in the power of God that is at work in us. The same one who blessed and empowered our Lord now blesses and empowers us.[32]

None of the preceding in any way works against the fact that Jesus was truly divine every second he lived in his incarnation. The New Testament teaches us that Jesus had access to his heavenly abilities throughout his life, and that he used these abilities at different points in his ministry.[33] We should not read the Spirit as subbing in for the divine nature of Christ, as if the God-man effectively removed his divinity from himself and grafted on the

---

Salvation in Christ, 314 (see chap. 6, n. 22). This helps us understand the connection between the ontology and function (life) of Christ.

[32] Jesus also gave commands to the apostles "through the Holy Spirit," a reference we likely understand as the handing down of the Great Commission. See Acts 1:1–2. This means "the risen Christ continues to have the Spirit upon him," a remarkable matter to consider. See Ware, *The Man Christ Jesus*, 42–43. The Son and Spirit are linked in ways the church has not always appreciated.

[33] See Bruce A. Ware, "The Man Christ Jesus," *Journal of the Evangelical Theological Society* 53, no. 1 (March 2010), 5–18.

Spirit in his human life. This did not occur. But in a way that expands our appreciation of both Jesus and the Holy Spirit, Jesus walked in fellowship with the third person of the Trinity. He drew power and strength from the Spirit. He preached in the Spirit. He obeyed the Father by the Spirit. Because of union with Jesus through the Spirit, so may we.

Jesus the Second Adam and the True Image

The biblical story begins with a covenantal head, Adam, and terminates with the greater Adam, Jesus Christ. In the scriptural framework, humanity has in Adam both a starting point and a figure of perfect fulfillment of God's original design. In 1 Corinthians 15, the apostle Paul traces this intertextual connection in his discussion of the resurrection:

> So it is with the resurrection of the dead: Sown in corruption, raised in incorruption; sown in dishonor, raised in glory; sown in weakness, raised in power; sown a natural body, raised a spiritual body. If there is a natural body, there is also a spiritual body. So it is written, The first man Adam became a living being; the last Adam became a life-giving spirit. However, the spiritual is not first, but the natural, then the spiritual. (1 Cor 15:42–46)

We take note of this passage for several reasons. First, Paul treats the first Adam as a historical figure. The text makes most sense when we treat the first man as Adam, for this initial figure enjoyed "natural" existence before any other. Adam does not here refer to a generic representative of the human race, but to the man made first by God in Eden, the husband of Eve, the first woman. We make this link because the text does, recognizing the first man as Adam. Second, this figure, bearing the name Adam, "was from the earth" and created from "dust" (15:47).[34] This man's "image" we have borne (15:49). Like our father Adam, we return to the dust, dying in hamartiological solidarity with him (15:48). Adam's destiny is our own.

The good news for all who trust Christ is this: we may claim the destiny of the second Adam. Both of these figures explain the nature of the human race. The story of the first Adam shows us why we die, sin, and experience all the sad effects of "corruption" (15:42). The story of the second Adam explains how we may rise from the dust and inherit a "spiritual body" that cannot suffer decrepitude (15:44). We love the dust as the children of the first Adam, but humanity does not meet its rightful end in the dust. Humanity may climb the skies to live forever with God by trusting in the second Adam. Born image-bearers in Adam's likeness, we bear the image of "the man of heaven" through faith in Christ (15:49). He is the one whose birth charts "a new beginning in the life of humankind," as Henri Blocher comments.[35] We are members of a new humanity. We were like Adam, but by the

---

[34] See Gordon D. Fee, *The First Epistle to the Corinthians*, The New International Commentary on the New Testament (Grand Rapids: Eerdmans, 1987), 791–92.

[35] Cf. Blocher, *Original Sin*, 132 (see chap. 2, n. 13).

grace of God, the Spirit is remaking us in the image of Christ (15:49). It is not that Adam was a false image; he represented the person of God in the earth, and we do too. To see a human being is to see a living picture of a transcendent Creator. But Adam fell away. To see God's true son, we must receive the second Adam, the Messiah who effectively forms a new humanity by his blood.

The apostle Paul straightforwardly identifies Christ as "the image of God" (2 Cor 4:4).[36] We do not look to Adam for healing, hope, and salvation. We look to Adam to see God's original intentions for his creation.[37] We see in Adam the compulsion that still resides in humanity after the fall—the instincts to procreate, take dominion of the earth, and rule. Though these instincts surely misfire in sinful mankind, we yet see the glory of God in the purposefulness of the human race. Surely, we fell away from God through Adam; but we did not lose our spiritual capacities, our brains were not emptied of all thinking ability, and we have not stopped (as a collective race) filling the earth

---

[36] This is "the opening phrase of a christological hymn." Victor Paul Furnish, *II Corinthians: A New Translation with Introduction and Commentary*, The Anchor Bible, vol. 32A (New York: Doubleday, 1964), 222.

[37] Murray Harris contends that the use of "image language" speaks to both representation and divine expression: "Given passages such as Phil. 2:6; Col. 1:19; 2:9, we may safely assume that for Paul εἰκών here, as in Col. 1:15, signifies that Christ is an exact representation *(Ebenbild)* as well as a visible expression of God. ἐστιν is a timeless present, indicating that Christ is eternally the perfect reflection of God or at least that in his glorified corporeality Christ remains forever God's visible expression." Harris, *The Second Epistle to the Corinthians*, 331 (see chap. 1, n. 43).

with offspring. Though we may not consciously glorify the Lord in our unbelieving state, we still give some measure of honor to the Creator by our human existence. Mankind made in the image of God is distinct from all the created order by virtue of this ontological identity. This does not change following the fall; we are fully human and nothing can alter that fact, try as we do to thwart the design of God.

Adam shows us a crucial part of who we are, but to know what God would have us be we cannot look to Adam. We must look to Christ. Like Adam, he had no sin nature, but he also had no capacity to fall away from the Lord. His humanity is the perfect kind; Jesus is the second Adam, the greater Adam. It is not merely possible that he will honor the Lord; the divine Son of God became a man in order to rout the devil and restore God's honor (1 John 3:8). Like Adam, he faced a major temptation from Satan, hearing the very words of the serpentine one, but he overcame the enemy and trusted the word of the Lord. Like Adam, Jesus had a mission of obedience from God that he fulfilled in the Spirit's power.[38] Adam brought us down, back to the ground from which he came; Jesus lifts us up through his obedient life and death.[39] Made for communion, breathed into

---

[38] Cortez elegantly links Christ, the Spirit, and the fulfillment of the *imago Dei*: "in Jesus we see that being human fundamentally involves manifesting God's own glorious presence through the indwelling power of the Spirit." Cortez, *ReSourcing Theological Anthropology*, 115.

[39] Brandon Crowe argues that the obedience of Christ is of vital importance in his salvific mission: "Jesus is portrayed in the Gospels as the last Adam whose obedience is necessary for God's people to

by God himself, Adam chose to trust the antiwisdom of the anti-god. Jesus restores spiritual communion with God by vivifying us spiritually, awakening our souls to worship the Lord.

Adam was the firstborn in physical terms. Scripture never devalues Adam; his is a tragic tale, but the Lord did not obliterate Adam even after he fell away. The firstborn mattered, and he still stood as the head of the human race. But the entirety of the biblical narrative swayed and groaned and labored under the long-delayed hope of a greater Adam, a faithful son who would perfectly honor his Father. So it was that Christ came. Adam was the firstborn in a physical sense; Christ, Paul teaches us, is the firstborn in a spiritual sense (Col 1:15). He "is the image of the invisible God, / the firstborn over all creation," the one who rules over the world as God originally intended.

Paul is not teaching that Jesus was made by the Father.[40] He has no beginning date, just as he has no expiration date.[41] Jesus is

---

experience the blessings of salvation." Crowe, *The Last Adam*, 2 (see chap. 1, n. 42). Crowe reminds us of the need to connect the ontology of the *imago Dei* (and especially the true image) with the resulting function, worshipful obedience.

[40] The affirmation of eternal generation in no way signifies the "making" of Jesus. See Fred Sanders and Scott R. Swain, eds., *Retrieving Eternal Generation* (Grand Rapids: Zondervan, 2017), 27–146.

[41] "Does **firstborn** imply that Jesus is merely the most supreme created being? Hardly! The main point is surely Jesus's function in bringing creation into being and his sovereignty over the entire created order. That authority encompasses the material and immaterial realms, the earthly and heavenly spheres, human and angelic creatures. Moreover, if Paul had wanted to suggest that Jesus was the first of God's creatures to be formed he would have used the adjective *prōtoktistos* ([πρωτόκιστός]

the crowned and reigning king of all that is, raised to the throne by the Father, resplendent during his obedient life through the power of the Spirit. Adam was made to inhabit a living throne, but he crashed back into the dust. Jesus came to earth as the second Adam, and he inaugurated a kingship in his ministry—his kingly power enacted once and for all time in his death on the ironic throne of the cross—that none can overcome.[42]

These resplendent theological truths speak to the core desires of the human heart. We crave a figure who will rule justly and rightly. Jesus alone fits this bill. Jesus alone has the power to overcome evil and build a lasting kingdom. We must trace and track every facet of his life and ministry, seeing in his teaching and his miracles the obvious signs of his deity as well as the tangible enfleshment of his rule. Adam was made to rule, but subjected himself to the anti-rule of the anti-ruler. We all live under the natural sway of Satan as a result. But Jesus comes to enact a new rule, the rule of the kingdom of God, the very embodiment of heavenly righteousness on the earth (Mark 1:15).

This rule requires the overcoming of darkness by Christ and the instantiation of godliness in Christ and his people. The kingdom, after all, is "in our midst" (Luke 17:21).[43] We cannot physi-

---

'created first') or the noun *prōtoplastos* ([πρωτόπλαστος] 'first made')." Michael F. Bird, *Colossians and Philemon*, New Covenant Commentary Series (Cambridge: Lutterworth, 2009), 53.

[42] See Treat, *The Crucified King*, 47–49 (see chap. 5, n. 28).

[43] Not only is the message of the kingdom here, but the very kingdom itself. See I. Howard Marshall, *Luke: Historian and Theologian*, New Testament Profiles (Downers Grove, IL: InterVarsity, 1998), 130–31.

cally claim a portion of the earth for the kingdom of Christ, but we may in ourselves become the living display of the kingship of the Son.[44] Whenever we trust in Christ, we bow to the rule of God and act to advance this heavenly kingdom wherever we go and whatever we do. Through the Spirit, we ourselves overcome darkness and instantiate godliness by growing in Christlikeness. He is our goal, and we behold his glory and are changed from degree to degree into his representation.

We may easily err when "kingdom building." We do not add anything to the kingdom; we cannot transform the earth—through environmental stewardship or more equable communities or more virtuous political policies—into a lasting outpost of the kingdom. The kingdom, frankly, is not primarily about us or the transformation of our surroundings. The kingdom centers in the king, Christ Jesus. His kingly rule advances through the kind conquering of gospel grace in the human heart. We do not build a lasting city here, but we await the day when we will enter the New Jerusalem (Heb 13:14). Our focus on kingdom work as believers, then, is the making of disciples (Matt 28:16–20). This is the heart of the Great Commission. This does not render

---

[44] The Christian faith is strikingly *personal*. This does not deny the concept of nature, but it does remind that the holy Godhead is made up of three *persons*. God in the biblical account is a personal God. For an engaging discussion of the person vs. nature debate, cf. Marc Cortez, "Personal Being: John Zizioulas and the Christological Grounding of Human Personhood" in *Christological Anthropology in Historical Perspective*, 163–89 (see chap. 1, n. 36).

culture and society unimportant, but drives the church to never flag in its expressly spiritual mission.[45]

Jesus, the second Adam, the greater image, shows us the *telos* (τέλος) of our humanity. We are being remade now in the image of the true man.[46] We find freedom in God, not in sin. We live truly when we worship the Lord, not when we worship the creation and ourselves. We flourish when we obey and submit to our Maker and Redeemer, not when we rebel against any constituted authority. We all in some way seek a king, but there is only one worth following. Jesus is a king unlike any other, for he rules by grace and his subjects dwell with him in a world of love. The kingdom of God, contrary the way the world looks and thinks, is not far off. It is among us and in us, and none can stop its advance.

Union with Christ as the Great Blessing of the Christian

The true man, Jesus Christ, has not come simply to be adored from afar by his people. The true man has drawn near to us. By his death and resurrection, Christ has made possible our full union

---

[45] This spiritual mission will always have "physical" and tangible effects in the immediate environment of the believer and the corporate body, the church. See Carl F. H. Henry, *The Uneasy Conscience of Modern Fundamentalism* (Grand Rapids: Eerdmans, 1947).

[46] Although we were made in God's image, our renewal by Christ is so propulsive that it will result in us (and not only Christ) being the image of God. See Kilner, *Dignity and Destiny*, 273 (see chap. 1, n. 12).

with him.[47] In his Upper Room discourse, Christ expounds this revolutionary relationship:

> I am the true vine, and my Father is the gardener. Every branch in me that does not produce fruit he removes, and he prunes every branch that produces fruit so that it will produce more fruit. You are already clean because of the word I have spoken to you. Remain in me, and I in you. Just as a branch is unable to produce fruit by itself unless it remains on the vine, neither can you unless you remain in me. I am the vine; you are the branches. The one who remains in me and I in him produces much fruit, because you can do nothing without me. (John 15:1–5)

The believer has a vital, living, relationship with Jesus Christ. Christianity is centered in Christ, or it is nothing. Christians are centered in Christ, deriving spiritual life directly from him, or they are not his. Those who know Jesus produce the "fruit" of holiness because they have trusted the word spoken to them by God. Faith is not a mystical meshing with the universe, a blind leap into a spiritualized sea; faith is a full-hearted trusting of the

---

[47] "The truth is that John is speaking of the union of believers with Christ, apart from whom they can do nothing. This union, originating in his initiative and sealed by his death on their behalf, is completed by the believers' responsive love and obedience, and is the essence of Christianity." C. K. Barrett, *The Gospel according to St. John: An Introduction with Commentary and Notes on the Greek Text*, 2nd ed. (Philadelphia: Westminster, 1978), 470.

promises of God made and realized in Christ. Faith, the gift of God, has Christ as its object and salvation as its hope.

Faith unites us with Jesus Christ. We remain in him. No believer will fall away from the Lord, but as in so many cases in the New Testament, Jesus calls the called to never assume their growth in godliness, their perseverance in the faith. Instead, the believer—anchored by the grace of God—must take care to "remain" in Christ and thereby yield "much fruit." Union with Christ involves a walk with Christ, a daily spiritual communion with him, that results in a banquet table filled with holy provisions. Jesus is the Savior who grants his followers access to him and living union with him. In terms that stretch the boundaries of our minds, we Christians live "in him."[48] Once we were "in Adam," belonging to the realm of death. Now we "reign in life through the one man, Jesus Christ," as the apostle Paul notes (Rom 5:17). He is ours; we are his.

Life, spiritual life, flows to us through our iron-clad union with Christ. Once we were creatures of darkness. We loved the shadows. We denied the glory of God and the over-spilling splendor of Jesus Christ. Even if we counted ourselves religious or spiritual, in our lostness we did not know Christ, we did not receive his teaching as the truth, and thus we did not honor him

---

[48] "To 'remain' in Jesus has a deeper significance than simply to continue to believe in him, although it includes that; it connotes continuing to live in association or in union with him." George R. Beasley-Murray, *John*, Word Biblical Commentary, vol. 36 (Nashville: Thomas Nelson, 1999), 272.

as he deserved. He was not our passion, and we did not recognize him as the alpha and the omega of all things. But now, through the visitation of divine mercy, we love Christ. He is our surpassing treasure. He has brought us into the family and the household of God. We were death-filled people in our past, and like the natural man, we thought we had joy in the dust. But now, in Christ, united to him, we love life. We breathe deeply and drink insatiably from the wells of living water. God breathed once into Adam and made him a living being; God has breathed his Spirit into us, regenerating us through conversion, and we have become living beings in Christ.

Humanity yearns for this kind of connection; we all want what only union with Christ affords. We speak today, for example, of *inclusion* and *unity*. But doctrine, the teaching of God's Word, is the only pathway to meaningful unity. Christ is the only figure who can unite the disaffected. Christ alone joins once-hostile people in organic, even mystical, union. Union with Christ is not formless and gauzy, but neither does it fail to be robustly spiritual. It is a wonder. Through faith and repentance, we are Christ's own body. He loves us. He will not abandon us. He shed his blood and consented to the breaking of his body, and he gave up his spirit for us.[49]

---

[49] On the importance of this doctrine for ministry, see J. Todd Billings, *Union with Christ: Reframing Theology and Ministry for the Church* (Grand Rapids: Baker Academic, 2011).

Conclusion: The Doctrine of Christ as the Solution to Disenchanted Humanity

What a race humanity is. What a story the Bible charts. Made by God an enchanted being, humanity chose to grovel in the ground beside the serpent. Yet in God's kindness, Adam's children may rise again. The Lord is not in the business of merely engaging humanity, as if he wishes to offer us a slightly better mode of existence. The Father has initiated the project of anthropological reenchantment, making us a new humanity in Christ through the power of the Spirit. In Adam we are fully human, but we are not truly human. In Christ we become truly human, for we are remade in the image of the true man.[50]

In order to understand humanity, we must grasp afresh the different theological dimensions of the doctrine of mankind. These dimensions, as the book has argued, are nine in number. They together shape and make up part of a properly biblical anthropology and Christological anthropology (which is in truth what this book offers).

First, the Scripture teaches an *ontological anthropology* (1). That is, humanity is given substance and meaning by God. Anthropology should not be understood primarily in psychological or emotional

---

[50] Cortez nicely distinguishes between the concepts of "full humanity" and "true humanity," both of which factor into a faithful biblical anthropology. In terms of Jesus, "Not only does he *become* truly human, but he exemplifies humanity in such a way that Paul calls his readers to contemplate and emulate what they see." Cortez, *ReSourcing Theological Anthropology*, 170.

terms, but in personal terms. God has made the human race in his image and established the nature of man as spiritual, ordered around and toward him. But here we must lay hold of *hamartiological anthropology* (2). The human race is not unblemished and untarnished. To understand humanity, we must understand our depraved natures as the result of Adam's historical fall. We have gone awry and died in Adam. Despite this truth, we nonetheless claim a *vocational anthropology* (3). Mankind has something to do—namely, work. Though traditional anthropology may omit coverage of this theme, seeing it as an outgrowth of ethics, a biblical theology of the human person necessitates that we understand in God-centered perspective the labor given us by God for his glory.

The human person is given the gift of *sexual anthropology* (4). We are not solely or even fundamentally sexual beings, but we have sexual capacities, and pleasure and fulfillment of this kind was given to us by God. Sadly, we rarely more exercise our ability to worship than in the realm of sexuality, finding in fallen sexual practices (neopaganism, to speak most currently) not only happiness but identity. The gospel redirects our sexual instincts Godward, disciplining and ordering them. Though diversity is another gift of God, we eschew a theologically *unitive anthropology* for a divided one (5). We see race and ethnicity—however precisely we construe these concepts—as problematic rather than doxological. Despite our sinful tendencies, the Lord is building one new man in Christ even now.

Our technologically saturated cultures urge us to deny a *creaturely anthropology* (6), but the church holds to it nonetheless. We use our powers of invention and creativity for the honor of

God, but we must resist technological delusions and the false visions of humanity they spawn. The Bible teaches us an *ethical anthropology* (7), enabling us to understand our consciences and our inherent thirsts for justice. Justice, we learn in the Old and New Testaments, is not a problem for the Christian, but a blessing given by God that makes us tremble for those who will face it. Instead of a self-immortalized vision of our humanity, the church happily confesses a *contingent anthropology* (8). Man is not the measure of all things; we are limited creatures, and we are both bound by time and sure to die. For this reason, we give unbounded praise to God that ours is a *teleological anthropology* (9). We as a redeemed people are headed somewhere; we know Christ now, and we will worship him as reenchanted beings for all of eternity.

This doctrine is a biblical anthropology. It stands in stark contrast to a secular or skeptical anthropology. It is a doctrine of man derived from and dependent upon the Word of God. We construct our doctrine unashamedly from the Scripture. The church is not playing from a weak position in promoting biblical doctrine; it is standing upon the solid ground of divine revelation. There is no surer surface on which to rest. Every other system of thought is built upon sand. This vision of anthropology is protological and eschatological. It begins with the first Adam, a real historical man made by God's own hand, and it comes to completion in the second Adam, who renews us in his own image. Adam is of immense importance to the biblical story and to our doctrine of man, but the heart of biblical anthropology is not Adam. Adam is the type, and Christ is the archetype.

Our doctrine of man is thus Christological and covenantal. We offer the world Christological anthropology, and the Christ we offer is the one whose blood is the blood of the new covenant, which once and for all time washes clean the chosen of God. Such a system must also be both pneumatological and paterological,[51] for we need the Spirit to take on the character of Christ, a pattern of holiness found in the life and ministry of Christ himself. The Spirit strengthens and empowers us even as the Spirit strengthened and empowered Christ. This pneumatological work gave great glory to the Father. The faithful obedience of the Son—in the power of the Spirit—to the will of the Father brought the great plan of salvation designed by the Father to completion (Eph 1:15–23). All this is one work of the Godhead; all this fulfills the great plan of redemption that involves fully all three members of the Trinity. So far from seeing anthropology as an isolated doctrine, dealing merely with the finer points of human existence, we see that sound anthropology is in truth inseparable from sound theology.[52] We

---

[51] On *pneumatology*, see Sinclair B. Ferguson, *The Holy Spirit*, Contours of Christian Theology (Downers Grove, IL: InterVarsity, 1996). On *paterology*, see Ryan L. Rippee, *That God May Be All in All: A Paterology Demonstrating That the Father Is the Initiator of All Divine Activity* (Eugene, OR: Pickwick, 2018).

[52] We remember with the use of terms such as *theology* that the God with whom we have to deal—the God who deals with us—is not an abstract standard of holiness but a personal God. For a fruitful discussion of the distinctions between the biblical God and less personal metaphysics, see Kevin J. Vanhoozer, "Theological Conceptualization (*Begriff*): Varieties of Theism and Pantheism," in *Remythologizing*

simply cannot understand humanity apart from God; we cannot understand the soteriological plan of God, the covenantal heart of the will of God, apart from God's choicest creation, mankind.

The doctrine of man, understood in proper theological perspective as one part of a greater whole, is enchanting. It is rigorously personal; it restores humanity to our God-given purpose and design, but more than this, it remakes us in the image of Christ, the true man. Once, through the evil ministrations of Satan and the eager cooperation of the sinful heart, we were disenchanted beings. We embraced our disenchantment. We loved the dust. We found delight, or thought we did, in sin. We took secularism or skepticism or man's wisdom for our philosophy and found ourselves enticed by the serpent's antiwisdom. We had no god, or at least we thought we had no god. In some form we worshipped the creation, and the lies of neopaganism crept into our surroundings and targeted our hearts and minds. We thought we were beasts when God had made us the crowns of his creation.

Now we have seen the God-man. We have found the one who brings light back into our eyes and hope back into our souls. We see through the Scripture that humanity is a being loaded with potential and promise and dignity and value. We find this in Adam, but we see it especially in Jesus Christ, the true human. Jesus Christ is the one who shows us our *telos*: to offer obedient

---

Theology: Divine Action, Passion, and Authorship, Cambridge Studies in Christian Doctrine (New York: Cambridge Univ. Press, 2010), 81–138.

worship to God. Truly, he is the new humanity, and he is leading a new exodus to the new heavens and new earth. He is the salvation and ontological restoration we so desperately need; his new covenant blood washes us clean, makes us new creations, and gives us new names.

This, and no other, is the reenchantment of our humanity.

ACKNOWLEDGMENTS

I am thankful for Willie Mackenzie, my editor at Christian Focus. My thanks go out to Jason Allen and Jason Duesing of Midwestern Baptist Theological Seminary, each of whom supported me considerably in this endeavor. The trustees of MBTS granted me a yearlong sabbatical which proved invaluable in the writing of this book. I am grateful for that. In addition, numerous faculty colleagues offered encouragement, wisdom, and friendship throughout the writing process.

The students of the Residency, PhD matriculants all, heard versions of this material and interacted helpfully with me over it. MBTS students Mike Brooks, Taylor DiRoberto, Ronni Kurtz, Sam Parkison, Phil Ort, and Austin Burgard offered assistance and research help to me in various ways. I wish to thank Erik Wolgemuth, my literary representative, for his friendship and partnership in this project.

I cannot fail to thank Rick Holland, my pastor at Mission Road Bible Church, for his role in my life. Sound preaching of the Word of God is a blessing almost unlike any other. The congregation of MRBC—led by faithful elders—provided great feedback after I presented material on anthropology to them. Few things more bolster a teacher of Scripture than churches that take joy in confessing the faith delivered to the saints without apology or fear.

My wife, Bethany, was a great help to me in every way as I wrote this book. I cannot imagine writing without her kind words, good counsel, and daily support. Thank you to Andrew and Donna Strachan, my father and mother, for all they did to nurture my faith and my mind; and to Rachel, for her sisterly love.

This book is dedicated to Bruce Ware, my father-in-law. He shaped me greatly during my time at Southern Seminary. His brilliant intellect married with his deep faith gave me the model of the God-centered theologian that I needed. Beyond my MDiv, I have learned much from Dr. Ware about being a husband, father, churchman, and man of God.

Above all, I am grateful to God, who has given us the greatest of gifts in his Son, and who is the rewarder of all who diligently seek him.

ALSO BY OWEN STRACHAN

With Gavin Peacock, *The Grand Design: Male and Female He Made Them* (Christian Focus, 2016).

Forthcoming with Gavin Peacock, a trilogy on biblical sexuality (Christian Focus, 2020):

What Does the Bible Teach About Lust? A Short Book on Desire

What Does the Bible Teach About Homosexuality? A Short Book on Biblical Sexuality

What Does the Bible Teach About Transgenderism? A Short Book on Personal Identity

NAME INDEX

Bente, F., 108
Bergen, Robert D., 292
Berger, Peter, 181
Bergler, Thomas E., 327
Berkhof, Louis, 80, 83, 87, 322, 358
Bethancourt, Phillip, 341
Beveridge, Henry, 12
Billings, J. Todd, 377
Bird, Michael F., 372
Blocher, Henri, 59, 61–62, 63, 235, 368
Blomberg, Craig, 115, 261
Blom, Philipp, 43, 266
Bock, Darrell L., 128, 351
Bolt, John, 251, 263, 270
Boswell, 185
Bovon, François, 354
Bowles, Nellie, 132
Boyd, Greg, 222
Bradley, Anthony, 217
Brand, Chad, 125
Brandt, Walther I., 160
Bratt, James D., 98
Bromiley, G. W., 27, 257
Broyles, Craig C., 121, 296
Bruce, F. F., 33, 103, 150, 234, 268
Bruckner, James K., 255
Burk, Denny, 179, 194, 357–58, 359
Bussey, O., 27
Butler, Trent C., 221, 222
Byrne, Rhonda, 46

Calvin, John, 12, 26, 68, 197, 307
Cameron, Andrew J. B., 74

Campbell, Constantine, 306
Cantarella, Eva, 191
Carpenter, Eugene, 120
Carpenter, Joel A., 266
Carson, D. A., 74, 198, 264, 308, 349
Cassuto, Umberto, 100
Castleberry, Grant, 198
Chafe, William H., 219
Chanski, Mark, 146
Ciampa, Roy E., 178, 206, 338, 344
Clines, David, 30
Cole, Graham A., 228, 230
Cole, Henry, 58
Colson, Chuck, 181
Conley, Dalton, 216
Copan, Paul, 222
Cortez, Marc, 29, 31, 356, 370, 373, 378
Craigie, Peter C., 173
Cranfield, C. E. B., 324
Crisp, Oliver, 363
Crouch, Andy, 281
Crowe, Brandon D., 33, 370–71
Cuilleanáin, Cormac Ó, 191
Culver, Robert Duncan, 80, 81

Danker, Frederick W., 218
Dau, W. H. T., 108
Davids, Peter H., 215
Davis, Dale Ralph, 291, 294
Dawkins, Richard, 52
DeJonge, Michael P., 59
Dempster, Stephen G., 298
Deresiewicz, William, 117

van Buren, Paul, 7
VanderLeest, Steven H., 259
VanDoodewaard, William, 14
Vanhoozer, Kevin J., 241, 337, 381
Van Til, Cornelius, 270
Vasholz, Robert I., 186–87
Veith, Gene Edward, Jr., 109
Vos, Geerhardus, 252, 302
Vriend, John, 35, 251, 263, 270

Walker, Andrew T., 180
Walker, Mark, 267
Wall, Robert W., 113, 157–58
Waltke, Bruce K., 300
Walton, John H., 22–23, 77, 119, 183, 186, 250
Ware, Bruce A., 32, 136, 261, 360, 366
Warfield, B. B., 57, 358
Waters, Guy Prentiss, 306

Wellum, Stephen J., 60, 77, 91, 123, 235, 236, 259, 304, 357, 359
Wenham, Gordon J., 15, 21, 76, 183, 185, 214, 223, 290, 304
Whitefield, George, 266
Williams, Jarvis, 234
Willimon, William H., 180
Wilson, A. N., 43
Wilson, Gerald H., 327
Wingren, Gustaf, 105
Winter, Bruce, 166
Wolfe, Tom, 117–18, 253
Wolterstorff, Nicholas, 19
Woolhouse, Roger, 168
Woudstra, Marten H., 221
Wright, N. T., 102
Wu, Frank H., 217

Zaspel, Fred G., 57
Zizioulas, John, 373
Zwingli, Ulrich, 261

SUBJECT INDEX

husbands, 62, 66, 75, 77, 135, 142,
148–53, 157–58, 160, 162,
165, 176, 180, 249, 290–91,
368, 386
identity, 3, 9, 29, 33, 44, 59–60,
135, 150, 156, 162–63, 167–
73, 175, 202, 215, 225, 231,
307, 309, 358, 370, 379
ideology, 144, 167, 168, 170–71,
182, 202, 258, 273, 276–78
idolatry, 92, 131, 181, 189, 204,
212, 246, 253, 256
image, 7, 13–14, 17, 25–35, 38, 41,
49, 53, 99, 114, 148–49, 164,
187, 201, 228, 245, 286, 359,
367–68, 374, 379–80, 382,
386
image-bearers, 5, 15, 20, 25–27,
30–32, 36, 80, 145, 218, 223,
265, 368
imago Dei, 4, 8, 13, 20–21, 28–31,
34, 36, 38, 42, 47, 49, 53, 170,
174, 177, 315, 352, 369–71
Jesus, 4–5, 23–24, 33–35, 38, 41,
60, 89, 109, 122–24, 127, 144,
152, 155–56, 163, 170, 180,
193, 198–99, 204, 226–27,
229, 231, 233–39, 242–43,
256–57, 259–60, 262–63,
267, 269, 304, 310, 312, 315,
334–35, 337–38, 340–41, 345,
347, 350–57, 359–67, 370–76,
382, 387
justice, 5, 44, 74, 93, 126, 147, 242,
285–87, 289–90, 293, 295–96,
299, 300–308, 311–12, 336,
348, 360–61, 380

justification, 36, 69, 74, 94, 102,
121, 204–5, 215, 217, 241,
258, 275, 300, 306
kindness, 128, 215, 220, 296, 317,
378
kingship, 268, 310, 361, 372–73
knowledge, 12–13, 25–26, 40,
56–57, 59, 62, 67, 94, 113, 149,
190, 267, 270, 329, 361
leadership, 61, 72, 78, 101, 135,
137, 139, 162, 226, 293, 332,
385
leisure, 125, 129–30, 336
life, 2–3, 11–12, 16, 18–19, 21–22,
27, 35, 37–38, 41, 46, 48, 63,
75–76, 80–81, 88, 90, 101,
104, 111, 113, 115–17, 121,
123–24, 130, 132–33, 135–36,
140–44, 148, 150–52, 155–56,
158, 160–61, 163, 165, 167,
173, 175, 200–201, 207, 214–
15, 220, 226, 241, 247, 254,
258, 260, 262, 267, 272–73,
276, 278, 282, 286, 290, 294,
300, 312–13, 321–22, 325,
327, 331–32, 337, 340–43,
348–55, 358, 360, 362, 365–
68, 370, 372, 375–76, 381,
386
lordship, 134, 268, 323
lust, 42, 44, 186, 188, 190, 192–93,
195, 197–99, 278
manhood, 132–33, 138–41, 148,
160–61, 164, 169, 175, 276
mankind, 4–6, 8–9, 13, 15–17,
19–20, 22, 27–30, 38, 41–43,
47, 49–50, 53–54, 57–59,

wholeness, 44, 168
wickedness, 68, 70, 74, 80, 86–87,
    92–93, 184, 191–92, 206, 221,
    223, 225, 261, 296–98, 300,
    303, 306, 308, 326, 365
wisdom, 20, 48, 51, 65–67, 73,
    82, 90–91, 132, 142, 171, 180,
    229, 255, 322, 327–28, 331,
    350, 352–54, 360–61, 382
womanhood, 132, 138, 141, 144,
    148, 160, 169, 175
womb, 198, 282, 294, 296, 350
wonder, 6, 13, 19, 21, 53, 91, 110,
    118, 155, 189, 247, 249, 329,
    336, 352, 377
work, 1–2, 4, 6–7, 13–14, 17, 20,
    23, 25, 27, 31–32, 36, 47, 86,
    93, 95–104, 106–9, 111–12,
    114–20, 123–26, 130, 133–34,
    138, 142, 152, 155, 157–59,
    163–64, 176, 192, 195–97,

211, 213, 231, 235–43, 247–
    48, 251–52, 255, 259–60, 265,
    269, 277, 282, 287–88, 297,
    300–301, 308–9, 312, 316,
    328, 330–31, 335, 341–42,
    352–53, 357, 359, 361–62,
    364–66, 373, 379, 381
workaholism, 97, 130
work-life, 116
worship, 32, 34–42, 44, 47, 49,
    96–97, 100, 104, 112, 120,
    124, 176, 186–87, 189–90,
    192, 199, 201, 203, 208,
    212–13, 222–24, 230, 234,
    244, 252, 256, 278, 286, 300,
    310–11, 328–29, 352, 371,
    374, 379–80, 382–83
worth, 2, 47, 50, 53, 94, 127, 208,
    243, 248, 253, 310, 349, 374
wounds, 72, 240, 291–92, 333
youth, 188, 229, 282, 327

SCRIPTURE INDEX

3:12 *72*
3:13 *73*
3:14–19 *76*
3:15 *76, 222, 340, 349*
3:16 *77, 138, 288*
3:17 *78*
3:17–19 *138*
3:19 *21, 78, 338*
3:21 *71, 249*
4 *287*
4:1 *183*
4:7 *138*
4:8–12 *288*
4:13 *290*
4:17 *250*
5:1–2 *30*
5:9 *30*
6–14 *104*
7 *302*
9 *18*
9:31 *18*
11 *214, 250*
11:1–4 *250*
11:1–9 *212*
11:5 *251*
11:7 *251*
11:7–8 *254*
15:6 *303*
18 *183*
18:25 *307*
19 *185*
19:1 *183*
19:4–9 *183*
19:8 *183*
41:55 *289*
50:20 *335*

Exodus

5:5 *118, 120*
12:7 *261*
12:13 *261*
12:22–23 *261*
12:26 *160*
14:10 *289*
14:21–31 *302*
15:3 *140*
17 *222*
18:4 *135*
19–40 *120*
20:8–10 *119*
20:11 *14*
21:10 *141*
22:22 *289*
22:23 *289*
22:26 *289*
22:27 *289*
31 *255*
31:3–5 *255*
31:6–11 *255*
32:4 *256*
36:6 *331*

Leviticus

16 *85*
16:15–22 *303*
18:20–25 *185*
18:22 *92, 173, 184–86*
18:23 *186*
18:26 *185*
18:27 *185*
18:29 *185*
18:30 *185*
19:33–34 *215*
20:13 *173, 184–85*

25:8–12 *126*
27–30 *173*

Numbers
19:2 *358*
21:21–35 *222*

Deuteronomy
6:4 *90*
6:4–9 *160*
6:6–9 *140*
7 *92*
7:25 *173*
8:3 *63*
18 *92*
18:12 *173*
22:5 *92, 172, 174, 181*
22:24 *289*
22:27 *289*
24:2–4 *173*
28:11–12 *114*

Joshua
1–12 *221*
3:9–11 *221*
7 *85*

Judges
4:3 *289*
4–5 *146*
4:6–8 *146*
4:9 *147*
4:21 *147*
19:22 *185*

1 Samuel
1–2 *146*
1:4–8 *291*
1:6–7 *294*

1:9 *294*
1:11 *294*
1:14 *294*
2 *293*
18:1 *39*

2 Samuel
23 *290*
23:8 *140*
23:8–39 *340*

1 Kings
2:1–4 *139*
2:2 *165*
21 *290*

2 Chronicles
3:16–17 *107*

Esther
4 *146*

Job
1 *222*
8:8–9 *327*
10:8–9 *22*
27:3 *22*
34:15 *21*

Psalms
4:7 *121*
4:8 *121*
8:3–6 *2*
8:4–5 *6*
14:2–3 *86*
20:2 *135*
20:7 *256*
23 *8*
23:2 *122*

ABOUT THE AUTHOR

Owen Strachan is associate professor of Christian theology at Midwestern Baptist Theological Seminary. He is the director of the Residency, the residential PhD program of MBTS, and leads the Center for Public Theology. He earned a PhD from Trinity Evangelical Divinity School, an MDiv from The Southern Baptist Theological Seminary, and an AB from Bowdoin College.

Strachan has published sixteen books, including *The Pastor as Public Theologian* (with Kevin Vanhoozer), *The Colson Way*, and *The Essential Jonathan Edwards* (with Douglas Sweeney). He has written academic journal articles for *Themelios*, *Trinity Journal*, *Midwestern Journal of Theology*, and the *Journal of Biblical and Theological Studies*, as well as popular articles for the *Atlantic*, *First Things*, *Christianity Today*, and the *Washington Post*.

Strachan is the president of Reformanda Ministries, a theological resource ministry. He is a member of the editorial committee of the *Journal for the Evangelical Theological Society*, a contributing writer for the Gospel Coalition, and a senior fellow of the Council on Biblical Manhood & Womanhood (CBMW).

Formerly the president of CBMW, Strachan speaks regularly for churches and conferences. A member of Mission Road Bible Church in Prairie Village, Kansas, Strachan is married to Bethany and is the father of three children.